Black Liberation and Socialism

Black Liberation and Socialism

Ahmed Shawki

Chicago, Illinois

To Kaya & Smitch

Published in 2006 by Haymarket Books
P.O. Box 180165
Chicago, IL 60618
773-583-7884
www.haymarketbooks.org

ISBN 1-931859-26-4 (10-digit)
ISBN 978-1931859-264 (13-digit)

Cover design by Josh On and Amy Balkin
Cover photograph: Malcolm X waits at Martin Luther King press
conference, March 26, 1964. Courtesy Library of Congress

Trade distribution:
In the US, Consortium Book Sales and Distribution, www.cbsd.com
In Canada, Publishers Group Canada, www.pgcbooks.ca
In the UK, Turnaround Publisher Services, www.turnaround-uk.com
In Australia, Palgrave Macmillan, www.palgravemacmillan.com.au
All other countries, Publishers Group Worldwide, www.pgw.com

This book has been published with the generous support of the
Wallace Global Fund.

Library of Congress Cataloging-in-Publication Data
is available from the publisher

Entered into digital printing, November 2017.

Contents

Acknowledgments

This book has been a long time in the making, and would not have been possible without the contributions of many people who helped improve the manuscript. I owe them special thanks. I am, of course, responsible for any errors that remain. In particular, I want to thank: Anthony Arnove, Paul D'Amato, Lance Selfa, Lee Sustar, Keeanga-Yamahtta Taylor, Alan Maass, Joel Geier, Sharon Smith, Julie Fain, Sherry Wolf, Jessie Kindig, Dao X. Tran, Tristin Adie, and Eric Ruder.

Introduction

Hurricane Katrina, which hit the Gulf Coast at the end of August 2005, left areas of Mississippi, Louisiana, and Alabama devastated. Katrina exposed the priorities of the U.S. government, as thousands of people were abandoned to fend for themselves. Hurricane Katrina also exposed—or rather, exposed again—the simple fact that African-Americans in the United States are the victims of deeply rooted racism. As the images of devastation and desperation were broadcast across the country and around the world, the chief of the U.S. government's agency charged with dealing with such disasters, the Federal Emergency Management Agency, blamed the victims of the hurricane for the situation they were in. After all, argued Department of Homeland Security Secretary, Michael Chertoff, they should have left town as advised by local authorities.[1] Leaving aside that evacuation orders went out late, the simple fact that a good portion of New Orleans' poor—largely Black—didn't have the means to leave town, or had nowhere to go, was not a matter of concern. The message being sent by the Bush administration was clear: If you're poor and Black you are plain out of luck. You are not a priority.

Less than a month later, at a mass demonstration of opposition to war and the occupation of Iraq, a Black woman held up a sign that evoked the now well-known phrase used by Muhammad Ali, the heavyweight boxing champion. When asked by a reporter why he was applying for conscientious objector status instead of going to fight the U.S. war against Vietnam, Ali replied, "I ain't got no quarrel with them Viet Cong."[2] He added pointedly, "no Viet Cong ever called me nigger."[3] The sign held at the antiwar demonstration in September 2005 read: "No Iraqis left me on a roof to die." This woman was not alone in making the connections among the unnatural effects of Hurricane Katrina, the priorities of the system, and the war in Iraq. Many resources that could have been mobilized to cushion the impact of Katrina were not available because they were diverted—funds, equipment, and people—to the war and occupation of Iraq. Thousands if not millions understood what many signs at the September 2005 antiwar demonstration spelled out, "Make levees, not war."

With their disgraceful mishandling of the aftermath of Katrina, George Bush and his administration stood naked in front of the world. This has fuelled a tremendous anger already brewing in the United States against the way this society works—or *doesn't*—for the majority of people. As many writers have suggested, it is a grave mistake to think that U.S. society is stable, or that the promise of neoliberalism is the solution for most people. The United States is headed for an inevitable and tumultuous conflict.

And as in every other period of radicalization in the past, Blacks will be at the heart of the effort to change the United States. The aim of this book is twofold: (1) to give an overview of some of the main ideological and political currents in the struggle for Black liberation in the United States; and (2) to argue the case that both historically and in the future, socialist ideas and organization are an integral part of this struggle.

In today's political climate, many may find this idea untenable. But it is irrefutable that the United States has gone through waves of radicalization on a mass scale—when millions of people showed their opposition to the existing system and how it is run. In the late 1960s, radical politics, including Marxism, were integrally connected to the movements for social change in the United States. Key figures and organizations in the Black freedom struggle identified themselves with some form of socialist or Marxist politics. And the Black struggle had profound effects on U.S. society.

The mass mobilizations of the late 1950s and 1960s to end segregation in the South helped break the stranglehold of McCarthyism and conservatism that dominated U.S. politics. The civil rights movement smashed "Jim Crow" laws—the apartheid-like segregation laws introduced at the turn of the century—that denied Blacks the most basic rights. The Black Power movement of the late 1960s represented a further radicalization of the movement involving hundreds of thousands of activists, Black and white, in political activity and mobilization.

All kinds of political ideas flourished during this period. For the first time since the demise of Marcus Garvey's Universal Negro Improvement Association (UNIA) in the 1920s, Black nationalist ideas gained a hearing on a mass scale. By the late 1960s, sections of the movement underwent an even greater radicalization. The Black Panther Party and the League of Revolutionary Black Workers, for example, spoke of the need for revolution and declared themselves "Marxist-Leninist" organizations. It was commonly asserted, in however partial, confused, or ill-conceived ways, that reformism was a dead end and that only revolutionary politics could achieve Black liberation. Whatever weaknesses the movement had, it remains a tremendous source of inspiration and holds many lessons for us today.

Yet, more than three decades later, the situation has changed completely. While the officially sanctioned racism of Jim Crow is a thing of the past, there has been a steady erosion of the gains Blacks won in the 1960s. Still today, in 2006, the polarization between Blacks and whites in incomes, living standards, education, health care, and just about any other marker remains substantial.

The *State of Black America 2005*, an annual report published by the National Urban League, documents the continuing reality of racism and discrimination in the United States. The executive summary of the report points out:

> The biggest divide between Blacks and whites is economic status, nearly 20 percent worse than any other category.
>
> In 2005, Black unemployment remained stagnant at 10.8 percent while white unemployment decreased to 4.7 percent, making Black unemployment over 2.3 times more than whites.
>
> Home Ownership: The homeownership rate for Blacks is nearly 50 percent versus more than 70 percent for whites. While African Americans' mortgage denial and home improvement loans rates did improve, Blacks are still denied these types of loans at twice the rate of whites.
>
> Health: The health index showed slight declines compared to 2004 due to a faster increase in obesity rates for African Americans than whites....
>
> Education: Teachers with less than three years experience teach in minority schools at twice the rate that they teach in white schools.
>
> Social Justice: 2005 showed the equality gap between whites and Blacks in the criminal justice system is worsening, going from 73 percent to 68 percent. Blacks are three times more likely to become prisoners once arrested and a Black person's average jail sentence is six months longer than a white's for the same crime; 39 months versus 33 months.[4]

At the same time as these major inequalities have hardened, there was a corresponding retreat from left-wing ideas, leading to an almost complete absence of mass political activity today around these fundamental questions. The decline and disorientation of the left movements of the 1960s began in the late 1970s and has affected not just Blacks, but also the labor movement, and movements for women's and gay rights, among others.

By 1987, the activist and scholar Manning Marable wrote,

> the political mood across Black America ha[d] grown more pessimistic. Allies of the Black freedom struggle have abandoned their previous support for affirmative action and expanded civil rights legislation. Among Blacks there is a deepening sense of social alienation and political frustration, generated partially by the continued popularity of President [Ronald] Reagan, the conservative trend in the Democratic Party, and the intense economic chaos which plagues Black inner cities despite three years of national economic "recovery."[5]

And if the mood was pessimistic in the late 1980s, it is altogether bleaker today. There is a greater sense of alienation and powerlessness in Black America and an even greater fragmentation of organized forces—at the very time the need for an organized movement of resistance has grown more urgent.

Over the past three decades, the left has largely abandoned revolutionary politics in favor of some variety of reformism—what is often described as the politics of "realism." This development did not occur overnight. Many activists on the U.S. left, for example, supported Jesse Jackson's 1984 and 1988 presidential bids, arguing that the Rainbow Coalition was the historic continuation of the struggles of the 1960s. To quote Marable again,

> The essence of the Jackson campaign was a democratic, anti-racist social movement, initiated and led by Afro-Amer-

icans, which had assumed an electoral mode. Its direct historical antecedents—the Montgomery bus boycott of 1955–56, the formation of SNCC and the sit-in movement of 1960, the Birmingham desegregation campaign of 1963— were revived in a new protest form within bourgeois demo- cratic politics.[6]

Leaving aside the validity of this argument for now, what is clear today is that supporting candidates like Jackson, once seen as a means to achieve left-wing or radical aims, by 2004 had morphed into supporting anyone who declared he or she was opposed to the right wing, regardless of their actual positions. Thus, virtually the entire left in the United States called for, and worked for, a vote for Democrat John Kerry against President George W. Bush, despite the fact that Kerry had virtually identical positions to Bush on the war in Iraq, the USA PATRIOT Act, marriage rights for gays and lesbians, and a host of other questions.

In this way, much of the left radicalized in the 1960s and 1970s has migrated wholesale into the Democratic Party, the party that in the 1960s prosecuted the war in Vietnam and up- held Jim Crow in the South. In so doing, this left severed itself from the tradition of struggle that the 1960s revived.

This book seeks to reaffirm the need for a *struggle* against racism and the economic and political system that maintains it—capitalism. An examination of the history of the fight for Black freedom in the United States confirms the need for such a strategy. This elementary (but often forgotten or ig- nored) truth was summed up memorably by the abolitionist leader Frederick Douglass in 1857:

Let me give you a word of the philosophy of reform. The whole history of the progress of human liberty shows that all concessions yet made to her august claims, have been born of earnest struggle. The conflict has been exciting, agitating, all-absorbing, and for the time being, putting all other tumults to silence. It must do this or it does nothing. If there is no struggle there is no progress. Those who profess to favor freedom and yet deprecate agitation, are men who want crops without plowing up the ground, they want rain without thunder and lightning. They want the ocean without the awful roar of its many waters.

This struggle may be a moral one, or it may be a physical one, and it may be both moral and physical, but it must be a struggle. Power concedes nothing without a demand. It never did and it never will. Find out just what any people will quietly submit to and you have found out the exact measure of injustice and wrong which will be imposed upon them, and these will continue till they are resisted with either words or blows, or with both. The limits of tyrants are prescribed by the endurance of those whom they oppress. In the light of these ideas, Negroes will be hunted at the North, and held and flogged at the South so long as they submit to those devilish outrages, and make no resistance, either moral or physical. Men may not get all they pay for in this world, but they must certainly pay for all they get. If we ever get free from the oppressions and wrongs heaped upon us, we must pay for their removal. We must do this by labor, by suffering, by sacrifice, and if needs be, by our lives and the lives of others.[7]

This book also makes the case that such a struggle needs to aspire to the radical reconstruction of society if racism is to be overcome and Black liberation truly realized. This is not to suggest that advances, reforms, or real victories cannot be achieved under capitalism. Rather, it is only to underline that whatever reforms are won can, will, and many have been taken away—unless there is a fundamental restructuring of a system that relies on exploitation and oppression to survive.

This book is not a comprehensive history of the Black struggle in the United States. Nor is it a comprehensive history of all socialist currents and organizations and their relationship to the Black movement. Rather, its aim is to highlight some of the political issues—ideological and organizational—in the relationship between socialism and the struggle for Black liberation. The most commonly written-about example of the relation between socialism and Black liberation is the Communist Party (CP) in the 1930s. There is good reason for this. The CP was the largest and most influential left-wing party that was fully committed to fighting racism and had a sizeable Black membership. Its accomplishments—most critically in the 1930s—showed in practice that it was possible to forge unity between working-class Blacks and whites and advance their common interests. There are several important studies of the work of the CP in this period, notably by Robin Kelley and Mark Naison.[8]

But as important as the CP's work was during this period, it suffered from the fact that its perspective and outlook was shaped by the needs of the foreign policy of the Soviet Union rather than those of workers' interests in the United States—Black or white. This book looks more closely at a current that emerged from the Communist movement in the late 1920s—the Trotskyists—who have not been as carefully studied, but who helped shape and inform the politics and activities of several important currents both in the civil rights movements and in the Black Power movement.

Another aspect of this book should be explained. I chose to quote extensively from some of the key figures that are discussed in the book. I did so because I felt that those who were actually involved in the struggle best advance many of the arguments that I make in the book. It is also the case that their words are less well known than they should be.

Lastly, and on a more personal note, I want to acknowledge the significance of the 1960s struggle in helping shape a whole generation for the better. Even if many of the advances made in the 1960s have been rolled back today, the movement's impact cannot be measured only by its impact on government policy, or even by its effect on the economic and social conditions for Black people in the United States. One of the most important legacies of periods of mass struggle is that those involved are transformed—and that their actions also help shape and transform others. Speaking, or writing, for myself, the example of Muhammad Ali standing up to the U.S. war in Vietnam, or the outrage that exploded with Martin Luther King, Jr.'s assassination, had a profound and lasting impact. Growing up outside the United States, two images of this country were etched in my mind. One was the image of war—Vietnam, napalm, and the massacre at My Lai—captured so famously in the image of a naked young girl, running for her life, weeping in pain. The other is of the Black struggle, of courage and heroism, of a wronged people standing up to a juggernaut.

The United States is today's only military superpower. It is seen around the world as a bully abusing its power for profit and empire. But the United States of 2006 is no different from the United States of 1968 with regard to who prosecutes and who benefits from its wars. And, in reality, just like 1968, there isn't one United States of America, but two. The difference is that those forces that represent opposition to the U.S. war machine are weaker today than those of the late 1960s. So there are two questions to contend with: one in changing reality, the other, which flows from the first, in changing perception.

There is no doubt that the Bush administration and its policies are very unpopular with a very large segment of the population. Among Blacks, the Bush administration scores all-time lows—with an approval rating in the single digits.[9] But disapproval is one thing, active opposition is another, and organized oppositional politics and action yet another. For starters, the "official" opposition—the Democrats—offer no alternative and will not fight the Republicans. Indeed, they discourage any such idea. Second, the right wing is more confident, organized, and mobilized than other sections of U.S. society. Third, there has been a two-decade retreat on the part of the left in this country. This has meant that despite some quite substantial sentiment and opinion against Bush, there is not yet an instrument or organized means to express this. In addition, it must be said that the Democratic Party is unwilling to do anything that it feels will tar them with being "liberal." Its strategy for more than two decades has been clear and best summed up during the Clinton presidency in the strategy of "triangulation": To simply adopt the policies of the Republicans and repackage them. The result of this strategy has been to move politics in the United States to the right—and to sharply limit what is "acccptable" in mainstream politics.

This book argues that a different set of politics is needed—and that there is a rich legacy of struggle from which we can learn.

CHAPTER ONE

Slavery in the United States

Direct slavery is as much the pivot upon which our present-day industrialism turns as are machinery, credit, etc. Without slavery there would be no cotton, without cotton there would be no modern industry. It is slavery which has given value to the colonies, it is the colonies which have created world trade, and world trade is the necessary condition for large-scale machine industry. Consequently, prior to the slave trade, the colonies sent very few products to the Old World, and did not noticeably change the face of the world. Slavery is therefore an economic category of paramount importance. Without slavery, North America, the most progressive nation, would be transformed into a patriarchal country. Only wipe North America off the map and you will get anarchy, the complete decay of trade and modern civilization. But to do away with slavery would be to wipe America off the map. Being an economic category, slavery has existed in all nations since the beginning of the world. All that modern nations have achieved is to disguise slavery at home and import it openly into the New World.

—Karl Marx[1]

The labor of Blacks, forced to come to the New World as slaves, was essential to the economic development not only of the new colonies, whether in the Caribbean, Latin America, or North America, but also the major powers of the "Old

World." But slavery did not come innocent of ideological trappings. A historically distinct ideology designed to justify and maintain the oppression of the slaves developed with the rise of the Atlantic slave trade.

Racism and racial oppression have been features of everyday life for Blacks in the United States for more than 350 years. But the persistence of racism is not inevitable and racism, certainly in its modern form, has not always existed. Far from being the unavoidable result of interaction between different peoples, racism and racial oppression emerged in Europe's transition from feudalism to capitalism. Ancient and feudal societies before capitalism were able to do without this form of oppression.

Specifically, racism emerged in Western Europe and the New World as a consequence of the slave trade, as the ideological justification for slavery. Prejudice against strangers (xenophobia) and distinctions between "barbarian" and "civilized" existed, but did not take the form of modern racism. So for example,

> North American Indians whom European settlers first encountered had a conception of "outsider," i.e., non-members of the band, tribe, or nation. But the fact that it carried no racial connotation is shown not only by the practice of adoption of Indian captives of other nations into the tribe to replace lost loved ones, but also of the adoption of captured white Europeans as full-fledged members of the tribe. "Thousands of Europeans are Indians," complained Hector de Crévecoeur in his 1782 *Letters from an American Farmer*, but "we have no examples of even one of those Aborigines having from choice become Europeans!"[2]

As historian Frank Snowden has argued:

> Color prejudice has been a major issue in the modern world.... Notable, therefore, is the fact that the ancient world did not

make color the focus of irrational sentiments or the basis for uncritical evaluation. The ancients did accept the institution of slavery as a fact of life; they made ethnocentric judgments of other societies; they had narcissistic canons of physical beauty; the Egyptians distinguished between themselves, "the people," and outsiders; and the Greeks called foreign cultures barbarian. Yet nothing comparable to the virulent color prejudice of modern times existed in the ancient world. This is the view of most scholars who have examined the evidence and have come to conclusions such as these: the ancients did not fall into the error of biological racism; black skin color was not a sign of inferiority; Greeks and Romans did not establish color as an obstacle to integration in society; and ancient society was one that "for all its faults and failures never made color the basis for judging a man."[3]

The slave system that developed in the New World was different in fundamental respects. Chief among these was the fact that it was "racially" based—Africans were the slaves—even if the reasons for the enslavement of Blacks were economic and not racial. The initial attempts to meet the enormous—and ever-increasing—demand for labor in the New World included attempts to enslave Native peoples and whites. When these attempts failed, Africans became the chief source of labor.

"It has been said of the Spanish conquistadors," writes Eric Williams, one of the pioneering historians of New World slavery in *From Columbus to Castro: The History of the Caribbean*, "that first they fell on their knees, and then they fell on the aborigines."[4] So after claiming their colonies for God and the King, the Spaniards set about pressing into service the local indigenous population to pump out the colonies' wealth for the benefit of the Spanish crown.

The Indians were assigned in lots of fifty, a hundred, or more, by written deed or patent, to individual Spaniards to work on their farms and ranches or in the placer mines for gold dust. Sometimes they were given to officials or to parish priests in lieu of part of their annual salary. The effect was simply to parcel out the natives among the settlers to do with as they pleased.[5]

The results were devastating:

> The results are to be seen in the best estimates that have been prepared of the trend of population in Hispaniola. These place the population in 1492 at between 200,000 and 300,000. By 1508 the number was reduced to 60,000; in 1510, it was 46,000; in 1512, 20,000; in 1514, 14,000. In 1548 Oviedo doubted whether five hundred Indians of pure stock remained. In 1570 only two villages survived of those about whom Columbus had assured his Sovereigns, less than eighty years before, that "there is no better nor gentler people in the world."[6]

African slave labor proved more plentiful and cheaper than either Native Americans or white indentured servants and eventually slavery was confined exclusively to Blacks. According to Williams,

> Here, then, is the origin of Negro slavery. The reason was economic, not racial; it had to do not with the color of the laborer, but the cheapness of the labor. As compared with Indian and white labor, Negro slavery was eminently superior.... The features of the man, his hair, color and dentifrice, his "subhuman" characteristics so widely pleaded, were only the later rationalizations to justify a simple economic fact: that the colonies needed labor and resorted to Negro labor because it was cheapest and best. This was not a theory, it was a practical conclusion deduced from the personal experience of the planter. He would have gone to the moon, if necessary, for labor. Africa was nearer than the moon, nearer too than the more populous countries of India and China. But their turn was to come.[7]

Unfree Labor in the North American Colonies

The North American colonies started predominantly as private business enterprises in the early 1600s. Unlike the Spanish, whose colonies served to export precious metals back to the colonial center, settlers in the colonies that became Maryland, Rhode Island, and Virginia were planters.[8] The settlers' chief aim was to obtain a labor force that could produce the large amounts of indigo, tobacco, sugar, and other crops that would be sold back to England. From 1607, when Jamestown was founded in Virginia, to about 1685, the primary source of agricultural labor in English North America came from white indentured servants after the settlers failed to build a sustained workforce from the indigenous population.[9]

After their terms expired, many white indentured servants sought to acquire land for themselves. Black slaves worked on plantations in small numbers throughout the 1600s. But until the end of the 1600s, it cost planters more to buy slaves than to buy white servants.[10] Some Blacks who lived in the colonies were free, some were slaves, and some were servants. Free Blacks in Maryland, Massachusetts, New York, North Carolina, Pennsylvania, and Vermont had voting rights.[11] In the 1600s, the Chesapeake society of eastern Virginia had a multiracial character:

> There is persuasive evidence dating from the 1620s through the 1680s that there were those of European descent in the Chesapeake who were prepared to identify and cooperate with people of African descent. These affinities were forged in the world of plantation work. On many plantations Europeans and West Africans labored side by side in the tobacco fields, performing exactly the same types and amounts of work; they lived and ate together in shared housing; they socialized together; and sometimes they slept together.[12]

For most of the 1600s, the planters depended mainly on a predominantly white workforce of English, Scottish, and Irish servants.[13] But planters found the white workforce was becoming increasingly restive and expensive. As the 1600s was a time of revolutionary upheaval in England, many of the servants began demanding their rights. And those who finished their terms often became direct competitors to the planters in agriculture. With costs of servants increasing, planters asked colonial administrations to begin widespread importation of African slaves.

By the end of the seventeenth century, a planter could buy an African slave for life for the same price as a white servant with a ten-year contract. This decision to turn to a racially specified labor force had enormous human consequences. Between 1640 and 1800, more than four million West Africans were forcibly transferred to the New World.[14] Perhaps ten to fifteen million Black slaves made it to the Americas by the 1800s, an estimated one-third of the total captured in Africa.[15] The conditions of transport in the Middle Passage (the journey made by slave ships from Africa across the Atlantic) were horrendous, with human beings stacked and chained like firewood, and disease and suffocation killing hundreds of thousands.

Many, if not most, historians place race rather than the demand for labor as the central driving force for slavery. The crudest version of this argument says that slavery developed because of European racism.[16] The more sophisticated version is almost identical except that it acknowledges the need for labor and concludes that slavery was settled upon as a solution, and in particular the enslavement of Africans because of the depths of racism.[17]

But these arguments invert the process. As historian Barbara Fields has argued:

Probably a majority of American historians think of slavery in the United States as primarily a system of race relations—as though the chief business of slavery were the production of white supremacy rather than the production of cotton, sugar, rice, and tobacco. One historian has gone so far as to call slavery "the ultimate segregator." He does not ask why Europeans seeking the "ultimate" method of segregating Africans would go to the trouble and expense of transporting them across the ocean for that purpose, when they could have achieved the same end so much more simply by leaving the Africans in Africa. No one dreams of analyzing the struggle of the English against the Irish as a problem in race relations, even though the rationale that the English developed for suppressing the "barbarous Irish" later served nearly word for word as a rationale for suppressing Africans and indigenous American Indians.[18]

The dominant historical view of slavery places ideas—in particular, racial ideas—as the motor force of history. This view of history thoroughly underestimates the material connection between capitalism and the development of racism. Colonial slavery, however, was intimately tied to capitalist development, and was not a remnant of an older mode of production. As Karl Marx put it:

> The discovery of gold and silver in America, the extirpation, enslavement and entombment in mines of the indigenous population of that continent, the beginnings of the conquest and plunder of India, and the conversion of Africa into a preserve for the commercial hunting of black skins, are all things which characterize the dawn of the era of capitalist production. These idyllic proceedings are the chief moments of primitive accumulation.[19]

Slavery and the American Revolution

U.S. slavery developed primarily in the rice and tobacco plantations of the Southern colonies. Slavery also existed in the North, although it was largely peripheral to the Northern economy. By 1776, slaves composed 40 percent of the population of the colonies from Maryland south to Georgia, but well below 10 percent in colonies to the North.[20] Blacks made up one in five of the total population at the time of the American War of Independence in 1776.[21]

The American Revolution did not end slavery, despite the growth of a powerful current in favor of abolition. The original draft of the Declaration of Independence in June 1776 included an attack on the slave trade as "a cruel war against human nature itself," but it was abandoned in the final version. Northern merchants were themselves involved in the slave trade, and the use of slavery had become widespread, especially in the Southern states.[22]

It is a paradox of the American Revolution that it cast off the chains of colonial rule, but shackled one-fifth of the population of the newly independent states in the chains of slavery. Thus American democracy and American racism emerged as "Siamese twins," as Fields described them. In feudal societies of kings, lords, vassals, and serfs, slavery did not demand an elaborate justification, as it seemed to fit with the natural, hierarchical, and unequal order of things. But in a society that proclaimed "all men are created equal," a systematic explanation for why some people were denied rights that others were entitled to needed to be developed. "That is why the slave society of the United States was the only one in the hemisphere that developed a systematic pro-slavery doctrine," Fields concluded. "You don't find that anywhere else. Bondage does not need justifying as long as it seems to be the natural order of things. You need a radical affirmation of bondage only where you have a radical affirmation of freedom."[23] Frederick Engels made much the same point, noting the fundamental contradiction: "It is significant," he wrote, "that the American Constitution, the first to recognize the rights of man, in the same breath confirmed the slavery of the colored races existing in America: class privileges were proscribed, race privileges sanctified."[24]

The leaders of the American Revolution were clear that an end to the tyranny of the British king did not mean an end to the tyranny of class rule—certainly not when they were the dominant class. Alexander Hamilton represented the views of the most aristocratic among the new ruling order:

> All communities divide themselves into the few and the many. The first are the rich and wellborn, the other the mass of the people. The voice of the people has been said to be the voice of God; and however generally this maxim has been quoted and believed, it is not true in fact. The people are turbulent and changing; they seldom judge or determine right. Give therefore to the first class a distinct, permanent share in the government.... Can a democratic assembly, who annually revolve in the mass of the people, be supposed steadily to pursue the public good? Nothing but a permanent body can check the imprudence of democracy.[25]

One of Hamilton's proposals at the Constitutional Convention of 1787 was the selection of a president and Senate for life. The Convention didn't take his suggestions for the creation of a "permanent body" to rule and check the "imprudence of democracy." But it did severely limit popular participation in elections.[26] Senators were to be elected by state legislations, the president was to be elected by electors chosen by the state legislators, and the Supreme Court was to be appointed by the president. Ten of the original thirteen states limited the right to vote for members of the House of Representatives to property owners.[27]

These limitations on the rights of the "mass of the people" were not simply an expression of the aristocratic beliefs of the Founding Fathers; nor were they primarily concerned with elections in their own right. They were, rather, an expression of the growing conflict between those who were rich and powerful and the vast majority who were neither. By 1787, the elites were acutely aware of the need to establish a strong central government to protect their interests—and to suppress popular rebellions.

The threat from below was very real. In the summer of 1786 an uprising in western Massachusetts by discontented farmers—Shay's Rebellion—underlined the point. As one farmer put it:

> I have been greatly abused, have been obliged to do more than my part in the war; been loaded with class rates, town rates, province rates, Continental rates and all rates...been pulled and hauled by sheriffs, constables and collectors, and had my cattle sold for less than they were worth....
>
> The great men are going to get all we have and I think it is time for us to rise and put a stop to it, and have no more courts, nor sheriffs, nor collectors nor lawyers.[28]

The rich and powerful that ruled America decided to close ranks and try to resolve their differences in order to establish a strong, central state. A veteran of George Washington's army, General Henry Knox, founded an organization of army veterans who would be on alert for signs of rebellion from below. As Knox wrote to Washington in 1786 of Shay's Rebellion:

> The people who are insurgents have never paid any, or but very little taxes—But they see the weakness of government; They feel at once their own poverty, compared with the opulent, and their own force, and they are determined to make use of the latter, in order to remedy the former. Their creed is "That the property of the United States has been protected from the confiscations of Britain by the joint

exertions of all, and therefore ought to be the common property of all. And he that attempts opposition to this creed is an enemy to equity and justice, and ought to be swept off the face of the earth."[29]

At the Constitutional Convention of 1787, the rich and powerful gathered to debate and settle their differences. The convention brought together fifty-five men, many of whom were slaveholders and some of whom considered themselves abolitionists. The question of slavery loomed large. As James Madison put it, in many of the debates "the institution of slavery and its consequences formed the line of discrimination."[30] The Constitution was a compromise between slaveholding interests in the South and moneyed interests in the North.

The Southern ruling class knew that its wealth and power derived almost exclusively from their ownership of slaves. The South Carolina delegation expressed this sentiment with the utmost clarity and with no hint of embarrassment. Without slaves, stated General Pinckney, "South Carolina would soon be a desert waste." Speaking against ratification of the Constitution, Rawlin Lowndes, a delegate from South Carolina, stated, "Without Negroes, this state would degenerate into one of the most contemptible in the union.... Negroes are our wealth, our only natural resource."[31]

Michael Goldfield writes,

Although the Continental Congress rejected the South Carolinian attempt to place the adjective *white* in the Constitution, it acceded or compromised on almost every other demand. Yet, this complete capitulation in accepting the legality of slavery did *not* eliminate it as a major issue. Sectional disputes on how to regard Negro slavery came up over taxation (1783) and representation (1787). The Founding Fathers made a final compromise on July 12, 1787, by assigning three-fifths representation for both purposes. The three-fifths compromise had momentous consequences.[32]

As Donald Robinson puts it, the three-fifths compromise "gave constitutional sanction to the fact that the United States was composed of some persons who were 'free' and others who were not." Furthermore, he argues, it established a new idea, "new in republican theory, that a man who lived among slaves had a greater share in the election of representatives than the man who did not. With one stroke, despite the disclaimers of its advocates, it acknowledged slavery and rewarded slave owners. It is a measure of their adjustment to slavery that Americans in the eighteenth century found this settlement natural and just."[33]

The main provisions in the Constitution regarding slavery can quickly be summarized: First, Congress was prohibited from outlawing the importation of slaves before the year 1808.[34] Second, states were obliged constitutionally to return all fugitives from slavery to their owners.[35] Third, for purposes of electoral representation and taxation three-fifths of the slaves and the free population would be counted.[36] Later in the Constitutional Convention, the delegates agreed upon the method for electing presidents. Rejecting direct elections (because the voters couldn't be trusted), the delegates agreed to set up an electoral college to select the president. Then, it was decided, each state would elect the president by casting a fixed number of winner-take-all electoral college votes equivalent to its total of representatives in the House. This in turn would be proportional to the state's population—artificially boosted in the South by the three-fifths clause. Enslaved and denied a vote, Blacks added political power to their Southern white oppressors.

In order to abate the sensibilities of some of the delegates at the Convention, the words "slave" and "slavery" do not appear in the final document. Instead the document refers to slaves as "other persons" and persons "held to service or labor." Luther Martin, a Maryland attorney who strongly argued against ratification, noted that his fellow delegates "anxiously sought to avoid the admission of expressions which might be odious in the ears of Americans." But, they were "willing to admit into their system those things which the expressions signified."[37]

The Constitution was made more palatable when the first Congress, responding to pressure and criticism, passed a set of amendments known as the Bill of Rights. These amendments give the appearance that the new government was not in fact run in the interests of the rich, but rather was an institution that rose above class interests and was the guardian of everyone's freedom to speak, to publish, to assemble, and to be tried fairly. This packaging of the amendments was designed to garner popular support for the government. The difference between appearance and reality was made clear soon enough, however. The First Amendment of the Bill of Rights, passed in 1791 by Congress, provides that "Congress shall make no law...abridging the freedom of speech, or of the press." Yet, only seven years after the First Amendment became part of the Constitution, Congress passed a law doing just that—the Sedition Act of 1798, passed under John Adams' administration. As one historian put it, "The fears of men like Adams and Hamilton had been aggravated by the social unrest of the 1780s and particularly by Shay's Rebellion in 1786. This event, however shocking it was, paled in significance when compared with the French Revolution."[38] The law made it a crime to say or write anything "false, scandalous and malicious against the government, Congress, or the United States or either house of the Congress of the United States or the United States President, with intent to defame said government, or either house of the said Congress, or the said President, or bring them...into contempt or disrepute, or to excite against them...the hatred of the good people of the United States."[39]

In 1790, Adams had already complained that "too many Frenchmen, after the example of too many Americans, pant for equality of persons and property." Years later he recalled that the idea of a democratic government in France had always struck him as "unnatural, irrational and impracticable." As he said then, "the French Revolution I dreaded."[40]

Some antislavery proponents believed that slavery would die a slow death as a result of the 1808 slave trade ban. But the enormous growth in demand for cotton—in large part due to the growth of the textile industry in Britain—ensured that the opposite took place. The prohibition by Congress against the importation of slaves after 1807 could not slow the expansion of the cotton plantations in the fifteen Southern states. Slavery had become too entrenched. In any case, the prohibition of the importation of slaves was quite different to the prohibition of slavery. Even pro-slavery advocates supported an end to the slave trade as a prudent measure to reduce the possibility of slave rebellions. The slave system would instead rely on the internal reproduction and trade in slaves.

Members of the ruling class, who had in the past expressed hostility to slavery, came to make their peace with its slow disappearance in the Northern states. In 1790, 698,000 slaves were in the United States; by the close of the century, the number had reached 893,000. An estimated 35,900 slaves still lived in the North: the Emancipation Laws[41] had usually freed the children of slaves rather than slaves themselves. In New York, for instance, the Emancipation Law of 1799 freed no living slave; it merely provided for the liberty of any child born to a slave mother and only after he or she had served the mother's master until adulthood as compensation for the owner's future loss of property rights.[42]

Thomas Jefferson and James Madison illustrate the quandary of the antislavery wing among U.S. rulers. In private communications, Jefferson continued to express his opposition to the enslavement of so many Blacks. But, he was quick to add, the price of any change would be even greater: "We have the wolf by the ears, and we can neither hold him, nor safely let him go. Justice is in one scale, and self-preservation in the other."[43]

James Madison, who followed Jefferson as president, did not let his personal reservations about slavery cloud his understanding of the economic significance of the slave system. Responding to a critic of slavery, he declared his total agreement "as to the evil, moral, political, and economical," of slavery. But he suggested that there could be "much improvement" in slave culture "particularly where slaves are held in small numbers, by good masters and managers." He appealed to his critic to reconsider. After all, he argued, the risks of running a plantation were considerably smaller than those of a speculation on stocks or bonds: "look at the wrecks everywhere giving warning of the danger." How else would the United States expand agriculturally? Madison asked: If into large landed property, where there are no slaves, "will you cultivate it yourself? Then beware of the difficulty of procuring faithful and complying laborers. Will you dispose of its leases? Ask those who have made the experiment what sort of tenants are to be found where an ownership of the soil is so attainable."[44]

Until the early 1790s, cultivation of cotton had been overwhelmingly concentrated in the coastal regions. The invention of Whitney's cotton gin in 1793 made it possible to shift production and processing much farther inland. By 1860, the slave population in the Southern states had grown to almost four million. U.S. exports of raw cotton grew from five hundred thousand pounds in 1793 to eighteen million pounds in 1800 and eighty-three million pounds by 1815.[45] As Marx put it in *Capital*:

> While the cotton industry introduced child-slavery in England, in the United States it gave the impulse for the transformation of the earlier, more or less patriarchal slavery into a system of commercial exploitation. In fact the veiled slavery of the wage laborers in Europe needed the unqualified slavery of the New World as its pedestal.... Capital comes dripping from head to toe, from every pore, with blood and dirt.[46]

Antebellum Society

The plantation system that developed in the South was different in several respects to slavery in the Caribbean and Latin America. These differences shaped the kind of resistance that developed among slaves. Unlike Brazil, for example, where slaves who successfully escaped their plantations could find uninhabited areas and establish communities of escaped slaves, this was less likely in the United States. In the South, slaves were a minority in most states. The majority of slaves also lived on plantations whose owners had twenty or fewer slaves, in contrast to the mass plantations of the Caribbean.[47]

The Southern society that the slave economy created was highly unequal and culturally backward. The South's wealth, already highly concentrated among the planter class, became increasingly so in the half century before the Civil War. In 1800, one-third of white families in the region owned slaves; in 1860, only one-quarter did. In 1860, half of Southern slaveholders owned fewer than five Blacks, while 72 percent owned fewer than ten each and held approximately one-fourth of all slaves.[48]

Only a small minority of white families in the prime cotton-producing counties dominated staple output: the top 10 percent of farms there contributed over 68 percent of total cotton production. Of the farms in these counties 28 percent produced no cotton at all; half of them held no slaves.[49] The wealth of the combined Southern states was greater than either France or Germany in 1860, and income for the wealthiest of the planter class—defined as owning fifty slaves or more—was more than sixty times the per capita income of the day.

Yet, only a few thousand families made up this planting elite, and over two-thirds of the white Southern population owned no slaves at all.[50] And unlike the successful slave revolt of Saint Domingue, where Toussaint L'Ouverture successfully used splits among the slaveholding powers to his advantage, both the North and South were committed to slavery until the 1860s.

It is important to point out that the majority of the South's population did not have any direct interest in slavery. Fully two-thirds of Southern whites didn't own any slaves at all.[51] Only 1,733 white families owned more than 100 slaves each before the outbreak of the Civil War.[52] But instead of opposing slavery, the majority of whites accepted the racist ideology of the planter class, thus tying them to the slave masters. The great abolitionist Frederick Douglass, himself a former slave, explained the reasons: "The hostility between the whites and Blacks of the South is easily explained. It has its root and sap in the relation of slavery, and was incited on both sides by the cunning of the slave masters. Those masters secured their ascendancy over both the poor whites and the Blacks by putting enmity between them. They divided both to conquer each."[53]

Slavery not only oppressed Black slaves, it also ensured the subordination of the poor whites, Douglass argued:

> The slaveholders...by encouraging the enmity of the poor, laboring white man against the Blacks, succeeds in making the said white man almost as much a slave as the Black slave

himself.... Both are plundered, and by the same plunderers. The slave is robbed, by his master, of all his earnings, above what is required for his physical necessities; and the white man is robbed by the slave system, of the just results of his labor, because he is flung into competition with a class of laborers who work without wages.... At present, the slaveholders blind them to this competition, by keeping alive their prejudice against the slaves, *as men*—not against them *as slaves*. They appeal to their pride, often denouncing emancipation, as tending to place the white working man, on an equality with Negroes, and, by this means, they succeed in drawing off the minds of the poor whites from the real fact, that, by the rich slave-master, they are already regarded as but a single remove from equality with the slave.[54]

What Douglass describes in the South was mirrored in the North among white workers. While slavery flourished in the South, the Northern economy was entering a period of rapid expansion. The emerging labor movement of the 1830s was blunted by nativism and racism. The bulk of "native" workers reacted violently to the mass migrations of Irish workers in the 1840s and 1850s. Historian Mike Davis described the reaction of native-born workers to Irish immigrants: "[The Irish] were met by the universal hostility of a native working class which rioted against them, evicted them from workplaces, refused them admission into trade unions, and tried to exclude them from the franchise."[55]

Both native and immigrant labor competed for jobs, and accepted the argument that the emancipation of slaves would "flood" the labor market with four million Blacks. Free Blacks in the North (who numbered 250,000) were excluded from all the existing trade unions. The question of slavery was thus also crucial to the working class in the North. Marx put it succinctly: "In the United States of America, every independent workers' movement was paralyzed as long as slavery disfigured a part of the republic. Labor in a white skin cannot emancipate itself where it is branded in a black skin."[56]

The status of free Blacks in the North was largely determined by conditions in the South and the threat of enslavement loomed large, especially after Congress passed the Fugitive Slave Act in 1850.[57] But while the position of Blacks in the United States was determined by slavery, not all Blacks were affected equally. Even under slavery, a small Black elite that tied its interests with capitalism and set itself against those of the mass of slaves developed. According to scholar and civil rights activist Earl Ofari, "It has been estimated that in 1830 there were 3,777 Black slave masters in the United States."[58] While many of these slave owners purchased slaves in order to emancipate them, others hired them out for profit. In Louisiana there arose a class of wealthy Black and mixed-race planters, which, although never as numerous or as influential as the white planters, owned slaves just the same.[59] Historian Manning Marable explains:

> Even before the Civil War, there were a number of southern Blacks who had access to property and considerable privileges. A group of over eight hundred free Blacks in New Orleans possessed property and private businesses worth nearly $2.5 million in 1836, plus titles to a total of 620 slaves. By 1860 New Orleans's free Creole and Black elites were worth over $9 million. North Carolina free Blacks owned about one million dollars' worth of personal property and real estate in 1860, and Virginia's free Blacks controlled 60,000 acres of farm property.[60]

This elite was tiny in comparison to the Southern slaveocracy, but nevertheless constituted the early class differentiation of the Black population. Moreover, as will become clear, the relatively insecure position of the Black elite—and skilled Blacks generally—became the material basis for the adoption of separatist Black capitalist solutions that at the same time sought accommodation within U.S. capitalism.

CHAPTER TWO

Abolitionism

The three decades leading to the Civil War saw the birth and growth of a mass social movement for the abolition of slavery. The abolitionist movement became a significant force in U.S. politics; it involved tens of thousands of active members, and mobilized and influenced even greater numbers. The abolitionist movement remains one of the most important social movements ever seen in this country. This chapter is not meant to be a comprehensive history of abolitionism in the United States. Rather, it aims to highlight some of the key features of the movement: its explosive growth from a marginal movement to one involving tens of thousands; its political diversity as illustrated in the debates and competing approaches within the movement; and its points of intersection and divergence with the currents of Black separatism and radicalism both before and after the Civil War.

In its early years, the abolitionist movement was marginalized, ridiculed, and attacked. As Michael Goldfield notes: "At first, abolitionists were denounced throughout the country, especially in New England. They were stoned, had their meetings broken up, were arrested, and were threatened to death."[1] Abolitionists were unpopular in both the North and South. As Goldfield reports: "Let us look first at their strongest opponents. Leonard Richards has analyzed anti-abolitionist mobs in Cincinnati, Ohio, and Utica, New York, concluding that the rank and file overwhelmingly consisted of commercial and property men, in stark contrast with the composition of the abolitionist ranks in both cities. Herbert Aptheker argues 'the most avid opponents of Abolitionism were the rich—slaveowners and their lackeys, the merchants and their servitors, the dominant figures in politics, the press, the churches, and the schools.'"[2] The Ohio legislature passed a resolution condemning the abolitionists as "wild, delusive, and fanatical."[3] Yet by 1838, one abolitionist estimated that there were more than 1,400 antislavery societies, with at least 112,000 members.[4] Thousands of activists, both Black and white, dedicated themselves to the eradication of slavery.

The new abolitionist movement that began to take shape in the 1830s was quite different to its predecessors. The earlier generation of abolitionists was politically conservative and timid. In 1827, twenty-four abolition societies with a membership of 1,500 existed in the free states, and the slave states had 130 societies with a membership of 6,625.[5] As Benjamin Quarles points out, "These earlier abolitionists had a religious orientation, a moderate and conciliatory tone, and...a colonizationist outlook. With branches in the slaveholding South, these reformers counted in their ranks an imposing roster of men of means and high public position. No Negroes or women held membership in their societies."[6]

These early abolitionists believed that slavery would gradually disappear of its own accord. Writes Quarles: "With rare exceptions...these early abolitionists were gradualists, trusting what they conceived as the slow but inevitable operation of religious and equalitarian principles. They felt that slavery was not to be abolished overnight but that it would certainly disappear in the fullness of time."[7] Moreover, the previous generation of abolitionists was not particularly hostile to slaveholders in the South and often crafted its appeal to them by making reference to the slaveholders' own best interests.

Many historians date the beginning of the modern abolitionist movement to the publication of William Lloyd Garrison's *Liberator*, in 1831. In contrast to the earlier generation of abolitionists, Garrison called for an immediate end to slavery. The first issue of Garrison's publication made clear how it would approach the struggle against slavery: "I will be as harsh as truth, and as uncompromising as justice. On this subject, I do not wish to think, or speak, or write with moderation.... I am in earnest—I will not equivocate—I will not excuse—I will not retreat a single inch—and I will be heard."[8]

Along with the *Liberator*, Garrison launched the New England Anti-Slavery Society in 1832. Twelve people, all white, attended the founding meeting and declared the organization's purpose to be the abolition of slavery and the improvement of the economic conditions of Northern Blacks. In December 1833, Garrison and sixty other abolitionists founded the American Anti-Slavery Society in Philadelphia.

The influence of the abolitionist movement grew, but so too did the number of factions within the movement. Almost immediately, the abolitionist movement split into gradualist and militant wings. The issue of Black membership in abolition societies and the call for "social equality" for Blacks (i.e., whether the movement should go beyond advocating the abolition of slavery to embracing equality of Blacks and whites in all spheres of life) similarly divided abolitionists. The militant wing of the abolitionist movement was itself divided over several questions, including the role of women in the abolitionist movement; the relationship between abolitionists and labor unions; the use of force or of "moral suasion"; and proposals for Black emigration. Of these, the latter two will be discussed in detail here.

The debate over "moral suasion" versus force built to its climax in John Brown's 1859 raid on the federal armory in Harpers Ferry. On one side of the abolitionist movement were those who insisted that campaigns of education were necessary to persuade politicians and, in some cases, even slaveholders themselves, to abolish slavery. On the other side of this debate were those like Brown, who believed that only struggle would overthrow slavery.

The Role of Black Abolitionists

While the contribution of Garrison and the American Anti-Slavery Society to the "second generation" of abolitionists was fundamental, it may be more correct to assign the pivotal role to David Walker, who published his antislavery *Appeal* in 1829.[9] A clothing dealer in Boston, Walker was also an agent for *Freedom's Journal*, the first Black newspaper in the United States. His writings share many of the themes later developed by other nineteenth-century Black intellectuals. "We are the most degraded, wretched, and most abject set of beings that ever lived since the world began," wrote Walker. He targeted whites, like Thomas Jefferson, who spoke against slavery, but were themselves slaveholders and held that Black people were inferior to whites:

> For let no one of us suppose that the refutations which have been written by our white friends are enough—they are *whites*—we are *Blacks*. We, and the world wish to see the charges of Mr. Jefferson refuted by the Blacks *themselves*, according to their chance; for we must remember that what the whites have written respecting this subject, is other men's labors, and did not emanate from the Blacks.[10]

Walker named four factors for the condition of Blacks: slavery, ignorance, "the preachers of Jesus Christ," and the influence of the American Colonization Society—an organization of whites that sought to repatriate Blacks to Africa.[11] Walker argued that Blacks had to fight for economic and political rights in the United States and therefore should oppose schemes of emigration.

> Let no man of us budge one step, and let slave-holders come to beat us from our country. America is more our country, than it is the whites.... The greatest riches in all America have arisen from our blood and tears—and will they drive us from our property and homes, which we have earned with our *blood*?[12]

Walker died in August 1830, soon after the publication of the third edition of his *Appeal*. Copies of his tract were found in Georgia, Virginia, and Louisiana.[13] Although his public career was short, his influence was large. The abolitionist movement was to receive its most consistent support from Blacks, and Black abolitionists weighed in on all the central questions in the movement discussed above. But they also brought particular insight to the questions of the relations of Blacks and whites in the movement and to the movement's position on emigration to Africa.

Henry Highland Garnet, another Black abolitionist, was deeply influenced by Walker's ideas. Born a slave in Maryland in 1816, he escaped with his family to New York City. Garnet's address at the National Negro Convention held in Buffalo, New York, in 1843, echoed the sentiments of Walker:

> Brethren arise, arise! Strike for your lives and liberties. Now is the day and the hour. Let every slave throughout the land do this, and the days of slavery are numbered. You cannot be more oppressed than you have been—you cannot suffer greater cruelties than you have already. *Rather die freemen*

than live to be slaves. Remember that you are four millions!...
Let your motto be resistance! resistance! resistance![14]

Like Walker, Garnet stressed Black resistance to slavery.
His evolving political perspective illustrated in microcosm all
the key questions the movement confronted. He helped bring
to a head the debate among Black abolitionists concerning
the question of moral suasion and armed resistance. Garnet, like other Black nationalists after him, initially opposed
schemes of separation like the proposals to emigrate to Africa. "America is my home, my country, and I have no other,"
he explained in 1848.[15] Yet Garnet was to change his position,
as did several other Black abolitionists, on emigrationism
after 1850.

Martin R. Delany's *The Condition, Elevation, Emigration,
and Destiny of the Colored People of the United States* is widely
considered as the first manifesto of Black nationalism in the
United States, making Delany "the founding father of Black
nationalism."[16] A Harvard-trained physician, Delany's early
political activity included a stint in 1846 as coeditor of Frederick Douglass' abolitionist newspaper, *North Star*, and as a pas-
sionate opponent of the American Colonization Society. The
American Colonization Society—with a Congressional appro-
priation of $100,000 in 1819—purchased a strip of land three
miles wide and 36 miles long on the west coast of Africa. This
strip of land was named Liberia—and its capital was named
Monrovia, in honor of then-president James Monroe. However, with the passage in 1850 of the Fugitive Slave Act (FSA),
which gave slaveholders the right to recapture escaped slaves
even in free states and territories, Delany grew quite pessimistic about the prospects for either coexistence with whites
or for abolishing slavery itself. The FSA created a force of federal commissioners empowered to pursue fugitive slaves in

any state and return them to their owners. No statute of limitations applied, so that even those slaves who had been free for many years could be (and were) returned.

"We love our country," Delany wrote in 1852, "dearly love her, but she doesn't love us—she despises us, and bids us be gone, driving us from her embraces."[17] In a similar vein, he wrote to William Lloyd Garrison, "I am not in favor of caste, nor a separation of the brotherhood of mankind, and would as willingly live among white men as Black, if I had an *equal possession and enjoyment* of privileges; but shall never be reconciled to live among them, subservient to their will—existing by mere sufferance, as we, the colored people, do, in this country."[18]

Delany became the most vocal advocate of emigrationism among Black abolitionists. He continued to oppose the American Colonization Society's attempt to colonize Liberia, which he referred to as "a poor miserable mockery—a burlesque on a government,"[19] and instead argued for resettlement in the Western Hemisphere—including such locations as Canada, the West Indies, Central and South America.[20]

Delany went further than Garnet in developing a Black nationalist approach and aims for the movement. He argued at an 1854 national emigration convention (an outgrowth of the pro-emigration Negro Convention Movement established in 1817):

> Let it then be understood, as a great principle of political economy, that no people can be free who themselves do not constitute an essential part of the *ruling element* of the country in which they live.... The liberty of no man is secure who controls not his own political destiny.... A people, to be free, must necessarily be *their own rulers*: that is, *each individual* must, in himself, embody the *essential ingredient*—so to speak—of the *sovereign principle* which composes the *true*

basis of his liberty.[21]

The struggle for Black freedom, argued Delany, was not "a question of rich against the poor, nor the common people against the higher classes," that is, a class struggle, "but a question of white against Black—every white person, by legal right, being held superior to a Black or colored person."[22]

Delany's call for Black emancipation aimed at creating a Black elite to replace a society ruled by whites. Foreshadowing the type of appeal that Booker T. Washington later became known for, Delany argued: "Let our young men and women prepare themselves for usefulness, trading, and other things of importance.... Educate them for the store and the country house...to do everyday practical business."[23] By 1860, Delany's battle cry had become "Africa for the Africans."[24]

Delany was also aware that any colonization of Africa would have to involve the assistance or support of one of the "Great Powers." Delany looked to Britain and France for assistance in the colonization project. "The National Council shall appoint one or two special commissioners, to England [and] France, to solicit...the necessary outfit and support."[25] After all, he argued, Africa was ready for colonization: "The land is ours—there it lies with inexhaustible resources; let us go and possess it."[26]

Douglass and Radical Abolitionism

The preeminent Black abolitionist of this period was Frederick Douglass. More than any other abolitionist of the time, Douglass tied the antislavery struggle to a general struggle against oppression in all forms; and, unlike the emigrationists, Douglass saw the Black struggle as being rooted in the United States.

Douglass was born a slave in 1817. At age sixteen, he recounts in his autobiography, he resisted a whipping by the plantation's overseer. "I was a changed being after that fight," he wrote. "I had reached the point at which I was not *afraid to die*. This spirit made me a freeman in *fact*, though I still remained a slave in *form*. When a slave cannot be flogged, he is more than half free."[27] Douglass escaped in 1838, and soon became active with William Lloyd Garrison's abolitionist group. Over the next ten years, he became the most renowned Black abolitionist in the United States. During this period, on most questions, Douglass lined up squarely with Garrison. Like Garrison, he strongly objected to Henry Garnet's 1843 call for insurrection, arguing it would only end in disaster. Likewise, he opposed all plans for emigration. Following Garrison, Douglass argued that because the U.S. constitution was a pro-slavery document, holding office or participating in electoral activity would be immoral and sanctify slavery itself.

Nevertheless, differences between Garrison and Douglass had already emerged. In 1847, Douglass had started publication of his own newspaper, the *North Star*, despite Garrison's objections. "The man who has suffered the wrong is the man to demand redress," argued Douglass. "He who has endured the cruel pangs of Slavery is the man to advocate Liberty."[28] Other differences of substance emerged. Douglass began to reassess the tenets of Garrisonian abolitionism. He soon came to reject the idea that nonviolent resistance could end slavery. He told a Boston audience in 1849 that he would "welcome the intelligence to-morrow, should it come, that the slaves had risen in the South, and that the sable arms which had been engaged in beautifying and adorning the South were engaged in spreading death and devastation there."[29] Douglass also came to reject some of Garrison's views on politics and political activity. Instead of the wholesale rejection of political activity advocated by Garrison, Douglass came to see political action as another arena of action for the abolitionist movement, describing such action as a "legitimate and powerful means for abolishing slavery."[30] Indeed, he came to believe that political action was necessary, and that the federal government had a responsibility to eradicate slavery. He also argued against Garrison's slogan of "No union with slaveholders." For abolitionists to push for a secession from the slave states would deprive slaves of their allies and slavery would continue even if the north had washed its hands of it, Douglass argued.[31] Until 1849, Douglass claimed to be loyal to Garrison's credo. But it was clear that Douglass had begun to shake off some of the limitations of Garrison's politics. In 1851, he made public his break with Garrison on several key questions at the annual convention of the Anti-Slavery Society.

Douglass also extended his analysis of how racism was used to divide white from Black in the slaveholding South to the North, as well. Garrison and his leading followers tended to be upper-middle-class Northerners who reflected the outlook of their class. Their elitist views left little room for a broader critique of American society, much less any sympathy for working people or their organization. In contrast, Douglass grasped the class dynamic of racism in U.S. society. The "poor laboring white man" was "almost as much a slave as the Black slave himself," Douglass argued. Explaining this view, he added, "The white slave had taken from him by indirection what the Black slave had taken from him directly and without ceremony. Both were plundered by the same plunderers."[32]

Though Douglass had considerable illusions about Republicanism, he shared none of Garrison's glorification of Northern society, had none of his sympathy for the very rich, and saw clearly how the North was complicit in the slavery of the South. He put the case most forcefully in a speech on the Fourth of July, delivered in 1852:

What, to the American slave, is your 4th of July? I answer; a day that reveals to him, more than all other days in the year, the gross injustice and cruelty to which he is the constant victim. To him, your celebration is a sham; your boasted liberty, an unholy license; your national greatness, swelling vanity; your sounds of rejoicing are empty and heartless; your denunciations of tyrants, brass fronted impudence; your shouts of liberty and equality, hollow mockery; your prayers and hymns, your sermons and thanksgivings, with all your religious parade and solemnity, are, to him, mere bombast, fraud, deception, impiety, and hypocrisy—a thin veil to cover up crimes which would disgrace a nation of savages. There is not a nation on the earth guilty of practices more shocking and bloody than are the people of the United States, at this very hour.[33]

Douglass' denunciation of the hypocrisy of U.S. "democracy" did not, however, lead him to join forces with those who supported emigration as a solution to slavery and racism. Douglass opposed the idea of emigrationism as well as the emphasis that Garnet and Delany put on race. He once said that he thanked God for making him a man, whereas Delany thanked God for making him a Black man.[34] Douglass believed that slavery was an aberration from the revolutionary traditions that the United States was founded upon. Douglass had illusions about what could be achieved under bourgeois democracy. He served in a number of government posts after the Civil War even while the U.S. government stepped back from granting Blacks full citizenship. But in the pre-Civil War years, his politics were considerably more consistent and clearer than those of the early Black nationalists.

This short review of debates in the abolitionist movement, particularly among Black abolitionists, allows us to make several observations about the character of the Black struggle and Black nationalism. These themes would recur over the next century in subsequent movements for Black civil rights. First, the political paths that both Garnet and Delany took demonstrated that Black nationalism was not primarily a reflection of their primary aspirations or a reflection of any material base for a Black nation. Rather, their adoption of sep-aratism was a *reaction* to white racism. When the prospect for Black and white unity seemed possible in fighting racism, as in the Civil War period, both abandoned their emigration-ist positions. With the defeat of Reconstruction in 1877 (see Chapter Four), they returned to separatist politics. Similarly, the only period when Frederick Douglass flirted with emigra-tionism was at the lowest point following the defeat of Recon-struction, when he considered the possibilities of any other form of struggle to be very dim.[35]

Second, separatism and assimilation have to be seen as the expression of the contradictory position in which the small Black elite under slavery found itself. This class aspired to fully become part of American capitalism, and therefore im-pelled it to seek assimilation, but the existence of slavery and racism placed severe limits on this process, forcing the elite into a separatist position. Finally, as Wilson Moses points out, in the pre-Civil War period there was no clear-cut distinction between Black nationalism and assimilation. Nationalists like Delany "were dedicated to Christianizing and 'civilizing' the African continent and actively solicited the support of whites to accomplish this goal. Avowed integrationists, like Doug-lass, were willing to participate in all-Black institutions, and defended their right to do so."[36]

Revolutionary Abolitionism

Despite its often on-target criticisms of the largely white-led abolitionist movement, the politics that Garnet and Delany represented didn't offer a militant strategy to confront slavery and racism. On this score, Douglass, the avowed integrationist, was in the vanguard. In breaking with the Garrisonian politics of "moral suasion," Douglass came to the conclusion that armed force would be necessary to rid the country of slavery. Above all, throughout his career Douglass never lost sight of the importance of struggle. It was this commitment to struggle that led Douglass to see *both* the necessity of Black self-activity *and* the need for unity with whites who sought to fight slavery. He thus moved from advocacy of moral suasion to advocating armed resistance. "The slaveholder has been tried and sentenced," he declared in 1857. "He is training his own executioners."[37]

One of the abolitionists who influenced Douglass to question the idea of nonresistance, or moral suasion, was John Brown. Brown's conviction that slavery was actually a state of war made an impression on Douglass. Douglass writes of Brown, "[T]hough a white gentleman, is in sympathy with a Black man, and as deeply interested in our cause, as though his own had been pierced with the iron of slavery."[38]

John Brown stood out as a white abolitionist who was never charged with racism. Writes Quarles, "Brown's relationships with Negroes had been close, continuous, and on a peer basis.... Apparently no Negro who ever knew Brown ever said anything in criticism of his attitude or behavior toward colored people. Brown's attitude toward slavery and his grim and forceful response to it were shaped by many things, of which his own personal experiences with Negroes was not the least."[39]

Brown had distinguished himself as an antislavery fighter in the 1850s in Kansas, where a civil war between pro-slavery and antislavery forces raged in the decade before the outbreak of the nationwide Civil War. The attempt of Brown and eighteen other armed men to capture the federal armory in Harpers Ferry, Virginia, with the intent of arming slaves in the South for an insurrection, was certainly the boldest blow struck against slavery before the Civil War. Although Douglass demurred from participation in the failed 1859 raid, he defended Brown, even after Brown and his comrades were executed for treason and insurrection:

> Did John Brown fail? He certainly did fail to get out of Harpers Ferry before being beaten down by United States soldiers; he did fail to save his own life, and to lead a liberating army into the mountains of Virginia. But he did not go to Harpers Ferry to save his life.
>
> The true question is, Did John Brown draw his sword against slavery and thereby lose his life in vain? And to this I answer ten thousand times, No! No man fails, or can fail, who so grandly gives himself and all he has to a righteous cause. No man, who in his hour of extremest need, when on his way to meet an ignominious death, could so forget himself as to stop and kiss a little child, one of the hated race for whom he was about to die, could by any possibility fail.
>
> Did John Brown fail? Ask Henry A. Wise in whose house less than two years after, a school for the emancipated slaves was taught.
>
> Did John Brown fail? Ask James M. Mason, the author of the inhuman fugitive slave bill, who was cooped up in Fort Warren, as a traitor less than two years from the time that he stood over the prostrate body of John Brown.
>
> Did John Brown fail? Ask Clement C. Vallandingham, one other of the inquisitorial party; for he too went down in the tremendous whirlpool created by the powerful hand of this bold invader. If John Brown did not end the war that ended slavery, he did at least begin the war that ended slavery. If we look over the dates, places and men, for which this honor is claimed, we shall find that not Carolina, but Virginia—not Fort Sumter, but Harpers Ferry and the arsenal—not Col. Anderson, but John Brown, began the war that ended Amer-

ican slavery and made this a free Republic. Until this blow was struck, the prospect for freedom was dim, shadowy and uncertain. The irrepressible conflict was one of words, votes and compromises.

When John Brown stretched forth his arm the sky was cleared. The time for compromises was gone—the armed hosts of freedom stood face to face over the chasm of a broken Union—and the clash of arms was at hand. The South staked all upon getting possession of the Federal Government, and failing to do that, drew the sword of rebellion and thus made her own, and not Brown's, the lost cause of the century.[40]

CHAPTER THREE

The Civil War

The election of Abraham Lincoln, the Republican Party's presidential candidate in 1860, was greeted with horror by the Southern slaveholders. For the Southern ruling class, a Republican presidency was a "revolution" threatening "to destroy their social system," above all slavery.[1] Rather than submit to Republican rule, they decided to secede from the Union. In February 1861, a convention of slave owners established the Confederate States of America (CSA), and elected a provisional government. The secession of eleven slave states precipitated a crisis that led to the outbreak of war between North and South.

The Civil War was a titanic four-year struggle that had a profound effect on the United States. Often described as the "first modern war," it completed the bourgeois revolution[2] of 1776. The war abolished slavery and "as a continuation of the bourgeois revolution begun during the Revolution/founding period, swept away those obstacles to pure market relations in the North and West and established the dominance of the cash nexus in social relations, making this perhaps the most purely bourgeois of all countries."[3] The revolutionary nature of the war stemmed from the increasingly irreconcilable coexistence of Southern slave labor and an expanding Northern capitalism based on free wage labor. "The present struggle between the South and the North," wrote Karl Marx shortly after the outbreak of war, "is...nothing but a struggle between two social systems, the system of slavery and the system of free labor. The struggle has broken out because the two systems can no longer live peacefully side by side on the North American continent. It can only be ended by the victory of one system or the other."[4]

These two systems, of free labor and slave labor, had co-existed for decades. Far from being incompatible, they had been a necessary complement to one another. Capitalist development in the North depended on a slave South, which in turn fuelled the growth of slavery. "Northern merchants helped finance and export the Southern cotton crop" to the British textile industry. British capitalists provided credit for Northern exports and for imports of British-made manufactured goods.[5] But there was a growing contradiction between the two economies. The rapid growth of Northern industry and agriculture, combined with large-scale immigration, transformed the North and its relation to the South. A new coalition of forces emerged, united in its opposition to the expansion of slavery. Composed of industrial capitalists, Midwest farmers, workers, and artisans, this coalition formed the basis of the new Republican Party. The chief slogan the Republicans advanced was "free soil, free labor," embodying the aspiration of a modern economy based on widespread property ownership ("free soil") and artisanal enterprise ("free labor"). The main impediment to achieving either of these goals, argued the Republicans, was the slaveocracy's domination of government and the continued expansion of slavery into new territories. For Northern capital, slavery had become an impediment to capitalist development. Consolidation of political and economic power required limiting the further expansion of slavery.

The South was economically backward compared to the North, but its political power was greater. Of sixteen presidents elected between 1788 and 1848, half were Southern slaveholders.[6] The slaveholders' power stemmed from the Constitution's provision that three-fifths of the disenfranchised slave population would be counted in determining a state's representation in Congress and the allocation of electoral votes.

The economic divergence between North and South grew more stark in the decades leading up to the war. As the historian James McPherson describes it, "More striking was the growing contrast between farm and nonfarm occupations in the two sections. In 1800, 82 percent of the Southern labor force worked in agriculture compared with 68 percent in the free states. By 1860 the Northern share had dropped to 40 percent, while the Southern proportion had actually increased slightly, to 84 percent."[7] When it came to race, the demographics were clear: "[T]he most crucial demographic difference between North and South resulted from slavery. Ninety-five percent of the country's Black people lived in the slave states, where Blacks constituted one-third of the population in contrast to their 1 percent of the Northern population."[8]

The North-South conflict also expressed the growing competition between American and British capitalism. On the eve of the Civil War, the South's output of cotton amounted to three-quarters of the world's output. Cotton was the country's most important export and source of foreign exchange, with most of the profits from shipping, warehousing, and manufacturing ending up in Northern hands. During the cotton boom of the 1850s, Southern planters demanded the South build its own fleet to ship cotton directly to England so it wouldn't have to depend on Yankee shippers.[9] The fortunes of the Southern ruling class were therefore completely tied to British, not Northern, capitalism. Northern capital could only fully establish itself by imposing its interests over those of the South. Above all, this meant breaking the slaveholders' control of the state.

The Republican Party was able to unite otherwise antagonistic classes against the slaveocracy. The Republican Party, however, did not oppose slavery as such—only its expansion. Lincoln's 1860 election campaign repeatedly stressed that the Republican Party did not wish to end slavery or grant social and political rights to Blacks. Lincoln's views are representative of the Republican Party's approach: "I will say then, that I am not, nor ever have been in favor of bringing about in any way the social and political equality of the white and Black races—that I am not nor ever have been in favor of making voters or jurors of Negroes, nor of qualifying them to hold office, nor to intermarry with white people."[10] So long as there were Blacks in the United States, he added, "there must be the position of superior and inferior, and I as much as any other man am in favor of having the superior position assigned to the white race."[11] "All I ask for the Negro," Lincoln explained, "is that if you do not like him, let him alone. If God gave him but little, that little let him enjoy."[12]

Lincoln's initial response to secession included several attempts to avoid an escalation of the conflict. He was especially concerned to maintain the loyalty of the border slave states, insisting that restoration of the Union could be achieved without any challenge to slavery. Indeed, as historian Cedric Robinson writes,

> As late as August 1862, in a meeting with Black leaders, Lincoln appealed for support for voluntary emigration. "Not a single man of your race is made the equal of a single man of ours...."

The abolitionists were sorely disappointed in the president. Wendell Phillips, perhaps the leading white abolitionist orator, who had cautiously championed Lincoln's election ("not an abolitionist, hardly an antislavery man, Mr. Lincoln consents to represent an antislavery idea"), now characterized him as "stumbling, halting, prevaricating, irresolute, weak, besotted."[13]

In August 1862, Horace Greeley, the editor of the *New York Tribune*,[14] wrote to Lincoln, "We think you are strangely and disastrously remiss."[15] In a public reply, Lincoln explained, "My paramount object in this struggle *is* to save the Union, and is *not* either to save or to destroy slavery.... What I do about slavery and the colored race, I do because I believe it helps to save the Union."[16]

Since the 1960s, many historians have clearly exposed the myth that Lincoln "fought the war to free the slaves," stressing his belief in colonization, his desire to conciliate with the South, and his attempts to limit the scope of the conflict. This is indeed a necessary critical corrective to the mythic view of Lincoln. By the same token, however, many of these historians fail to grasp the revolutionary character of the Civil War and the period of Reconstruction that followed it. A revisionist effort that began as a challenge to the dominant racist histories of the Civil War is today used to justify pessimistic and conservative ideas. As Eric Foner argues, historians who began by challenging the portrayals of Reconstruction as a "tragic era," now portray

change in the post–Civil War years as fundamentally "superficial." Persistent racism, these postrevisionist scholars argued, had negated efforts to extend justice to Blacks, and the failure to distribute land prevented the freedmen from achieving true autonomy and made their civil and political rights all but meaningless. In the 1970s and 1980s, a new generation of scholars, Black and white, extended this skeptical view to virtually every aspect of the period. Recent studies of Reconstruction politics and ideology have stressed the "conservatism" of Republican policymakers, even at the height of Radical influence.... Summing up a decade of writing, C. Vann Woodward observed in 1979 that historians now understood "how essentially nonrevolutionary and conservative Reconstruction really was."[17]

Such interpretations of the Civil War and Reconstruction downplay the significance and impact of these events, and crucially dismiss the possibility of any outcome other than the one that occurred. But the importance of this period is precisely that it showed that racism was not immutable and that ideas can change rapidly in periods of social upheaval. Lincoln, for example, was forced to move left during the course of the war, much as Oliver Cromwell and Maximilien Robespierre did during the English and French Revolutions. As James McPherson describes Lincoln, "Although it may seem like an oxymoron, Lincoln can best be described as a conservative revolutionary. That is, he wanted to conserve the Union as the revolutionary heritage of the founding fathers. Preserving this heritage was the *purpose* of the war; all else became a means to achieve this end."[18]

Karl Marx's assessment of the situation was astute. Describing Lincoln as "a first-rate, *second-rate* man," Marx wrote, "All Lincoln's acts appear like the mean pettifogging conditions which one lawyer puts to his opposing lawyer. But this does not alter their historic content.... The events over there [the United States] are a world upheaval."[19] An assault on slavery was the inevitable precondition for a Union victory. "Events themselves," he wrote in 1861, "drive to the promulgation of the decisive slogan—emancipation of the slaves."[20]

That "events themselves" forced the war to take on the

character it did was admitted by Lincoln himself: "I claim not to have controlled events, but confess plainly that events have controlled me."[21] A number of factors made emancipation the key question of the war. The role of slaves in the Southern economy was decisive. Summing up the views of both sides at the start of the war, historian Cedric Robinson writes:

> The majority of the civilian and military leaders on both sides expected a quick, three-month conflict. They antic- ipated no major battles, rather a few decisive skirmishes that would demonstrate the cause of secession as being too tenuous militarily (as loyalists anticipated) or the Union as without the resources or resolve to end the rebellion (as Southerners hoped). That the war extended into a pro- tracted struggle spelled the end of only one side, however: the slave regime was undone. Being a slave regime, con- stantly on alert for threats from the domestic enemy, the white South had the advantage in military readiness and the habit of mobilizing armed militias. But they mistakenly imagined that they could call up a good portion of the white males without disrupting the economy; that Black coerced labor would release sufficient free laborers and small farm- ers for war duties; that their human property would manage the production of staple crops, construct fortifications, trans- port supplies, and serve as support in the battle camps; that slaves would go on, according to the Southern racist mantra, being dependent, loyal, and simple.[22]

Almost any comparison of forces appeared to favor an easy victory for the North. Its population numbered twenty-two million, compared with nine million in the Confederacy, four million of them slaves. In every measure of economic strength, the North also proved dominant. But the North's initially half-hearted prosecution of the war—and above all its refusal to appeal to the four million slaves behind enemy lines—soon led to significant losses and demoralization. Radical elements within the Republican Party began to urge the war be turned into a war for emancipation, and raised the demand that Blacks be brought into the Union Army. Reluctantly at first, and later more decisively, Lincoln began to move toward abolition.

In September 1862, Lincoln issued a preliminary Emancipation Proclamation. It was conceived primarily as a military move. It gave the South four months to stop rebelling and threatened to emancipate their slaves if the Confederates continued to fight. At the same time, it promised to leave slavery untouched in states that came over to the North.

Of course, the Confederacy did not surrender. In response, Lincoln lifted the four-month time limit and issued the Emancipation Proclamation of January 1, 1863. The proclamation read in part: "That on the 1st day of January, AD 1863, all persons held as slaves within any State or designated part of a State the people thereof shall then be in rebellion against the United States shall be then, thenceforward and forever free."[23] Even at this time, the Emancipation Proclamation was essentially a military measure. In the words of radical historian Richard Hofstadter, the proclamation had "all the moral grandeur of a bill of lading. It contained no indictment of slavery, but simply based emancipation on 'military necessity.'" This led a cynical *London Spectator* writer to put it bluntly: "The principle is not that a human being cannot justly own another, but that he cannot own him unless he is loyal to the U.S."[24]

The Proclamation did not affect 450,000 slaves in border states loyal to the Union (Delaware, Kentucky, Maryland, and Missouri), or in Southern territory occupied by the Union Army (in Louisiana, Tennessee, Virginia), but it declared the more than three million Southern slaves "are henceforth and shall be free."[25] The practice of returning escaped slaves to their former owners was halted, and slaves joined the Union

Army in the thousands. By the war's end, 189,000 slaves had served in the army, out of a force of 2.1 million.[26]

The new policy transformed the course of the war. "A single Negro regiment would have a remarkable effect on Southern nerves," Marx predicted correctly. "A war of this kind must be conducted on revolutionary lines while the Yankees have thus far been trying to conduct it constitutionally."[27]

But by 1863 Lincoln was clearly tying the Emancipation Proclamation to the North's military success. "My enemies pretend I am now carrying on this war for the sole purpose of abolition," Lincoln wrote in 1863. "So long as I am President, it shall be carried on for the sole purpose of restoring the Union. But no human power can subdue this rebellion without the use of the emancipation policy, and every other policy calculated to weaken the moral and physical forces of the rebellion. Freedom has given us two hundred thousand men raised on Southern soil. It will give us more yet. Just so much it has subtracted from the enemy."[28]

The transformation of the Civil War into a war of emancipation was greeted enthusiastically by Blacks, abolitionists, and the nascent socialist movement. Frederick Douglass took to the pages of his newspaper, *Douglass Monthly*, to urge Blacks to enlist in the Union Army:

> The chance is now given you to end in a day the bondage of centuries, and to rise in one bound from social degradation to the place of common equality with all other varieties of men. Remember Denmark Vesey of Charleston—remember Nathaniel Turner of Southampton, remember Shields Green, and Copeland, who followed noble John Brown, and fell as glorious martyrs for the cause of the slave—Remember that in a contest with oppression, the Almighty has no attribute which can take sides with oppressors. The case is before you. This is our golden opportunity.[29]

Blacks proved themselves to be able and brave fighters. In fact, James McPherson concludes that the North would not have won the war as quickly as it did without Black soldiers— and it may not have won the war at all.[30] The courage and fighting spirit of the Black soldiers also affected their white comrades. A surgeon in a Black artillery regiment, writing to his wife, spoke of how the term "rabid Abolitionist" used to be considered an insult. "[B]ut now, if you will substitute the adjective earnest, which is all that was meant *then* by *'Rabid'* it is a title of honor. *We are all Abolitionists*, unless we are copperheads, which is *now* a contemptuous epithet."[31]

But despite the great advances made in the fight against racism, its legacy also found expression in brutal race riots. Needing to replenish the ranks of the Union Army, the federal government initiated the military draft in 1863. In response to the enforcement of conscription in July 1863, thousands of New York workers, most of them Irish immigrants and their descendents, protested by launching a virtual insurrection and pogrom against Blacks. Tired of the war and its financial burden, they were hostile to conscription. But their hostility to the rich, who could buy a deferment for $300, was combined with anti-Black hatred. The five-day riot was one of the most violent and graphic examples of the hold racist ideas exercised, even among groups of workers who were themselves the victims of racist pogroms. The New York riots against Blacks in 1863 left more than 100 dead.[32]

That racism persisted should not blind us to how the victory of the North over the South smashed the hideous system of slavery and marked a dramatic advance for freedom and equality. The key to the Civil War was the role that the Black slaves themselves played in achieving their own emancipation. As W. E. B. Du Bois puts it in his seminal work, *Black Reconstruction*:

The Negro became in the first year contraband of war; that is, property belonging to the enemy and valuable to the invader. And in addition to that, he became, as the South quickly saw, the key to Southern resistance. Either these four million laborers remained quietly at work to raise food for the fighters, or the fighters starved. Simultaneously, when the dream of the North for man-power produced riots, the only additional troops that the North could depend on were 200,000 Negroes, for without them, as Lincoln said, the North could not have won the war.

But this slow, stubborn mutiny of the Negro slave was not merely a matter of 200,000 Black soldiers and perhaps 300,000 other Black laborers, servants, spies and helpers. Back of this half million stood 3 1/2 million more. Without their labor the South would starve. With arms in their hands, Negroes would form a fighting force which could replace every single Northern white soldier fighting listlessly and against his will with a Black man fighting for freedom.[33]

The surrender of Southern forces in 1865 spelled the end of slavery. But another war broke out, North and South, to determine the position freed Blacks would now occupy.

CHAPTER FOUR

Reconstruction and Populism

The Civil War destroyed slavery in the South, but it did not immediately establish a new political and economic order in its place. The next three decades witnessed an intense, often violent, political struggle to determine the character of the South. In the end, white supremacy was reestablished, but this was not a foregone conclusion.

Today, it is widely accepted that all whites had an interest in disfranchising the newly freed Black population and that poor whites provided the main impetus for reaction. C. Vann Woodward argues "the escalation of lynching, disfranchisement and proscription reflected concessions to the white lower class" on the part of the upper class.[1] Restricting Black rights was a precondition for lower-class whites winning rights for themselves, according to Woodward. "The barriers of racial discrimination mounted in direct ratio with the tide of political democracy among whites."[2] Various left-wing academics share the basic thrust of this analysis, and therefore draw the inevitable conclusion that racist ideology among the mass of whites was the cause of continued Black oppression.[3] The political conclusion of such an approach is simple: the majority of whites, if not all whites, have a stake in maintaining racism. The prospects for Black and white unity are therefore slim, if not altogether excluded.

This analysis, however, never asks the central questions: Whose interests did white supremacy serve? Why did so many poor whites accept racism? And, if we understand that slavery gave rise to racism, why did racial oppression survive its abolition?

A careful look at the era of Reconstruction shows that there was a significant challenge to racism, and the reimposition of white supremacy was the result of a conscious and sustained campaign by the ruling class. Jack Bloom argues cogently that Reconstruction unfolded in a "revolutionary" period. The Civil War had destroyed the class system of the Old South, unleashing a fight over what type of society would replace it. Many different possibilities for a new racial order clashed. Therefore,

> It was not a foregone conclusion that whites would join in concert against Blacks. White small farmers had long borne their own grudges against the wealthy slaveholders, and the economic squeeze they felt after the Civil War reinforced their anger against the upper class. The newly freed slaves had similar interests. Separately, each group constituted a problem for the planters; together, especially with the support of the federal government, they were a genuine threat to the existence of the landed aristocracy.[4]

The South was devastated by the Civil War. As Eric Foner writes in *Reconstruction:*

> Even apart from the disorganization caused by the end of slavery, however, the widespread destruction of work animals, farm buildings, and machinery, and the deterioration of levees and canals, ensured that the revival of agriculture would be slow and painful. So too did the appalling loss of life.... Thirty-seven thousand Blacks, the great majority from

the South, perished in the Union Army, as did tens of thousands more in contraband camps, on Confederate Army labor gangs, and in disease-ridden urban shanty-towns. Nearly 260,000 men died for the Confederacy—over one-fifth of the South's adult white male population. Many more were wounded, some maimed for life. (Mississippi expended 20 percent of its revenue in 1865 on artificial limbs for Confederate veterans.) The region, moreover, was all but bankrupt, for the collapse of Confederate bonds and currency wiped out the savings of countless individuals and the resources and endowments of colleges, churches, and other institutions.[5]

This was the situation that confronted Andrew Johnson, who assumed the presidency after President Abraham Lincoln's assassination in April 1865. Johnson, a former slaveholder and the only senator from a seceding state to remain loyal to the Union, led a retreat from any notion of Black equality. Johnson was not interested in the plight of the newly emancipated slaves. He appointed provisional governors for the Southern states and conferred a blanket pardon to any former Confederate who took an oath of loyalty to the Union. Wealthy Confederate officials and owners of property valued at more than $20,000 were excluded, but they could apply for individual pardons, which Johnson granted generously.[6] After establishing a new government and acknowledging the illegality of secession and the abolition of slavery, each state could resume its place in the Union. Johnson denied the franchise to Blacks and ordered that former slaves be evicted from plantations they had occupied at the end of the war.

Blacks resisted any policy designed to scale back the full freedom they had been fighting for. When they were forced to sign exploitative labor contracts with employers, Blacks resisted en masse. Writes Cedric Robinson, "the army frequently arrested Blacks striking against the near slavery of labor contracts and used force against Blacks unwilling to surrender land they were now cultivating."[7]

By the summer of 1865, Johnson's direction was clear. Johnson is quoted as saying to the California Senator, John Conness, "White men alone must manage the South," and declaring "This is a country for white men, and by God, so long as I am President, it shall be a government for white men."[8]

Slavery had been the source of wealth and power for the planter class in the antebellum South. After the war, the Southern ruling class had two choices to respond to the labor shortage. It could try to transform the plantation economy using capital-intensive methods of production—as in the case of Britain and the North—and thereby increase the productivity of labor. Or it could impose a sharp limitation on labor mobility—through formal laws and informal practices and terror—to keep workers tied to the land and limit their access to other employment.[9]

Given a free hand, the old Southern ruling class began to re-establish itself. For the planter class, obtaining and controlling cheap labor were crucial. "Black Codes" were enacted to regulate the lives of Blacks, which, insisted a Louisiana Republican, were aimed at "getting things back as near to slavery as possible."[10] The laws required Blacks to possess written evidence of employment. In Mississippi, any Black person who failed to sign a labor contract or left a job could be arrested for vagrancy and forced to work for a white person who would pay the fine. Several states passed laws limiting the right of Blacks to carry firearms. Blacks were also prohibited by law from hunting, fishing, and grazing livestock. Virginia and Georgia made theft of a horse or mule a capital crime. North Carolina even made "the intent to steal a punishable crime, decreeing that all attempted thefts, even if unsuccessful, should be treated as larceny."[11]

A wave of violence was unleashed against Republicans, both Black and white. Among those assassinated in this campaign of terror were Arkansas Congressman James M. Hinds, three members of the South Carolina legislature, and several men who had served in state constitutional conventions.[12] Ex-Confederate Army officers in Pulaski, Tennessee, formed a secret organization called the Ku Klux Klan in 1865, aimed at reestablishing white supremacy. Initially formed as a social club for former Confederate Army officers, it made its true aims clear at its first convention, held in Nashville. The secret order pledged its members to "maintain[ing] the purity of white blood, if we would preserve for it that natural superiority with which God has ennobled it."[13] Summarizing their aims, Eric Foner writes that the Klan "aimed to reverse the interlocking changes sweeping over the South during Reconstruction: to destroy the Republican Party's infrastructure, undermine the Reconstruction state, reestablish control of the Black labor force, and restore racial subordination in every aspect of Southern life."[14]

Blacks and radical Republicans increasingly began to voice opposition to Johnson's accommodation to the South. The split between moderates and radicals deepened. Many Republicans who supported Johnson's program began to urge a different policy. These included Northern capitalists who believed that the end of the war would quickly lead to their control of the South. Expressing this view, General Philip Henry Sheridan wrote in 1865:

> There are without doubt many malcontents in the State of Louisiana and much bitterness but this bitterness is all that is left for these people, there is no power of resistance left, the country is impoverished and the probability is that in two or three years there will be almost a total transfer of landed property, the North will own every Railroad, every steamboat, every large mercantile establishment and everything which requires capital to carry it on.... The slave is

> free and the whole world cannot again enslave him, and with these facts staring us in the face we can well afford to be lenient to this last annoyance, impotent ill feeling.[15]

Sharing Johnson's leniency toward the leaders of the Old South, Sheridan continued, "The poor whites and Negroes of the South have not the intelligence to fill the offices of governors, clerks, judges, etc., and for some time the machinery of State Gov[ernmen]ts must be controlled by the same class of whites as went into the Rebellion against us."[16]

But the plan backfired. Once the Civil War ended, the Republican coalition began to disintegrate. The Democratic Party began to make headway among Northern farmers and layers of workers who had grown disillusioned with the Republicans. The Democrats

> identified the Republican [P]arty as an agent of economic privilege and political centralization, and a threat to individual liberty and the tradition of limited government.... And the party benefited from widespread resentment over the use of troops to suppress strikes, a dramatic illustration of what many workers perceived as the federal government's partiality toward capital....
>
> The potent cry of white supremacy provided the final ideological glue in the Democratic coalition. Sometimes the appeal to race was oblique. The Democratic slogan, "The Union as It Is, the Constitution as It Was," had as its unstated corollary, Blacks as they were—that is, as slaves. Often, it was remarkably direct. "Slavery is dead," the *Cincinnati Enquirer* announced at the end of the war, "the negro is not, there is the misfortune."[17]

The growth in Democratic support in the North was paralleled by its strength in the South—especially as Blacks were not permitted to vote. In state elections in the North, the Democrats polled 45 percent in 1865, 45.4 percent in 1866, and 49.5 percent in 1867.[18] Republicans, fearing a Democratic presidential victory in 1868, began to support granting Blacks the right to vote.

In 1867, the Radical wing of the Republican Party took control of Reconstruction policy. Legislation enfranchising Southern Blacks was enacted; at the same time, 100,000 whites who refused to sign a loyalty oath were disenfranchised and another 200,000 prohibited from holding public office.[19] Radical Reconstruction was a blow to white supremacy and continued the process begun during the Civil War. As W. E. B. Du Bois put it in *Black Reconstruction*: "The inevitable result of the Civil War eventually had to be the enfranchisement of the laboring class, Black and white, in the South. It could not, as the South clamored to make it, result in the mere legalistic freeing of the slaves."[20]

The principal base of support for the Republican Party in the South was among Blacks, but it also began to recruit whites on a class basis. An appeal from the Georgia Republican Party read:

> Poor white man of Georgia, be a man! Let the slaveholding aristocracy no longer rule you. Vote for a constitution which educates your children free of charge; relieves the poor debtor from his rich creditor; allows a liberal homestead for your families; and more than all, places you on a level with those who used to boast that for every slave they were entitled to three-fifths of a vote in congressional representation.[21]

Across the South, the Reconstruction governments experimented with unprecedented social reforms that benefited both Blacks and poor whites. In South Carolina, white farmers armed themselves to prevent foreclosures on their properties.[22] The military governor of the state halted foreclosures and closed debtors prisons. Free public education began to appear in the South for the first time.[23] Thus,

The new Reconstruction governments established conditions that were more favorable to the lower classes, Black and white. They set aside some of the Black Codes, tried to enact a free labor market, established the conditions and to some degree regulated the contracts for labor, and tried to protect Black civil rights. In some cases racial discrimination was specifically forbidden.[24]

Now able to vote, Blacks began to participate in large numbers in local and national elections. Fourteen Blacks were elected to Congress from six Southern states, and two from Mississippi were elected to the Senate.[25] (There was not a single Black representative from the North in Congress until the 1920s, and none in the Senate until the 1960s.) The demand for education also became central to Blacks, especially since 90 percent emerged from slavery illiterate.[26] "By 1869, there were nine thousand teachers in the South instructing the children of ex-slaves. By 1870, there were four thousand three hundred schools with close to 250,000 Black children in attendance."[27]

Despite these important reforms, Radical Reconstruction foundered because it was unable to solve the question of land reform in the South. While seizure and redistribution of plantation land was a chief demand of newly freed slaves and most Radical Republicans, the majority of Republicans would not countenance such an idea. "A division of rich men's lands," argued the *Nation,* "would give a shock to our whole social-political system from which it would hardly recover without the loss of liberty."[28]

The Southern planters also mounted increasing resistance to Reconstruction. In some cases, planters entered the new Republican Party organizations in order to subvert them and render them ineffective. Simultaneously, they launched a campaign against "negro domination" and projected the

Democratic Party as the party of whites in the South. Terror, intimidation, and fraud were used to prevent Blacks from voting. The Ku Klux Klan built its ranks on opposition to the Radicals' political program. As Allen Trelease puts it, "The Klan became in effect a terrorist arm of the Democratic Party, whether the party leaders as a whole liked it or not."[29]

The results of this violence and fraud can be seen in election results around the South. In Louisiana, many parishes with a Black majority went Democratic: In Natchitoches Parish, Louisiana, which had a Black majority, the vote was 2,800 Democratic, 0 Republican in 1878. In another majorityBlack parish, not a single Republican vote was counted for 1878. More than fifty Blacks were killed and dozens driven from their homes during the campaign.[30]

The planters' campaign for "redemption"—home rule without federal intervention—was successful because of the federal government's acquiescence. Reconstruction fell in a dirty deal cut in Washington back rooms over the disputed 1876 presidential election. The Republican-led federal government agreed to withdraw troops from the South if the South agreed to cast its Electoral College votes for the Republican candidate, Rutherford B. Hayes, rather than the Democrat Samuel J. Tilden, who had won the popular vote.

The Republican Party's abandonment of Reconstruction stemmed from two related developments. First, Northern capital had successfully extended its dominance into the South. Massive tracts of public land in the South had made their way into the hands of Northern railroads and speculators. More integrated into the rapidly expanding Northern economy, the Southern ruling class sought reconciliation with the North.

Second, Northern capitalists were eager to put an end to Reconstruction, especially in the wake of the depression of 1873 and a rising level of class struggle. Southern "redeemers" and Northern capitalists closed ranks in fear of a revolt from below. With the Paris Commune still fresh in his mind, a Northern Republican warned readers of the *New York Tribune* on June 21, 1871, that if the poor white population joined with the Black population, "so vast a mass of ignorance would be found that, if combined for any political purpose it would sweep away all opposition the intelligent class might make. Many thoughtful men are apprehensive that the ignorant voters will, in the future, form a party by themselves as dangerous to the interests of society as the communists of France."[31]

The Southern ruling class successfully defeated Reconstruction by using racism, terror, and fraud. The Republican Party's influence declined dramatically as the Democratic Party's hegemony extended. The ruling class no longer owned slaves but the plantation economy was still the cornerstone of the South. Despite an increase in the number of farms in the Deep South between 1860 and 1880, there was also a sharp decrease in the average amount of acres per farming unit.[32] By 1880, every Southern state showed an increase in its large plantations.[33] Sharecroppers, tenants, and farmers now worked the land under a crop-lien system. Typically, sharecroppers would rent several acres of land and pay the planter with a portion of the crop, usually one-half. Under the crop-lien arrangement, farmers lacking cash would sign over part of the coming year's crop in exchange for supplies from the local merchant or banker. Once in debt, few farmers ever escaped.

The South became even more dependent on one cash crop—cotton—than it had been before the Civil War. Farmers were not allowed to borrow seed to grow their own food, thus becoming even more dependent on the merchants, landowners, and bankers. This also led to increased cotton crops, which in turn helped drive prices down by flooding the market with too much product. These conditions not only affected

Black sharecroppers. From 1870, white sharecroppers outnumbered Black sharecroppers. In 1860, Blacks produced 90 percent of the cotton crop; by 1876, the figure had dropped to 60 percent; by 1900, they produced only 40 percent.[34]

The economic transformations that forced Black and white sharecroppers into similar positions also gave rise to efforts to organize them to fight side by side. Reverend J. L. Moore of the Florida Colored Farmers' Alliance argued that "the laboring colored man's interests and the laboring white man's interests are one and the same. Especially is this true at the South."[35]

In an effort to blunt the possibility of unity between Black and white farmers and sharecroppers, some Democrats adopted a different approach to Blacks. By the mid-1870s, the shrill cries of "Black domination" were replaced with attempts to tie Black votes to the Democratic Party. "The best friends of the colored men are the old slaveholders," claimed Wade Hampton, a leader of the "redeemers" in South Carolina. The Democratic Party election platform in Louisiana in 1873 promised "to exercise our moral influence, both through personal advice and personal example, to bring about the rapid removal of all prejudices heretofore existing against the colored citizens of Louisiana."[36] Throughout the South, conservative Democrats appealed for Black votes promising to safeguard Black rights. In Mississippi, politicians created organizations of Black Democrats and set about terrorizing Black Republicans. "They developed the policy of 'fusion,'" writes Jack Bloom, "in which they would divide up offices with the Black Republicans, each promising to support the other, thus leaving out the white farmers. Blacks were often conscious of what was happening, and many approved, feeling that with the defeat of Reconstruction their best hope lay not with the 'poor white trash' but with the 'well-raised gentlemen.'"[37] Disillusioned with the Republican Party, many Blacks concluded that supporting the Democratic Party was the only alternative. Some even argued that the interests of Blacks and ruling-class whites were the same. A Mississippi Black owner of several hundred acres of land and more than a hundred head of cattle, all acquired since the war, told a Senate committee in 1879 that he voted Democratic "because...I thought my interest was to stay with the majority of the country who I expected to prosper with."[38]

The most important challenge to one-party rule emerged in 1890 in the form of the Populist movement. Uniting Black and white farmers and sharecroppers in several Southern states, the Populist movement grew out of a class rebellion that also threatened to recast race relations in the South. The movement grew in the North and South in response to ever-worsening conditions faced by farmers. By the 1890s, farmers were losing their farms at unprecedented rates. Tenancy—families working land that now belonged to merchants, bankers, and speculators—involved one-quarter of all farms in Illinois, Indiana, Iowa, Kansas, Missouri, Nebraska, Ohio, Pennsylvania, and New Jersey. In the South, the figure was closer to half.[39] Farmers needed, in the words of Mary Lease, a Populist leader of Kansas, to "raise less corn and more hell."[40]

> Wall Street owns the country. It is no longer a government of the people, by the people, and for the people, but a government of Wall Street, by Wall Street, and for Wall Street. The great common people of this country are slaves, and monopoly is the master. The West and South are bound and prostrate before the manufacturing East. Money rules, and our Vice-President is a London banker. Our laws are the output of a system which clothes rascals in robes and honesty in rags. The parties lie to us and the political speakers mislead us....
>
> There are 30 men in the United States whose aggregate wealth is over one and one-half billion dollars. There are half

a million looking for work....

We want money, land and transportation.... We will stand by our homes and stay by our firesides by force if necessary, and we will not pay our debts to the loan-shark companies until the Government pays its debts to us. The people are at bay, let the bloodhounds of money who dogged us thus far beware![41]

The Populists aimed much of their fire at the financial and corporate interests that were ruining the farmer. Their program included regulation of the trusts, public ownership of the railroad and communications systems, revision of the lien laws in favor of the farmers, lowered interest rates, and extension of public schools. The Southern Populists were the most radical element in the Populist movement. While the Populists of the Far West and Midwest spoke of reform, Southern Populists talked of revolution. "While this system lasts," argued Georgia Populist Tom Watson, "there are no pure politics, no free men, in Georgia.... It is rotten to the core, and there is no remedy for it but destruction." He later proclaimed: "Men of the country! Let the fires of...this revolution grow brighter and brighter! Pile on the fuel till the forked flames shall leap in wrath around the foul structure of government wrong, shall sweep it from basement to turret, and shall sweep it from the face of the earth!"[42]

Many Southern Populists began to understand how racism had divided poor whites and Blacks and strengthened the ruling class. For the first time in the South, a movement emerged that consciously sought to break down the divisions between Blacks and whites. Tom Watson summed up this sentiment:

The Negro Question in the South has been for nearly thirty years a source of danger, discord, and bloodshed. It is an ever present irritant and menace....

> Never before did two distinct races dwell together under such conditions.
>
> And the problem is, can these two races, distinct in color, distinct in social life, and distinct as political powers, dwell together in peace and prosperity?...
>
> The white tenant lives adjoining the colored tenant. Their houses are almost equally destitute of comforts. Their living is confined to bare necessities. They are equally burdened with heavy taxes. They pay the same high rent for gullied and impoverished land.
>
> They pay the same enormous prices for farm supplies. Christmas finds them both without any satisfactory return for a year's toil. Dull and heavy and unhappy, they both start the ploughs again when "New Year's" passes.
>
> Now the People's Party says to these two men, "You are kept apart that you may be separately fleeced of your earnings. You are made to hate each other because upon that hatred is rested the keystone of the arch of financial despotism that enslaves you both.
>
> "You are deceived and blinded that you may not see how this race antagonism perpetuates a monetary system which beggars both."[43]

"The left [P]opulists," argues Bloom, "formulated and won support for a program unique in Southern history before or since. They proposed to organize a political coalition around the growing similarity of the economic conditions facing both Black and white farmers."[44] For instance, poor whites quickly found that the laws set up to disenfranchise Blacks—like the poll tax—also took the vote away from them.

"Left Populists" made numerous attempts to overcome racial divisions. In Georgia—a state that led all others in the number of lynchings—the Populists announced their intention to "make lynch law odious to the people."[45] This commitment was not simply verbal. In 1892, for example, when the Black Populist Reverend R. S. Doyle was threatened with lynching, two thousand white farmers responded to Tom Watson's appeal for help to defend Doyle. There were also many attempts to involve Blacks in the movement on an equal footing. In Kansas, the Populists ran a Black farmer for state auditor.[46] In many states, Blacks were elected to high offices in the Populist Party. In Georgia, Watson nominated a Black man to serve on the state executive council, and in Texas, a Populist convention elected two Blacks to serve on their state executive.[47]

By 1890, the Southern Alliance (the Southern wing of the Populist movement) claimed three million members, and the Colored Farmers' Alliance claimed more than 1.25 million Black members. The movement became a mass movement that threatened the stability of the Southern regimes. Thousands attended Populist meetings. In the early 1890s, the Populists defeated the Democratic Party in local and statewide elections.[48] "This country," reported the *Weekly Progress* of Charlottesville, Virginia, "is upon the edge of a great revolution...a test of strength is to be made in blood between labor and capital."[49]

For the Southern ruling class, the Populists were a threat to their class rule. And they responded with the same tactics to the Populists as they had to the advocates of Reconstruction. Above all, they resurrected a campaign of violence, fraud, intimidation, and vitriolic race hatred. The cry of "Black domination" was raised once more in an attempt to convince poor whites that racial supremacy was in their interest. Summarizing the period, one historian concludes:

> The agrarian struggles that gripped the South during the 1880s and 1890s were accompanied by widespread violence. As the Farmers Alliance and Populist movements fought to check corporate and banking domination of the South, racists employed terror as a means of retaining power for the

privileged few. Whereas the agrarian radicals would argue
that class was the crucial dividing line in society, the racists
would make white supremacy the all-important issue.[50]

Despite the violence and intimidation, the Populists continued to gain support. In 1894, the Populist candidates garnered almost 1.5 million votes nationally, an increase of 42 percent over 1892.[51] The recession of 1893 only fuelled the movement's growth. The 1896 elections, however, resulted in an abrupt collapse of the Populist movement. Reform Democrats, faced with a crisis, adopted the language of Populism and took a stand for "free silver." This "cheap money" policy was popular with indebted farmers.

The Populist rhetoric of Democratic Party presidential candidate William Jennings Bryan promised to lead "the masses against the classes."[52] But Bryan was by no means a Populist. "The People's Party," he said, was "plotting a social revolution and the subversion of the American Republic." But before suppressing Populists, he wanted their votes.

In the end, many Populists supported Bryan, arguing that a victory for William McKinley, the Republican candidate, would be worse. After McKinley narrowly won the election, the Populist alliance collapsed into warring factions. "Our party, as a party," Watson said, "does not exist any more. The sentiment is still there, the votes are still there, but confidence is gone, and the party organization is almost gone.... The work of many years is washed away and the hopes of many thousands of good people are gone with it."[53]

With the defeat of the Populist challenge, the Southern ruling class used a variety of devices—the poll tax, property qualifications, literacy tests—to sharply reduce the right to vote. Within a decade, Black disfranchisement was almost total in every Southern state. In Louisiana, 130,344 Blacks registered to vote in the 1896 elections. By 1904, it dropped to

1,342. In Alabama, a Black electorate of 100,000 before 1900 was reduced to 3,700.[54]

Disfranchisement was not the only restriction of Black rights. Statutes and laws decreeing segregation—or "Jim Crow" laws—of which there had been few until the 1890s—formally separated Blacks and whites in residentional areas, public parks and hospitals, and on trains and streetcars. They soon became the public rule rather than the exception.[55] Historian Harvey Wasserman writes, "[C]ourtrooms provided separate bibles and schools stored texts separately on the basis of which race used them. Some states passed laws forbidding Blacks and whites to fight, fish, boat, or play dominoes or checkers together."[56]

"How is the white man going to control the government?" asked Mississippi Governor James K. Vardaman in 1907. "The way we do it is to pass laws to fit the white man and make the other people [Blacks] come to them.... If it is necessary every Negro in the state will be lynched; it will be done to maintain white supremacy."[57] Many former Populist leaders joined the call for white supremacy. Tom Watson, who had dropped out of politics after the defeat of 1896, reemerged as a virulent racist and anti-Semite in 1904. Watson now endorsed lynching, arguing that "Black domination" was a "hideous, ominous, national menace." "Lynch law is a good sign," he wrote. "It shows that a sense of justice yet lives among the people."[58] In 1910, Watson bragged that he would no more hesitate to lynch a "nigger" than to shoot a mad dog. Even Booker T. Washington, the archetype of Black accommodation, was rejected by Watson. He closed a diatribe against Washington by saying: "What does Civilization owe the Negro? Nothing! Nothing!! Nothing!!!"[59]

The defeat of Populism and the turn to white supremacy by former Populists is often used to show the limitations of any strategy that seeks to unite Blacks and whites. The racism of poor whites is most often given as the principal cause of the movement's collapse. Robert Allen, for example, argues that "Like most other Southern Populists [Watson] was a white supremacist from the beginning and never really changed. He was willing to exploit the Black vote for the Populist cause."[60] Others argue that the Populist movement itself fuelled racism: "The net result of the Populist movement...seemed to be increased racial hatred and the embitterment of race relations."[61]

These traditional explanations focus on the ideology of poor whites. Michael Reich's objections are pertinent:

> This traditional explanation has two main weaknesses. First, it understates the role of conservatives and other powerful upper-class whites in the evolution of the harshest elements of post-Reconstruction racism....
>
> Second, the traditional explanation misstates the class basis of the disfranchisement movement, attributing a racist zeal to poor white Southerners who in fact were opposed to disfranchisement. Careful statistical analysis of Southern voting patterns by Morgan Kousser has shown that the extremism of the post-Populist era is attributable more to attempts from above by the upper class to prevent another Populist-like movement from arising than from a mass racist movement from below.[62]

The effect of these laws was to reduce both Black and white voting rights.[63] But far from agreeing to disfranchisement, the Populists generally opposed any restrictions on suffrage.

Traditional assessments of Populism fail to understand both the limitations of the movement *and* its tremendous potential. Moreover, they miss the most important point: for the Southern ruling class, the Populist movement was a challenge to their *class* rule. Their aim was to defeat *both* Blacks and whites, and they consciously fostered racism to do so. For all the appeals to the perils of "Black domination," the real danger was spelled out clearly by an editorial in the *Charlotte Observer,* June 27, 1900, hailing "the struggle of the white people of North Carolina to rid themselves of the dangers of the rule of Negroes and the lower class of whites."[64]

Once its position was secure, the ruling class would later allow white participation in primaries as a means of cementing white loyalty to white supremacism. But this "concession" did not represent a threat to their rule. By 1924, the grip of the Southern Democratic Party machines was so complete that only 6 percent of the electorate voted in the presidential election.[65] When Senator Cole Blease of South Carolina learned that Calvin Coolidge, the Republican candidate for president, had received just over 1,000 votes in South Carolina in 1924, he exclaimed, "I do not know where he got them. I was astonished to know that they were cast and shocked to know they were counted."[66]

Some have argued that the system of job segregation adopted in several Southern states was a direct benefit to whites. But the creation of "whites only" jobs by employers was a means to win the loyalty of workers and was only maintained as long as white workers' wages were kept at an absolute minimum. If white workers pressed for higher wages, the employers threatened to replace them with Black workers. As John Coffin, vice-President of the Southern Industrial Convention, explained in 1900, "If labor is reasonable, if labor will work for anything within reason, white labor will dominate the South forever; but they [management] will not submit to such outrages as have been frequently committed by organized labor."[67]

The defeat of Populism marked the victory of white supremacy in the South. Racist ideas—and racist violence— flourished. In June 1894, for example, the *Nation* reported the Right Reverend Hugh Miller Thompson, bishop of Mississippi, as justifying lynching because "the laws are slow and the jails are full."[68] But racism did not only flourish in the South. America's imperialist expansion in the 1890s was justified in terms that mirrored the ideology of Southern white supremacists. Various academics and pseudo-scientists produced studies showing the inferiority of non-whites. R. B. Bean of Johns Hopkins University published an article, "The Negro Brain," in which he concluded, "The Caucasian and the Negro are fundamentally opposite extremes in evolution.... It is useless to try to elevate the Negro by education or otherwise, except in the direction of his natural endowments.... Let them win their reward by diligent service."[69] As the twentieth century dawned, racism once again reigned supreme, North and South.

CHAPTER FIVE

Accommodation, Racism, and Resistance

The defeat of Reconstruction and the Populist movement saw the reemergence of two currents within Black politics: accommodation and emigrationism. The growth of both currents was rooted in the disillusionment that set in after the failure of Radical Reconstruction and represented a *retreat* from the struggle for Black rights in the United States. They both expressed the frustration and aspirations of the small and embattled Black middle class.

The most prominent spokesmen for separatism in this period were Alexander Crummell and Bishop Henry McNeal Turner. Crummell was born free in 1819. "Crummell typified the influences of Victorian civilization on the Black nationalist ideology and gave voice to a common belief that Africans were universally lacking in 'civilization,' which they would have to acquire in order to avoid the fate of the American Indian," writes historian Wilson Moses.[1] To this end, Crummell spent twenty years, from 1853 to 1873, in Liberia, where he found that "Darkness covers the land...human sacrifices, and devil-worship is devouring men, women, and little children."[2]

Unlike other proponents of emigration, Crummell remained aloof from the Civil War struggle and instead toured the United States to recruit missionaries, arguing that Black oppression stemmed from a lack of civilization and Christianity. Crummell dismissed the charge that his ideas were undemocratic: "All historic fact shows that force, that is, authority, must be used in the exercise of guardianship over heathen tribes. Mere theories of democracy are trivial in this case, and can never nullify this necessity."[3] After his return in 1873, Crummell said that it was pointless to fight for rights in the United States. Foreshadowing the views of later separatists, such as Nation of Islam leader Louis Farrakhan, Crummell said, "*What this race needs in this country is POWER....* And that comes from character, and character is the product of religion, intelligence, virtue, family order, superiority, wealth, and the show of industrial forces. THESE ARE THE FORCES WE DO NOT POSSESS."[4] Although he abandoned his attempts at emigrationist colonization in the 1880s, Crummell maintained his elitist contempt toward the mass of Blacks, arguing for the U.S. government to set up a protectorate state in Africa to "civilize" the Africans and urging the creation of a Black elite in the United States to "elevate the most abject and needy race on American soil."[5]

Bishop Henry McNeal Turner did not share Crummell's complete rejection of political struggle. Turner had thrown himself into the struggle for emancipation during the Civil War, and was appointed an army chaplain by President Lincoln in an effort to recruit Black soldiers. In 1868, he was elected to the Georgia state legislature, but when it convened, the first order of business was to disqualify Blacks from office. Denied his seat, Turner made an impassioned speech summing up the disillusionment he shared with thousands of Blacks in the possibility of achieving equality:

Never, in the history of the world, has a man been arraigned before a body clothed with legislative, judicial or executive function, charged with the offence [sic] of being a darker hue than his fellow men.... Cases may be found where men have been deprived of their rights for crimes or misdemeanors; but it has remained for the State of Georgia, in the very heart of the nineteenth century, to call a man before the bar, and there charge him with an act for which he is no more responsible than for the head which he carries upon his shoulders.... We [Blacks] have pioneered civilization here; we have built up your country; we have worked in your fields, and garnered your harvests, for two hundred and fifty years!... We are willing to let the dead past bury its dead; but we ask you now for our RIGHTS.... The Black man cannot protect a country if the country doesn't protect him; and if, tomorrow, a war should arise, I would not raise a musket to defend a country where my manhood was denied.[6]

Addressing the Black state representatives, Turner said, "White men are not to be trusted. They will betray you.... Do not fight for a country that refuses to recognize your rights.... Black men, hold up your heads.... This thing means revolution."[7]

Turner expressed the anger and frustration felt by many Blacks, but like Crummell was unable to provide consistent leadership or direction in the struggle. Turner first turned to advocacy of a return to Africa, leading him to support South Carolina Senator Matthew Butler's bill calling on the federal government to provide funds to transport any Blacks wishing to leave the United States.[8] But Turner found that emigration proved to be a difficult and utopian project, and he subsequently lost interest. Two decades later, when Populism held out the possibility of an interracial alliance of poor farmers, Turner and many other prominent Black Georgians instead supported the Democratic Party in 1892. In doing so, they helped to elect a governor who opposed lynching, but they helped to bolster a Democratic Party that was the principal force behind Black disfranchisement.[9]

Black separatism was one response to the disfranchisement of Southern Blacks. The other response was accommodation to the new order, typified by the rise of Booker T. Washington. Washington emerged as a national figure after his speech at the Cotton States and International Exposition in Atlanta, Georgia, in 1895. Washington's speech began by criticizing efforts to obtain Black equality during Reconstruction. "Ignorant and inexperienced," Washington asserted, "it is not strange that in the first years of our new life we began at the top instead of the bottom; that a seat in Congress or State Legislature was more sought than real estate or industrial skill; that the political convention or stump speaking had more attractions than starting a dairy farm or truck garden."[10] On another occasion, Washington argued that the South provided the most opportunities for Black advancement, and he urged that Blacks develop the skills necessary to advance economically.

Cast down your bucket where you are. Cast it down among the eight million Negroes whose habits you know, whose fidelity and love you have tested.... Cast down your bucket among those people who have, without strikes and labor wars, tilled your fields, cleared your forests, builded your railroads and cities, and brought forth the treasures from the bowels of the earth, and helped make possible this magnificent representation of the progress of the South.... In all things that are purely social we can be as separate as the fingers, yet one as the hand in all things essential to mutual progress.[11]

In an effort to reassure Southern whites, he pledged the complete fidelity of Blacks, whom he described as "the most patient, law-abiding, and unresentful people that the world has seen."[12]

Nor was social and political equality with whites an issue of contention, according to Washington. "The wisest among my race understand that the agitation of questions of social equality is the extremest folly."[13] He added, "As we have proved our loyalty to you in the past, in nursing your children, watching by the sick-bed of your mothers and fathers, and often following them with tear-dimmed eyes to their graves, so in the future, in our humble way, we shall stand by you with a devotion that no foreigner can approach, ready to lay down our lives, if need be, in defense of yours."[14]

Later dubbed the "Atlanta Compromise" by W. E. B. Du Bois, Washington's speech was the clearest exposition of the ideas of Black self-help and self-reliance. Washington's "Atlanta Compromise" speech echoed the move by the U.S. government to enshrine Jim Crow laws. It won Washington great praise from the white establishment. An editorial in the Atlanta *Constitution* noted, "The speech stamps Booker T. Washington as a wise counselor and a safe leader."[15] Then-president Grover Cleveland hailed the speech as a ray of "new hope" for Blacks.[16] Leading capitalists, including Andrew Carnegie, made substantial donations to Washington's Tuskegee Institute. The Institute was founded in 1881, financed through a grant from the Alabama legislature to establish a school to train teachers. Washington became a political boss and unofficial advisor to the government on Black affairs.

Washington's emphasis on industrial and agricultural training for Blacks included an unremitting hostility to trade unionism. As he put it, the Black worker "does not like an organization which seems to be founded on a sort of impersonal enmity to the man by whom he is employed."[17] The Black worker was "not inclined to trade unionism" and "is almost a stranger to strife, lock-outs and labor wars; [he is] labor that is law-abiding, peaceable, teachable...labor that has never been tempted to follow the red flag of anarchy."[18] "[T]he average Negro who comes to the town from the plantations does not understand the necessity or advantage of a labor organization, which stands between him and his employer and aims apparently to make a monopoly of the opportunities for labor."[19]

Blacks could prosper in the South only through hard work, Washington argued. If Blacks were occasionally mobbed and lynched, this was the result of the victim's "dense ignorance."[20]

Washington's policy of accommodation should not simply be seen as one of accommodation to "white America." It wasn't. Washington consciously bowed down to the white political and corporate magnates of the day, but he had quite another attitude when it came to *working-class* whites—and Blacks. Washington demonstrated his loyalty to the employers and hostility to integrated unionism in the Alabama coalminers' strike of 1908. The Alabama United Mine Workers (UMW) had an estimated twelve thousand members, half of whom were Black. In a clear effort to break their union, the United States Steel Corporation refused to renew its contracts and imposed large wage cuts. The miners called for a strike. The conflict was bitter, and the state government, U.S. Steel, and the company's hired thugs joined the state militia to crush the strike. Washington was solidly on the side of the employers; he opposed collective bargaining rights for the miners. The company fired the strikers and hired Black strikebreakers.

Initially, opposition to Washington's ideas among Blacks was limited. Crummell and Turner criticized Washington's accommodation, but they carried little influence, and both also shared many of his ideas about self-help. Although W. E. B. Du Bois would later lead an assault on Washington and the Tuskegee Institute, he was at first sympathetic to Washington's proposals. Less than a week after the Atlanta speech, Du Bois wrote Washington: "Let me heartily congratulate you upon your phenomenal success in Atlanta—it was a word fitly spoken."[21] This was not out of character for Du Bois who in the late 1800s shared many of Washington's assumptions. Du Bois, the leading Black scholar of his generation and first African American to earn a doctorate at Harvard University, lived a separate existence from the majority of African Americans of the time. As one historian writes, "Like Washington...Du Bois combined an enthusiasm for racial solidarity with one for economic development and the middle-class virtues."[22]

Initially Du Bois stressed racial solidarity as the precondition to the development of Black capitalism. "We must cooperate or we are lost. Ten million people who join in intelligent self-help can never be long ignored or mistreated," he asserted.[23] Like many of the leading intellectuals of the day, he accepted the importance of "the race spirit," which he regarded as "the greatest invention for human progress."[24] And while Du Bois was unwilling to acquiesce to the stripping away of all Black political rights, he was willing to compromise on the matter. Thus, he did not object to "legitimate efforts to purge the ballot of ignorance, pauperism and crime," and he conceded that it was "sometimes best that a partially developed people should be ruled by the best of their stronger and better neighbors for their own good," until they were able to fend for themselves.[25]

Du Bois and the NAACP

At first, Du Bois remained aloof from Black politics, supporting Washington's policy of separate Black economic development through industrial education and "non-engagement" in politics. But by 1903, Du Bois and the rest of the Black intelligentsia were compelled to take sides in the dispute between Washington and Boston newspaper editor William Monroe Trotter. A former Harvard classmate of Du Bois, Trotter had long accused Washington of being a "traitor" to Blacks. Trotter exposed Washington's use of his Republican Party connections to build a patronage machine at the expense of the Black masses. At a 1903 Boston meeting of the Washington-sponsored National Negro Business League, Trotter and his supporters heckled Washington. The scuffles that followed were reported with much exaggeration as "the Boston riot" in daily newspapers across the country.

After this incident, it was impossible for Washington to claim a monopoly on Black politics. He faced rising criticism from a number of Black middle-class intellectuals, especially from Du Bois who, in 1906, helped to organize a new activist organization, the Niagara Movement. Where Washington avoided all political struggle, the Niagara Movement plunged into the fight for civil rights, challenging segregation and other forms of racial discrimination.

The Du Bois-Washington debate was not only about abstract principles, as a 1906 anti-Black pogrom in Atlanta showed all too clearly. Hearing about the race riot while in Alabama, Du Bois purchased a shotgun and returned home to protect his family.

"If a white mob had stepped on the campus where I lived, I would have without hesitation have sprayed their guts over the grass," he wrote later.[26] Du Bois' growing concern for the dynamics of antiracist struggle was reflected in his next book, *John Brown*. In an era when scholars portrayed Brown as a deranged terrorist, Du Bois defended the militant abolitionist's violent tactics as progressive and historically necessary.

Washington's access to presidents and the inner circles of the Republican Party had benefited only a tiny elite within the Black middle class. Life for the mass of Black Americans was getting steadily worse—and not only in the Jim Crow South. For example, the race riot of 1908 in Springfield, Illinois, killed six Blacks and resulted in the expulsion of 2,000 Blacks from the city.[27]

The shock of the Springfield pogrom led to the formation of the National Association for the Advancement of Colored People (NAACP) in 1909. The NAACP, with its aims of stopping lynchings, securing voting rights, and ending Jim Crow segregation, was in many ways the antithesis of the Washington program. Du Bois folded the Niagara Movement into the NAACP. By 1910, Du Bois was probably the best-known Black leader in America after Washington. He was the only Black member of the interracial NAACP when the civil rights organization was formed. Giving up his academic career, he moved to New York to edit the organization's newspaper, the *Crisis*.

The election of Democratic President Woodrow Wilson in 1912 cut off Washington from his source of patronage and power. As a favor to his fellow Southern Democrats, Wilson systematically removed Black appointees from federal offices. Without federal patronage and clearly lacking any perspective to confront the racist attacks of the day, Washington's accommodationist politics began to lose their influence. By the time Washington died in 1915, Black leadership was clearly passing to the NAACP and similar civil rights groups.

Class Solidarity between Black and White

The NAACP's coalition between white liberal reformers and Black middle-class professionals was one of the few interracial ventures in a period of racial reaction and retreat. But it was not the only example of interracial cooperation, particularly among workers, even in the Jim Crow South. It is true that these were the exceptions, not the rule. But the exceptions are extremely important because they demonstrate that racism can be overcome in the process of struggle. Two examples of Southern unity among white and Black workers stand out in particular: the United Mine Workers (UMW) and the timber workers.

The United Mine Workers, founded in 1890 as one of the first industrial unions in the nation, counted more than 250,000 members by 1905. While the UMW exhibited some racism and segregation, the mineworkers also acted with a substantial level of interracial egalitarianism and solidarity in this period. By 1902, more than 20,000 of the UMW's members—most of them working in the bituminous coalfields in Alabama and West Virginia—were Black. They made up more than half the total number of Blacks organized in the AFL at that time. A significant number of Blacks were elected to leadership positions in integrated locals, and they helped organize both Black and white miners.[28]

The UMW exhibited more egalitarian race relations than most unions in the North. For example, District 20 of the UMW in Alabama succeeded in forcing coal operators to eliminate racial wage differentials, as well as the use of race to allocate workplaces. The same union forced Birmingham merchants to reverse their refusal to allow integrated union meetings in their halls. As one Black miner, O. H. Underwood, wrote in 1899, "I believe that the United Mine Workers has done more to erase the word white from the Constitution than the Fourteenth Amendment."[29]

The UMW record seems particularly impressive because it occurred in an era of increasing racial tension, rigid Jim Crow legislation, disfranchisement, and racial chauvinism, all of which were intensified in the effort to defeat Populism. Employers took advantage of the climate of racism following Populism's defeat. "With all these differences," a Senate-created Industrial Commission study of the mining industry concluded in 1901, "it is an easy matter for employers and foremen to play race, religion, and faction one against the other." Indeed, racism played a large part in the destruction of the union.[30]

Writes historian Michael Reich, "In 1904, the mining companies mounted a major offensive against the UMW in Alabama, refusing to renew union contracts and using Black strikebreakers with greater frequency than in any other industry. Employers moved to destroy unionism in Birmingham."[31] Coal operators that year refused to bargain a new contract with the UMW. In the resultant strike the mine owners imported Black strikebreakers, promising them better jobs if they would cross the picket line. Black workers stayed out, however, and convinced many Black strikebreakers to leave. Only the importation of labor from outside the area allowed coal operators to maintain production, and after sixteen months, the 9,000 strikers were defeated.

In 1908, the union countered with a two-month strike. Despite interracial solidarity on the picket line among the miners, this key strike was broken after the governor and many whites protested the organization of Blacks in the same union as whites. Upholding Jim Crow segregation, the governor ordered troops to cut down the tents in which the Black and white strikers lived, and forced the union to abandon the coalfields. The union did not survive such pressure. By the end of 1908, industrial unionism in bituminous coal was crushed in Alabama and West Virginia: after the strike failure, union membership dropped to the point where only 5 percent of the mine workers in the state were organized, and by 1915, less than 2 percent.[32]

In 1902, the International Longshoreman's Association (ILA) counted twenty thousand members, six thousand of them Blacks. A Great Lakes region officer of the ILA commented, "We have many colored members in our Association, and some of them are among our leading officials of our local branches. In one of our locals...there are over 300 members of which five are colored; of these two hold the office of President and Secretary."[33] According to a report from the New Orleans ILA office, "we are the only craft in that city who have succeeded in wiping out the color question. Our members meet jointly in the same hall and are the highest paid workmen in New Orleans."[34]

The 1919, twelve hundred Bogalusa, Louisiana, workers participated in the town's Labor Day parade. Bogalusa then boasted the largest lumber mill in the world, the Great Southern Lumber Company. Although Great Southern had made enormous profits during the First World War, its workers, both Black and white, still earned less than 30 cents an hour in 1919.[35] When the company decided to lock out the workers, they answered with the first strike in Bogalusa's history. Great Southern responded by bringing large numbers of Black workers from New Orleans as strikebreakers. "Many of these workers refused to stay and returned to New Orleans when they found that they were being used as strikebreakers," writes one historian of the strike.[36]

To break the strike, Great Southern "launched a huge campaign accusing the union of being integrated, and called for mob violence against the '[n——r] loving union.'"[37] This was despite the fact that Blacks were organized in a separate local at the impetus of Sol Dacus, the Black president of the Black local. But even the attempt to organize Blacks and whites to fight side by side in one union threatened the Great

Southern bosses. Great Southern spearheaded the creation of a vigilante squad, the Self-Preservation and Loyalty League (SPLL), composed of company supervisors, businessmen, and some army veterans. The SPLL declared Dacus the "bad Negro," and ordered him to leave Bogulusa. Dacus fled to the swamps, but returned later under the protection of the white-led Central Trades Assembly. Hearing of Dacus' return, SPLL thugs attacked the Trades Assembly headquarters, killing Dacus and three white trade unionists. SPLL gunmen were later acquitted of the unionists' murders.

"Whiteness" Triumphant?

Mainstream historians have largely ignored these examples of interracial solidarity. This is to be expected, of course, since they largely ignore any workers' struggles. On the other hand, there are those contemporary labor historians who write extensively about working people's struggles and interracial organizing, but often only with the aim of illustrating their thesis that unconquerable white supremacism among white workers explains the defeats of these attempts at interracial unionism. This academic trend focuses on the influence of "whiteness" on white workers to explain the defeats of interracial unionism.[38] In this reading, white workers consistently put their racial identity before all else, including their material interests. Yet this is a one-dimensional view that even the previous accounts of defeated strikes challenge. As the accounts of struggles in the mines, on the docks, and in the timber camps show, the issue of whether white workers will fight for their material interests and stand with their Black brothers and sisters, or opt for white supremacy, was not a fixed one, but contested. Moreover, these battles took place in a context in which employers, the state, armed militias, the Ku Klux Klan, the media, and the pulpit were fanning the flames of racism. To single out for blame the white supremacist ideology inside workers' heads is, at the very least, a selective reading of history—when every major institution of society was promoting white supremacy.

Frederick Douglass understood better than many historians who have written on the subject how white supremacist ideology became so dominant. He put it succinctly:

> Now where rests the responsibility for the lynch law prevalent in the South? It is evident that it is not entirely with the ignorant mob. The mob who breaks open jails and with bloody hands destroys human life are not alone responsible. These are not the men who make public sentiment. They are simply hangmen, not the court, judge, or jury. They simply obey the public sentiment of the South—the sentiment created by wealth and respectability, by the press and pulpit. A change in public sentiment can be easily effected by these forces whenever they shall elect to make this effort.[39]

If one does not take the approach of Douglass, one is left with the notion that combating racism in the workplace is futile. Clear away all the academic rhetoric, and one is left with the assertion that race and white racism are insurmountable barriers to the class struggle. Not only does this define white workers only by their "whiteness," it has the corollary effect of seeing the Black working class primarily as victims of white racism. According to Barbara Fields, a critic of "whiteness theory,"

> invocation of self-propelling "attitudes" and tragic flaws assigns Africans and their descendants to a special category, placing them in a world exclusively theirs and outside history—a form of intellectual apartheid no less ugly or oppressive, despite its righteous (not to say self-righteous) trappings, than that practiced by the bio- and theo-racists;

and for which the victims, like slaves of old, are expected to be grateful. They are the academic "liberals" and "progressives" in whose version of race the neutral shibboleths *difference* and *diversity* replace words like *slavery, injustice, oppression* and *exploitation*, diverting attention from the anything-but-neutral history these words denote.[40]

Ultimately, the literature on "whiteness" has no feel whatsoever of struggle, of dynamic, of change. As a result, it is a wholly inadequate way of understanding the relationship between race and class in U.S. history. But grasping the relationship between racism and the class struggle is essential, especially for understanding what came after the period covered in this chapter. In 1910, 70.2 percent of all Blacks lived in the rural South. Even after the First World War the majority of Blacks still lived in the South; Blacks accounted for only 2.2 percent of the non-agricultural employment outside the South—and the majority of these jobs were in household service.[41]

Following the "Great Migration" of Blacks to Northern cities in the early decades of the twentieth century (when approximately one million, or 10 percent of the total Black population of the country, moved from the rural South to the Northern cities), the presence of African Americans as a substantial section of workers in the main U.S. industries was established.[42] This social transformation of the Black population laid the basis for Marcus Garvey's Universal Negro Improvement Association, the first mass urban-based movement of Blacks, and, later, for the rise of the industrial unions and socialist and communist parties to which the African-American struggle for equal rights was crucial. We turn to these two developments in the subsequent chapters.

CHAPTER SIX

The Rise of Marcus Garvey

The end of the First World War was accompanied by a wave of strikes across the United States. Though the strikes were most commonly for wage increases and shorter working days, several important ones, including the Seattle general strike and the Boston police and steel strikes, threatened to transform this postwar strike wave into a generalized challenge to the employers and the state. The ruling class certainly viewed the strikes as a threat, and launched an anti-Communist crusade. Immigrant workers were singled out as "foreign agitators." In late April 1919, newspapers around the country warned, as one headline writer phrased it, of "Reds Planning to Overthrow U.S. on May Day."[1] May Day marches were either broken up, with numerous marchers arrested, or simply prevented from taking place. Judges issued injunctions to break strikes, and commonly impose severe limits on the number of pickets. A Toledo, Ohio, judge had the distinction of limiting the number of picketers—and adding that they had to be native-born.[2] Deportation became a favorite government tool, since laws provided for the deportation of immigrant "undesirables." Government officials were appalled at the release of two-thirds of arrested Wobblies (members of the radical

Industrial Workers of the World), and thus simply passed an act making membership in a radical organization a deportable offense. The government-sponsored red scare was a signal to employers to do whatever it took to break strikes.

1919 was also marked by brutal and bloody racial violence, which came to be known as the "Red Summer of 1919." From May to September of that year, major race riots broke out in Charleston, Knoxville, Omaha, Washington, Chicago, Longview, Texas, and Phillips County, Arkansas. All told, twenty-five riots took place.[3] The riots were primarily the result of violent, and often murderous, attacks on Blacks by white racists. Such attacks and lynchings were not new, but the rash of riots in 1919 was seen as different in a crucial respect: Blacks fought back. Black poet Claude McKay penned a battle cry:

> If we must die, let it be not like hogs
> . . . .
> Like men we'll face the murderous, cowardly pack,
> Pressed to the wall, dying, but fighting back![4]

The new Black militancy was the result of changes brought by the First World War. Labor shortages brought hundreds of thousands of Southern Blacks North during the war. A constant labor supply had traditionally been provided by successive waves of immigration, but the war had drastically curtailed immigration. The demand for labor became acute. Between 1910 and 1920, the number of Black industrial workers grew by nearly two-thirds from 550,000 to 900,000.[5]

During the war, an additional four hundred thousand Blacks entered the armed forces.[6] Both Black workers and veterans gained new confidence. As one newspaper editorial observed, "Out of this war the Negro expects—he demands—justice, and cannot and will not be content with less."[7] The gap between expectation and reality led to growing resentment and militancy among Blacks. Acute housing shortages, wartime inflation, and discrimination on the job were compounded by unemployment in 1919. Postwar demobilization resulted in mass layoffs and increased competition for jobs with white workers. The unwillingness of the American Federation of Labor (AFL) to organize Black workers played into the hands of employers, who consciously used racism to further divide Black and white workers. In several riots, job competition was the underlying cause. The bloody 1919 race riot in Chicago stemmed, in part, from Black and white job competition in the city's stockyards.[8]

The UNIA: A Mass Organization

It was in these conditions that Marcus Garvey built the Universal Negro Improvement Association (UNIA) into a mass organization—the largest Black nationalist organization to date at that time. Assessments of Garvey vary considerably. For Black nationalists, Garvey's success is evidence of the viability of nationalism. They see Garvey as the link between nineteenth-century nationalists such as Martin Delany and the nationalist revival of the 1960s. This assessment is shared by left-wing nationalists who are critical of many of Garvey's ideas, but stress his importance in establishing independent Black organization. The West Indian historian and critic C. L. R. James expressed this view in the 1980s, reversing his earlier hostility to Garvey: "Garvey was a remarkable man. Before Garvey there was no Black movement anywhere. Since Garvey there has been a continuous Black movement.... All of us stand on the shoulders of Marcus Garvey. There is plenty to say against Garvey, but nothing you can say against Garvey can ever weaken the things, the positive things, that Garvey did."[9]

It is worth emphasizing, however, that this assessment of Garvey was not shared by many of his contemporaries, including Black members of the Socialist Party and W. E. B. Du Bois, then the leader of the NAACP. Du Bois believed that "Garvey is financially more or less a fraud." He was suspicious of and hostile to Garvey whom he believed was under the influence of communists. In August 1920, Du Bois described Garvey as "a demagogue" in an unpublished interview and referred to Garvey's supporters as "the lowest type of Negroes.... They are allied with the Bolsheviks and the Sinn Feiners in their world revolution."[10] Du Bois' opinion of Garvey only hardened as time went on. "Marcus Garvey is, without doubt, the most dangerous enemy of the Negro race in America and in the world," Du Bois wrote. "He is either a lunatic or a traitor," he went on. "The American Negroes have endured this wretch all too long with fine restraint and every effort at cooperation and understanding. But the end has come. Every man who apologizes for or defends Marcus Garvey from this day forth writes himself down as unworthy of the countenance of decent Americans."[11]

It would have been hard to predict that Garvey would generate such raw feelings when he arrived in the United States in 1916. Here he hoped to build his recently formed and floundering organization, the UNIA. Born in Jamaica in 1887, Garvey entered politics inadvertently. A printer by trade, he became a foreman in one of Kingston's largest printing companies. When workers at the company voted for strike action in 1909, Garvey joined the walkout. The strike was defeated, and Garvey was fired for his role in the strike. During the next three years, he traveled across the West Indies and Latin America. He then moved to London, where he spent the next two years. Garvey's political ideas began to cohere during this period. Influenced by Egyptian nationalist Duse Mohammed Ali, Garvey learned of conditions in colonial Africa and began to relate them to those of Blacks internationally.

I asked myself "Where is the Black man's Government? Where is his King and his kingdom? Where is his president, his country, and his ambassador, his army, his navy, his men of big affairs?" I could not find them, and I declared "I will help to make them."... I saw before me then...a nation of sturdy men making their impress upon the human race. I could not remain in London any more.[12]

Five days after his return to Jamaica in July 1914, Garvey founded the UNIA. Under the slogan "One god! One aim! One destiny!" he defined the UNIA's tasks as "uniting all the Negro peoples of the world into one great body to establish a country and Government absolutely their own."[13] The aims and objectives of the UNIA were:

To establish a Universal Confraternity among the race; to promote the spirit of pride and love; to reclaim the fallen; to administer to and assist the needy; to assist in civilizing the backward tribes of Africa; to assist in the development of Independent Negro nations and communities; to establish a central nation for the race, where they will be given the opportunity to develop themselves; to establish Commissaries and Agencies in the principal countries and cities of the world for the representation of all Negroes; to promote a conscientious Spiritual worship among the native tribes of Africa; to establish Universities, Colleges and Academies and Schools for racial education and culture of the people; to improve the general conditions of Negroes everywhere.[14]

Garvey's nationalism did not lead him to oppose the major imperialist powers. Instead he praised them for helping to "civilize" Blacks. Garvey believed the UNIA could continue the colonial project, leading to the establishment of Black nations ruled by Blacks. "To do this," he argued, "we must get the co-operation and sympathy of our white brothers."[15] Garvey looked for support from several sources, including Britain. In a letter to the Secretary of State for the Colonies in September 1914, Garvey wrote, "We sincerely pray for the success of British arms on the battle fields of Europe and Africa, and at Sea, in crushing the 'Common Foe,' the enemy of peace and further civilization. We rejoice in British Victories and the suppression of foreign foes. Thrice we hail, 'God save the King! Long live the King and Empire.'"[16]

Garvey's efforts to build the UNIA met with little success. In 1916, he could claim only one hundred members. A supporter of Booker T. Washington's ideas, Garvey arrived in New York in March 1916 intending to raise funds for an industrial farm and trade school in Jamaica modeled after Washington's Tuskegee Institute. But Washington died shortly before Garvey arrived in the United States, forcing him to change his plans. He established a branch of the UNIA in Harlem, and set out to build the organization. At first it looked as though he would have as little success in Harlem as he did in Jamaica. Nervous and under pressure from hecklers, his first public speech ended with him fleeing the speakers' platform.

Garvey's fortunes soon changed dramatically, however. By 1920, Marcus Garvey was the most prominent Black figure in the United States, and in the early years of the decade, the organization claimed to have more than seven hundred branches in the United States, with 35,000 dues-paying members in New York City alone. The UNIA also claimed to have established branches in forty-two countries, and its newspaper *Negro World* was a widely read Black publication in the United States.[17] During this period, Garvey identified himself as a leader of Black resistance in the United States. In 1919, he urged Black supporters to "have a white man lynched for every Negro who was lynched."[18] In 1920, he claimed that the colors of the UNIA flag "showed their sympathy with the 'Reds' of the world, and the Green their sympathy for the Irish in their fight for freedom."[19] But the depths of Garvey's radicalism and identification with the left were quite shallow. The idea that "during the period 1918–1921 Garvey was profoundly sympathetic with the international left and with mass workers' movements against capital," as Manning Marable writes, is to overstate the case.[20] Judith Stein rightly stressed that Garvey adopted militant rhetoric in 1919 because he understood that it was necessary to attract members to the UNIA.[21] And while Garvey praised the Bolshevik Revolution for doing in Russia what he envisioned for Blacks, he quickly added: "We are not very much concerned as partakers in these revolutions."[22] In other words, Garvey tried to identify with the possibility of social change that the Bolshevik Revolution represented, without endorsing the socialist aims of the revolution.

Race Consciousness and the "Back to Africa" Movement

Modern-day commentators who exaggerate Garvey's sympathy with the left during this period also attempt to gloss over his subsequent development, without acknowledging the fundamental continuity in his ideas. This is not to say that Garvey's ideas did not change at all from 1916 to 1920. Influenced by events around him, Garvey moved away from the conciliatory and assimilationist approach of Booker T. Washington, and began to stress the importance of racial pride and racial purity. Garvey also began to argue more clearly for racial separation. He attacked other Blacks who believed that Black equality could be achieved in a white America:

> The professional Negro leader and the class who are agitating for social equality feel that it is too much work for them to settle down and build up a civilization of their own. They feel it is easier to seize on the civilization of the white man and under the guise of constitutional rights fight for those things that the white man has created. Natural reason suggests that

the white man will not yield them, hence such leaders are but
fools for their pains. Teach the Negro to do for himself, help
him the best way possible in that direction.[23]

Garvey's increased race consciousness was not accompanied by a rejection of the other ideas he shared with Booker
T. Washington, though. Black capitalism and self-help were
now combined with the slogan "Back to Africa." Toward that
end, the UNIA promoted racial consciousness and established a number of business ventures. The most important of
these was the Black Star Line endeavor, which Garvey set up
in 1919. The Black Star Line drew the savings of thousands of
Blacks into a plan to form a fleet of Black-owned cruise ships
for transoceanic travel, especially transit to Africa. Many of
Garvey's critics accused Garvey of trying to embezzle the
thousands of poor Blacks who invested money in this ven-
ture. Similar charges would become the excuse for government prosecution of the UNIA in 1921. In 1919, however, the
government was more concerned with the threat posed by
the wave of strikes sweeping the country and socialist agitation in support of the Russian Revolution. A Justice Department investigation at the time concluded that Garvey was the
"foremost pro-negro agitator in New York. It is apparent, however, that his pro-negroism is secondary to his scheme for the
solicitation of subscriptions for stock in the Black Star Line."[24]

UNIA supporters greeted the Black Star Line with considerable enthusiasm, especially after the purchase of its
first ship, the *SS Frederick Douglass.* The ship was docked on
the Hudson River for a few weeks, and evoked a massive response described in the following terms by Claude McKay:
"There was a wild invasion of Harlem by Negroes from every
Black quarter in America. Hordes of disciples came with
more dollars to buy more shares. The boat was moored at the
pier with its all-Negro crew. And the common people gladly

paid half a dollar to go aboard and look over the miracle. Loudly talking and gesturing, they inspected the ship, singing the praises of Marcus Garvey."[25]

Garvey had successfully tapped the aspirations of many Blacks, and the UNIA expressed their alienation from a society that oppressed them. He provided a vision of a different society, if only in embryonic form, through the UNIA, its businesses, its adoption of a flag and anthem, and its establishment of a government in exile (with Garvey as president). In an argument with C. L. R. James and others of his followers in the United States, the exiled Russian revolutionary leader Leon Trotsky stressed that Garvey's following was an expression of the aspiration for Black self-determination:

> The Black woman who said to the white woman, "Wait until Marcus is in power. We will know how to treat you then," was simply expressing her desire for her own state. The American Negroes gathered under the banner of the "Back to Africa" movement because it seemed a possible fulfillment of their wish for their own home. They did not want to actually go to Africa. It was the expression of a mystic desire for a home in which they would be free of the domination of the whites, in which they themselves could control their own fate.[26]

But the problem for Garvey was that while he could build on such aspirations, he could not satisfy them. This explains the meteoric rise *and fall* of the UNIA. As the postwar radicalization dissipated, the UNIA lost its mass base. The positive elements in Garvey's ideas in 1920—encouraging race pride and resistance—soon gave way to the most reactionary elements. Soon nothing was left but the emphasis on racial purity. Denouncing any sexual relations between the races, Garvey declared: "Miscegenation will lead to the moral destruction of both races, and the promotion of a hybrid caste that will have no social standing or moral background in a critical moral judgment of the life and affairs of the human race."[27]

For Garvey, political ideas and programs were irrelevant when it came to race. The UNIA, he announced, "has absolutely no association with any political party.... Republicans, Democrats, and Socialists are the same to us—they are all white men to us and all of them join together and lynch and burn Negroes."[28]

Garvey and Separatism

But despite this condemnation of whites, Garvey did not treat all whites in the same way. He began to identify white supremacists as the only true friends of Blacks because they understood the need for racial purity. On a trip south in 1922, he thanked whites for having "lynched race pride into the Negroes."[29] He met with the Ku Klux Klan's second in command in Atlanta, Georgia. According to Garvey's worldview, the Klan and other white supremacists shared common aims with the UNIA. "I regard the Klan, the Anglo-Saxon Clubs and White American societies, as far as the Negro is concerned, better friends of the race than all other groups of hypocritical whites put together."[30]

If some whites were better friends, others were more dangerous—above all socialists and Communists.

> It seems strange and a paradox, but the only convenient friend the Negro worker or laborer has, in America, at the present time, is the white capitalist....
>
> I am of the opinion that the group of whites from whom Communists are made, in America, as well as trade unionists and members of the Workers' party, is more dangerous to the Negro's welfare than any other group at present.[31]

He added, "The danger of Communism to the Negro in countries where he forms the minority of the population, is seen in the selfish and vicious attempts of that party or group to use the Negro's vote and physical numbers in helping to smash and over-throw by revolution, a system that is injurious to them as the white underdogs, the success of which would put their majority group or race still in power, not only as [C]ommunists but as white men."[32]

Garvey's hostility to socialists reflected his long-held admiration for capitalism: "Capitalism is necessary to the progress of the world, and those who unreasonably and wantonly oppose or fight against it are enemies of human advancement."[33] Garvey would draw even more reactionary conclusions a few years later. In 1937, Garvey gave an interview in London in which he claimed: "We were the first fascists...when we had 100,000 disciplined men, and were training children, Mussolini was still an unknown. Mussolini copied our fascism."[34] Later the same year, he declared that the "UNIA was before Mussolini and Hitler ever were heard of. Mussolini and Hitler copied the program of the UNIA—aggressive nationalism for the Black man in Africa."[35]

By the time he expressed his admiration for Hitler and Mussolini, few Black Americans paid much attention to what Garvey had to say. The U.S. government deported him in 1927, and the UNIA spiralled downward to collapse. Although Garvey and the UNIA espoused quite reactionary positions as the organization declined, the Garvey movement left behind thousands of Blacks who became activists in subsequent community, labor, and political struggles. Many of them or their children would emerge as key leaders in the struggles of the 1930s, 1940s, and 1950s.

CHAPTER SEVEN

The Socialist, Communist, and Trotskyist Parties

In the four decades before the Civil War, several communitarian and utopian socialist societies were established in the United States. Utopian socialism found fertile ground in the United States and was the dominant current among socialists until 1850. "During 1820–1850," wrote historian Philip Foner, "the American countryside was liberally dotted with communities established by searchers for the utopias promised by [Robert] Owen and [Charles] Fourier."[1]

In the 1850s, German immigrants, many of whom were exiles of the revolutions of 1830 and 1848, established a Marxist movement in the United States. Joseph Weydemeyer, a comrade and friend of Karl Marx and Frederick Engels, came to the United States in 1851 and was, until his death in 1866, the most important Marxist propagandist in the country. Weydemeyer and four friends formed the first explicitly Marxist organization, or *proletarierbund,* in the summer of 1852.[2] A number of other organizations were established by Marxists, perhaps most importantly the Communist Club of New York in 1857. Communists set up similar clubs in Chicago and Cincinnati the following year.[3]

Marxists and utopian socialists had fundamentally different approaches to the questions of slavery and racism. The first difference involved the attitude toward Blacks and their involvement in the movement. Robert Owen opposed slavery but was a supporter of emigrationism and excluded Blacks from his own colony, New Harmony, in Indiana. Blacks could be helpers "if necessary," Owen said, or "if it be found useful, to prepare and enable them to become associated in Communities in Africa."[4] In contrast, the Communist Club of New York invited Blacks to become members. Its constitution required all members to "recognize the complete equality of all persons—no matter of whatever color or sex."[5] In 1858, the Club unanimously adopted a resolution that stated, "We recognize no distinction as to nationality or race, caste or status, color or sex; our goal is nothing less than the reconciliation of all human interests, freedom and happiness for mankind, and the realization and unification of a world republic."[6] Another resolution demanded the repeal of all discriminatory laws, while another "favored the eligibility of all citizens...for office."[7]

The second difference that separated utopians from Marxists was their attitude to abolition. Slaveholders, unlike Blacks, could become members of Owenite communities, and they were not required to relinquish their slaves.[8] The Communist Club of New York expressly prohibited membership of slaveowners, but in addition expelled any member who expressed sympathy for the slaveholders' point of view. Finally, while opposing slavery, the utopians did not call for its immediate abolition. Indeed, they tended to argue that wage slavery in the North was worse than chattel slavery in the South. One such utopian, the Associationist William West, insisted that American workers "do not hate chattel slavery less, but they hate wage slavery more."[9] This view led many of the utopians to stay aloof—if not stand in outright opposition to the abolitionists' demands. In contrast, the Communist Club stood firmly in favor of abolition.[10]

In part, the strength of conviction of the Marxist current can be attributed to the attitude and position adopted by Karl Marx in favor of Black emancipation. "In the United States of America, every independent workers' movement was paralyzed so long as slavery disfigured a part of the republic. Labor in a white skin cannot emancipate itself where it is branded in a Black skin."[11]

At the Colored National Labor Union convention in 1869, the Black trade unionist Isaac Myers put forward a similar argument. "Slavery, or slave labor, the main cause of the degradation of white labor, is no more," he said. "And it is the proud boast of my life that the slave himself had a large share in striking off the fetters that bound him by the ankle, while the other end bound you by the neck."[12]

Despite their revolutionary understanding of the situation, however, the small size of the early Marxist groups, combined with a language barrier for many émigré Marxists, meant that, as Mike Davis observes, "their heroic efforts had little impact upon the mainstream of the labor movement."[13] With the outbreak of the Civil War, the Communist Club of New York virtually disappeared. The Club did not meet for the duration of the war because most of its members had joined the Union forces. Several Marxists became high-ranking Union army officers, having gained considerable experience in the Prussian military.

By 1867, organizers had revived the Communist Club of New York, and voted to become a section of the International Workingmen's Association (IWA), otherwise known as the First International. The IWA was formed in September 1864 and brought together a wide assortment of unionists, radicals, and socialists to establish a mechanism for international collaboration and coordination between different countries. But the organization was not to exist very long. In 1872, the International's headquarters were moved from London to New York. Only four years later, the International was dissolved—after a serious split developed in the organization between the Marxists, other socialists, and the anarchists.

The approach adopted by the Communist Club of New York on slavery and Black emancipation could have provided a solid foundation for later generations of socialists. Unfortunately, this was not to be the case. The early Marxists never broke out of their isolation, and remained largely on the fringes of the labor movement. As Karl Marx's lifelong collaborator, Frederick Engels, wrote in a letter:

> I think also the K[nights] of L[abor] a most important factor in the movement which ought not to be pooh-poohed from without but to be revolutionized from within, and I consider that many of the Germans there have made a grievous mistake when they tried, in the face of a mighty and glorious movement not of their creation, a kind of *alleinseligmachendes* [necessary to salvation] dogma and to keep aloof from any movement which did not accept that dogma.... What the Germans ought to do is to act up to their own theory—if they understand it, as we did in 1845 and 1848—to go in for any real general working-class movement, accept its *faktische* [actual] starting points as such and work it gradually up to the theoretical level by pointing out how every mistake made, every reverse suffered, was a necessary consequence of mistaken theoretical views in the original programme; they ought in the words of the *Communist Manifesto*, to represent the movement of the future in the movement of the present.[14]

If the German émigré socialist movement went to pieces, a frustrated Engels told Friedrich Albert Sorge, a German socialist émigré to the United States, "it would be a gain." Unfortunately, he concluded, "we can hardly expect anything so good as that."[15]

The Socialist Labor Party

The target of Engels' wrath was the *Sozialistiche Arbeiter-partei*, later renamed Socialist Labor Party (SLP). The SLP was the main socialist current in the United States from its founding in 1877 until 1900. The party emerged from the remnants of the IWA and was made up almost entirely of German immigrants. But the SLP was quite different from the early Communist Clubs in several respects. First, while the earlier generation of Marxists, most notably Sorge, helped found the SLP, virtually none of them were active in the organization by the 1880s. Second, the SLP's forerunner, the Workingmen's Party of the United States, was not a Marxist organization. Rather, it was formed at a unity conference of Lasalleans and Marxists. Third, the majority of the membership was composed of new immigrants from Germany, escaping Otto von Bismarck's repression. More than anything else, they saw the SLP as a wing of the German Social Democratic Party, the mass socialist party established in 1875. It was not until the 1890s, under the leadership of Daniel De Leon—an academic who became leader of the SLP—that a conscious effort was made to refocus the SLP on American conditions.

The SLP's founding meeting said nothing in relation to Blacks, but its 1879 convention platform declared the party in favor of "universal and equal rights of suffrage without regard to color, creed or sex."[16] While precise figures are not available, it is clear that the SLP attracted some Black support. One of the first Black people in the United States to publicly identify himself with socialism, Peter Clark, was a member of the SLP and one of the leaders of the 1877 railroad strike in St. Louis. When he joined the party's National Executive, he became the first Black person to assume a leadership position in a socialist party. Clark was one of two congressional candidates in Ohio's 1878 election.[17]

It is also clear that some members of the SLP were exemplary in their opposition to racism. Among the leaders of District Assembly 49 of New York's Knights of Labor were several white SLP members like Timothy Quinn, a master workman, Victor Drury, a former leader of the French section of the First International in the United States, and Thomas Maguire, an Irish-American socialist. The district's secretary treasurer was Frank Ferrell, one of the most well-known Black members of the Knights of Labor. Going against the massive anti-Chinese racism in the United States, the District Assembly 49 leadership argued for organizing Chinese workers into the Knights. They succeeded in organizing two groups of workers in New York, only to have the General Executive Board of the Knights refuse to grant them a charter. In a minority report, they argued that "the first and basic principle of the organization was the obliteration of lines of distinction in creed, color and nationality."[18] After the Chinese assemblies were dissolved, they were welcomed in District 49.

Another instance of District 49's fight against racism took place at the Knights of Labor 1886 convention. A few months before the convention, Quinn had sent a delegation to Richmond, Virginia, to see what hotels would be available for convention delegates. They concluded an agreement with a Colonel Murphy, a former Confederate officer. When he discovered that Ferrell was one of the delegates, he canceled the contract, arguing that "customs here must be respected." He offered to find accommodations for Ferrell at a "Black hotel."[19] District 49 unanimously rejected these terms and went to Richmond with tents, planning to sleep outdoors, rather than abandon their Black brother. Even the *New York Times* remarked, "The delegates are determined to fight the battle on the color line right in the midst of that part of the country where race prejudice is the strongest, and they will insist on carrying on what they claim is a fundamental principle of their Order—that the Black man is the equal of the white socially as well as politically, and that all races stand upon an equal footing in all respects."[20]

Unfortunately, as an organization, the SLP did not generalize from the example set by its members in District 49. Neither the party leadership nor its press had very much to say about Blacks or racism. They didn't even report on the struggles involving District 49.

Daniel De Leon's assumption of the SLP's leadership in the 1890s would transform the organization on many questions, including its relationship to Blacks. "Whatever his other weaknesses, De Leon deserves credit for bringing the Negro question to the attention of [the readers of the SLP newspaper] the *People*," writes Philip Foner. "While James Benjamin Stolvey is correct when he writes...of De Leon that the *People* did not at any time make the Negro question 'a special feature,' it was nevertheless the first American socialist paper to feature it at all."[21]

De Leon was an outspoken critic of the AFL's adoption of exclusionary Jim Crow policies and opposed the formation of segregated locals in the South. He played an important role in opposing racist attitudes in the Second (or Socialist) International, the federation of the world's socialist parties founded in 1889. De Leon argued against proposals for restrictions on immigration by "inferior races."

Where is the line that separates "inferior" from "superior"

races? What serious man, if he is a Socialist, what Socialist if he is a serious man, would indulge in "etc." in such important matters? To the native American proletariat, the Irish was made to appear an "inferior" race; to the Irish, the German; to the German, the Italian; to the Italian—and so down the line through the Swedes, the Poles, the Jews, the Armenians, the Japanese, to the end of the gamut. Socialism knows not such insulting iniquitous distinctions as "inferior" and "superior" races among the proletariat. It is for capitalism to fan the fires of such sentiments in its schemes to keep the proletariat divided.[22]

De Leon's opposition to racism flowed from his understanding that discrimination against one group of workers could only weaken all workers. Like most socialists in this period, though, he saw racism *only* as a class question. Black workers, he argued, were like white workers, and their problems were those of all workers. Racial oppression was simply a manifestation of class oppression. Therefore, he concluded, agitation around non-economic questions—segregation, lynching, or race riots—could only distract from the real struggle, the abolition of the wage system. De Leon's views on the struggle against segregation and for Black equality were also shaped by his completely sectarian and doctrinaire politics. That is, he only saw the struggle for the ultimate goal—the struggle for socialism—as meaningful. "De Leon would invariably remind his listeners," says Arnold Petersen, a national secretary of the party, "that there was no such thing as a race or 'Negro question'.... There was only a *social*, or *labor* question, and no racial or religious question so far as the Socialist and labor movements were concerned."[23]

De Leon's approach to "the Black question" represented his failure to understand oppression in general. De Leon's failure to understand this question led some in the SLP to challenge him. Thus, for example, Charles G. Baylor, a Black member of the SLP (actually, the only Black member of the SLP at the time), drafted a letter to De Leon at the height of the Populist revolt in 1895, expressing his desire to organize Southern Blacks into the SLP:

> [We should] make the expression of Southern and the worse-known American oppression of the Southern Negro a special feature of the *People*.... This attitude of the SLP and the *People* will give us and the paper not only a stronghold on the southern Negro population but in the colored population of the north. I believe that it alone [will] add 10,000 names to your subscription list.[24]

De Leon didn't answer Baylor's letter. Later he argued, unconvincingly, that Blacks constituted a special division within the ranks of labor, but "In no economic respect is he different from his fellow wage slaves of other races."[25]

In part, De Leon's attitude stemmed from his opposition to any struggle for reforms: "The essence of this revolution—the overthrow of Wage Slavery—cannot be too forcefully held up. Nor can the point be too forcefully kept in evidence that, short of the abolition of Wage Slavery, all 'improvements' either accrue to Capitalism, or are the merest moonshine where they are not sidetracks."[26]

The Socialist Party

While the Socialist Labor Party had the distinction of being the first Marxist party in the U.S., the Socialist Party founded in 1901 has the distinction of being the first socialist party to attract a mass following. Formed from the fusion of several smaller socialist groups, the Socialist Party (SP) was a peculiar organization, even by the standards of the Second International. Unlike the social democratic parties of Europe, the Socialist Party cannot be described as a mass working-class party. Founded in 1901, the SP was much broader (and looser) than any of the European parties. It was a heterogeneous organization, combining several tendencies in the working-class movement. Its radical wing emerged from mass working-class struggles, including the battles of the Western Federation of Miners led by "Big Bill" Haywood, and the railroad struggles that made the Indiana-born railroad union leader Eugene Debs a socialist. It had a right wing composed of municipal reformers based in several cities, led by Victor Berger. Its center was grouped around Morris Hillquit of New York, a former member of the SLP. Its biggest electoral support came from agrarian Midwestern and Western populists. And just before and during the First World War, a large number of new immigrants joined the SP, grouped around foreign language federations that had their own publications and were largely autonomous from the party. Despite this rather motley assemblage, the Socialist Party quickly became the largest and most important socialist organization in the United States as De Leon's SLP declined in influence and size in the late 1890s.

Leon Trotsky was unsparing when describing the character of the Socialist Party:

> To this day, I smile as I recall the leaders of American Socialism. Immigrants who had played some rôle in Europe in their youth, they very quickly lost the theoretical premise they had brought with them in the confusion of their struggle for success. In the United States there is a large class of successful and semi-successful doctors, lawyers, dentists, engineers, and the like who divide their precious hours of rest between concerts by European celebrities and the American Socialist Party. Their attitude toward life is composed of shreds and fragments of the wisdom they absorbed in their student days. Since they all have automobiles, they are invariably elected to the important committees, commissions, and delegations of the party.... They think that Wilson

was infinitely more authoritative than Marx. And, properly speaking, they are simply variants of "Babbit," who supplements his commercial activities with dull Sunday meditations on the future of humanity.[27]

The Socialist Party's approach to Black oppression mirrored the existence of different tendencies within the organization. There were those who professed a complete indifference to questions of racism and Blacks. Worse, was the right wing, which was openly racist. Victor Berger, the first socialist elected to Congress, wrote in 1902:

> There can be no doubt that the Negroes and mulattoes constitute a lower race—that the Caucasian and indeed the Mongolian have the start of them in civilization by many thousand years—so that Negroes will find it difficult ever to overtake them. The many cases of rape that occur whenever Negroes are settled in large numbers prove, moreover, that the free contact with the whites has led to the further degeneration of the Negroes, as of all other inferior races. The "Negro question" will one day give the Socialists a good deal of headache, and will never be settled by mere well-phrased resolutions.[28]

Berger was consistently racist, and argued at the party's December 1907 National Executive meeting that the SP should favor sharply curbing immigration. "Berger warned that we would soon have five million 'yellow men' invading the country every year. We already have one race question, said Berger, and if something was not done at once, 'this country is absolutely sure to become a black-and-yellow country within a few generations.'"[29] He was not isolated in his views and reflected a common view, especially within the right wing of the Second International, which favored colonization and believed in the "civililizing" mission of the Great Powers.

Balancing between the different factions was the SP's most famous propagandist, Eugene Debs, who, though a "romantic and a preacher," in the words of Trotsky, "was a sincere revolutionary."[30] Unfortunately, Debs' influence inside the SP was limited by his lack of interest in the day-to-day affairs of the organization.

Debs represented a different current, one that opposed Berger and the SP right wing. While on occasion Debs suggested that Blacks were not equal to whites because of the legacy of slavery, he opposed the view that Blacks were innately inferior. He opposed discrimination, and when he toured the South, encouraged Blacks to reject doctrines of "meekness and humility."[31] He argued that Blacks should join the Socialist Party and consistently refused to speak to segregated audiences. Philip Foner concludes:

> Compared with the racist Berger, Debs was a forthright supporter of Negro rights. Despite all the ideological weakness of his 1903 writings on the Negro question, these writings also demonstrate that as early as 1903 he clearly understood that "the history of the Negro in the United States is a history of crime without a parallel." His test for a socialist when it came to the Negro was simple: "Socialists should with pride proclaim their sympathy with and fealty to the Black race, and if any there be who hesitate to avow themselves in the face of ignorant and unreasoning prejudice, they lack the true spirit of the slavery-destroying revolutionary movement."[32]

Debs argued that Blacks were not seeking "social equality" with whites and that socialism would not force whites to associate with Blacks in private. The cry of "social equality" was a red herring raised by the ruling class to divide workers.

> The very instant that it [social equality] is mentioned the old aristocratic plantation owner's shrill cry about the "buck nigger" marrying the "fair young daughter" of his master is heard from the tomb and echoed and re-echoed across the spaces and repeated by the "white trash" in proud vindica-

tion of their social superiority.

Social equality, forsooth! Is the Black man pressing his claims for social recognition upon his white burden bearer? Is there any reason why he should? Is the white man's social recognition of his own white brother such as to excite the Negro's ambition to covet the noble prize? Has the Negro any greater desire, or is there any reason why he should have, for social intercourse with the white man than the white man has for social relations with the Negro? This phase of the Negro question is pure fraud and serves to mask the real issue, which is not *social equality*, BUT ECO-NOMIC FREEDOM.

There never was any social inferiority that was not the shriveled fruit of economic inequality.[33]

This didn't mean Debs closed his eyes to segregation or Jim Crow laws. No socialist worth the name could accept Jim Crow. "Absolute equality for white and Black, covering perfect uniformity not only in the opportunities for labor, but also in those public services such as education, transportation...entertainment, etc., which may be collectively rendered together with complete recognition of political rights," he wrote, "must be insisted on more strenuously by the socialist than ever they could have been by any abolitionist agitator."[34]

Debs shared De Leon's view that Blacks merited no special attention. His approach is summed up in his most often quoted statement on Blacks: "We have nothing special to offer the Negro, and we cannot make separate appeals to all the races. The Socialist Party is the Party of the whole working class regardless of color."[35] Yet simply leaving an understanding of Debs at that quote ignores the fact that Debs was far from passive when it came to confronting racism. In response to the 1910 Socialist Party congress report on immigration, which he termed "utterly unsocialist, reactionary, and in truth outrageous," Debs shifted his emphasis to the need to combat racism and to uphold full Black equality.[36] In the summer of 1915, Debs was one of the few voices to condemn D. W. Griffith's racist film *Birth of a Nation,* which glorified the Ku Klux Klan for having saved "civilization" by reestablishing white supremacy in the South. Debs called on socialists to picket the film, and himself joined the NAACP when they organized a picket in his hometown, Terre Haute, Indiana. He authored several articles denouncing white supremacy, lynching, and Black oppression. In 1915 and 1916, Debs worked closely with Oklahoma socialists to challenge new ruses by the Democratic Party to achieve Black disfranchisement. Calling on Black and white workers to defeat "the capitalist conspiracy" to disenfranchise Black voters, the Socialist Party succeeded in defeating several attempts by the Democrats to limit the voting rolls—an impressive achievement given the widespread success of disfranchisement in other parts of the country.

The racism of sections of the Socialist Party can be attributed to their lack of what Debs called "true revolutionary spirit." The right wing of the party was not only racist toward Blacks, but was also racist toward immigrants. Their racism was not simply an aberration in otherwise committed socialists, but was tied to their reformist politics.

The relationship between the search for respectability and the politics of the Socialist Party was well captured by one of the historians of socialism in the United States, Ira Kipnis. In summarizing the legacy of the SP, he writes:

> As prospects for electoral success seemed to grow, Right-wing Socialist leaders dumped increasingly large sections of the program in a desperate effort to win votes. Was middle-class America frightened by strikes, industrial unionism, free speech campaigns? Left-wing members of the party were expelled, industrial unionism dismissed as unimportant, im-

prisoned labor leaders abandoned. Were some Americans prejudiced against Negroes and the foreign-born? Negroes were attacked as "lynchable degenerates," and immigrants as saboteurs of America's high standard of living.[37]

In contrast, the left in the Socialist Party was the most consistent in fighting racism and segregation. Many of these socialists were active in the labor movement.

Especially important were the efforts of socialists to organize Black and white workers into a common organization—the Industrial Workers of the World (IWW). The IWW was established in 1905 as an alternative to the conservative craft unionism of the American Federation of Labor (AFL). Eugene Debs, Daniel De Leon, and "Big Bill" Haywood were among the many socialists in the IWW. The IWW considered the AFL "unreformable," proclaimed the need to organize on industrial rather than craft lines, and declared itself committed to organizing *all* workers, regardless of skill, color, sex, or national origin. At its founding convention in 1905, the IWW adopted the slogan "An injury to one is an injury to all" (a modification—and improvement—on the Knights of Labor motto "An injury to one is the concern of all"). The first section of its bylaws stated unambiguously: "no working man or woman shall be excluded from membership because of creed or color."[38]

The socialists who helped found and lead the IWW believed that the SP's emphasis on electoral respectability was a mistake and that the true power of workers lay in organizing at the point of production. This left wing, to its credit, emphasized action rather than speechifying. But this division produced a dichotomy between politics and economics, as well as electoral work and industrial work, and it left the SP in the hands of the right wing.

The IWW vigorously opposed racism in all its publications, and its unflinching opposition to all forms of discrimination was not only verbal. Unlike some unions before and since, the IWW practiced what it preached, even in the Southern states. The Wobblies, as IWW members called themselves, launched an impressive campaign to recruit Black workers in 1910, and at no time in its history did the IWW organize a segregated union.

Perhaps the best example of the IWW's activities was its organizing of lumber workers in the South. The Southern lumber industry employed 262,000 workers in 1910, more than half of whom were Black.[39] Despite the poor conditions of these workers, the AFL showed no interest in organizing them. In 1910, a group of lumber workers sympathetic to the Socialist Party and the IWW organized a local union. The union spread to other states and in 1911 a national union, the Brotherhood of Timber Workers (BTW), was established.

The BTW allowed Black workers to join but it did not challenge Southern segregation, forming separate "colored lodges" for its Black members. The employers responded quickly to the union's growth. Three hundred and fifty mills in three states were closed, and the union members were locked out. By the fall of 1911, between five thousand and seven thousand union members, Black and white, had been blacklisted.[40] Attempts to force workers to accept a substandard contract or to divide them on racial lines failed. The employers were forced to end the lockout and rehire the workers in February 1912.

Sympathetic to the IWW, the BTW decided to affiliate, and invited Bill Haywood to its 1912 convention in Alexandria, Louisiana, to address convention delegates. At the convention, Haywood expressed surprise that no Black workers were in attendance. BTW officials explained that the Black members were meeting separately because Louisiana law prohibited Blacks and whites from meeting together. Haywood answered:

> You work in the same mills together. Sometimes a Black man and a white man chop down the same tree together. You are meeting in convention to discuss the conditions under which you labor. This can't be done intelligently by passing resolutions here and then sending them out to another room for the Black man to act upon. Why not be sensible about this and call the Negroes into this convention? If it is against the law, this is one time when the law should be broken.[41]

Covington Hall, a Mississippi-born former adjutant general in the United Sons of the Confederate Veterans who had become a socialist and Wobbly, told delegates he supported Haywood's suggestion. "Let the Negroes come together with us, and if any arrests are made, all of us will go to jail, white and colored together."[42] The proposal was accepted. The Black and white lumber workers voted in favor of affiliation, and elected Black and white delegates to the upcoming IWW convention. That evening Haywood and Hall addressed a nonsegregated mass meeting at the Alexandria Opera House. This was an unprecedented event in the city's history. Even the Louisiana Socialist Party did not hold mixed meetings. Haywood noted the meeting had "a tremendous effect on workers who discovered that they could mingle in meetings as they mingled at work."[43] Philip Foner continues:

> [T]he feudal-minded lumber barons made intense efforts to destroy the unity of Black and white workers and to smash the union. They resorted to every weapon in the arsenal of anti-unionism: blacklisting of union members, Negro and white; eviction of union members from company houses; and spreading the charge throughout the South that the union was a revolutionary organization that sought, through its policy

of equality for Black and white, to undermine the entire fabric of Southern society. None of the measures succeeded. In November 1913, 1,300 unionists struck at the American Lumber Company in Merryville, Louisiana. The company brought in non-union workers, mostly Black, in an effort to break the strike. To keep strikers from talking to the scabs, the company housed them in quarters surrounded by a high barbed wire fence charged with electricity. But these efforts failed, and many of these workers refused to scab and instead joined the union. Foreign-born workers and Mexicans who were brought in to scab likewise refused to scab. The IWW announced: "It is a glorious thing to see, the miracle that has happened here in Dixie. This is coming true of the 'impossible'—this union of workers regardless of color, creed, nationality. To hear the Americans saying, 'You can starve us, but you cannot whip us'; the Negroes saying, 'You can fence us in, but you cannot make us scab!' Never did the Sante Fe Railroad, the Southern Lumber Operators' Association and the American Lumber Company expect to see such complete and defiant solidarity."[44]

Unable to break the strike, the employers and city authorities resorted to violence. Union leaders were arrested and deported from Merryville. Five union organizers were kidnapped, four of them brutally beaten and deported. The fifth, F. W. Oliver, a Black unionist, was murdered. Armed mobs attacked unionists and the union's headquarters were ransacked. "On February 19," recounts Philip Foner, "all remaining union men in Merryville were deported under penalty of death if they returned.... The union tried to get Governor Hall to halt the reign of terror. But the governor, charging that the union, by allowing Negroes to meet with whites in the same union halls, was seeking to destroy the Southern way of life, refused to act.... By the spring of 1914 the Brotherhood of Timber Workers was effectively destroyed."[45]

There are no reliable figures for the number of Black workers who joined the IWW. One estimate put the number of IWW cards issued between 1909 and 1924 at one million, 100,000 of which were issued to Black workers.[46] Whatever the exact number, the IWW provided a glimpse of the power a united working-class movement can exercise. Unfortunately, the ideas and practice of the IWW did not become the accepted norm inside the Socialist Party. Leaders of the party frowned upon the militancy of the IWW, and they successfully organized to expel Haywood and other IWW members in 1912. But there was another reason for the relatively limited influence of the IWW inside the Socialist Party: in rejecting the narrow electoral reformism of the right wing, the IWW dismissed "politics" in favor of economic struggles. This led them not only to see elections as irrelevant, but led to a general deprecation of the need to provide an overall political alternative to the right wing of the party.

The Communist Party

In August 1919, the Socialist Party of the United States split. At the heart of the split was the SP's attitude toward the successful 1917 Russian Revolution. The left wing of the SP supported the revolution and garnered a majority within the party. The right-wing minority, which controlled the party's apparatus, responded by expelling the majority.[47] Not one, but two, communist parties emerged from this conflict—the Communist Party (CP) and the Communist Labor Party. (The two would soon merge under pressure from leaders of the Russian Revolution and be renamed the Workers' Party in 1922.) Though they were largely made up of left-wing SP members and revolutionaries, neither of which accepted racists such as Berger in their ranks, both organizations initially shared the position advanced by Debs on racial oppression. The CP's position was summarized in the program adopted at its founding convention: "The Negro problem is a political and economic problem. The racial question of the Negro is simply the expression of his economic bondage and oppression, each intensifying the other. This complicates the Negro problem, but does not alter its proletarian character. The Communist Party will carry on agitation among the Negro workers to unite them with all class conscious workers."[48]

James P. Cannon, a founding member of the CP and later the leader of the Trotskyist movement in the United States, argued that the newly formed Communist Party had "nothing to start with on the Negro question but an inadequate *theory*, a false or indifferent *attitude* and the adherence of a few individual Negroes of a radical or revolutionary bent." This false theory, Cannon argued, stemmed from viewing the oppression of Blacks purely as "an economic problem, part of the struggle between the workers and capitalists; nothing could be done about the special problems of discrimination and inequality this side of socialism." In practice, he continued, this was "a formula for inaction on the Negro front, and—incidentally—a convenient shield for the dormant racial prejudices of the white radicals themselves."[49]

The CP's approach changed, however, largely because of two factors: the growth of the Black working class in the North and, crucially, the influence of the Russian Revolution. As Cannon put it:

> Even before the First World War and the Russian Revolution, Lenin and the Bolsheviks were distinguished from all other tendencies in the international socialist and labor movement by their concern with the problems of oppressed nations and national minorities, and affirmative support of their struggles for freedom, independence and the right of self-determination....
>
> After November 1917 this new doctrine—with special

emphasis on the Negroes—began to be transmitted to the American Communist movement with the authority of the Russian Revolution behind it. The Russians in the Comintern started on the American Communists with the harsh, insistent demand that they shake off their unspoken prejudices, pay attention to the special problems and grievances of the American Negroes, go to work among them, and champion their cause in the white community.

It took time for the Americans, raised in a different tradition, to assimilate the new Leninist ideas. But the Russians followed up year after year, piling up the arguments and increasing the pressure.... [S]lowly and painfully [the CPers began] to change their *attitude;* to assimilate the new theory of the Negro question as a *special* question of doubly-exploited second-class citizens, requiring a program of special demands as part of the overall program—and to start doing something about it.[50]

The "new theory" Cannon refers to was the approach developed by Lenin and the Russian Bolsheviks toward national struggles and movements for self-determination. It is worth reviewing Lenin's ideas on this question in some detail because they not only form the basis of the revolutionary Marxist position on nationalism, but they would also play an important role in the Communist Party's approach to Black oppression.

The Second International had no common position on the national question. The right wing of the Socialist Party in the United States, for example, supported the nationalism of its own ruling class but opposed any movements for self-determination in the colonized world. Gustav Noske similarly argued that the German Social Democratic Party would defend Germany "with as much determination as any gentleman on the right side of the House."[51] To right-wing reformists, socialism was not against colonies in principle.[52] Left-wing socialists such as Rosa Luxemburg, on the other hand, opposed any identification with the nationalism of their own state, but also opposed the slogan of self-determination. National independence, Luxemburg and other like-minded socialists argued, was the cry of a rising bourgeois class and should not become a demand of the workers' movement. "Socialism gives to every people the right of independence and the freedom of independent control of its own destinies," Luxemburg argued, but under capitalism, small nations could not attain real independence and became "only the pawns on the imperialist chessboard of the great powers."[53]

Lenin's view was a sharp break with both these positions. Revolutionaries, he argued, should support the right of self-determination as part of the struggle against imperialism. In the age of imperialism, capitalism would simultaneously reduce national differences, while giving rise to national struggles. "Developing capitalism knows two historical tendencies in the national question," Lenin wrote. "The first is the awakening of national life and national movements, the struggle against national oppression and the creation of national states. The second is the development and growing frequency of international intercourse in every form, the break-down of international barriers, the creation of the international unity of capital, of economic life in general, of politics, science, etc."[54]

The division of the world between oppressor and oppressed nations was the focal point of Lenin's position. Introducing the "Theses on the National and Colonial Questions" at the Second Congress of the Communist International, Lenin stated, "The characteristic feature of imperialism consists in the whole world, as we now see, being divided into a large number of oppressed nations and an insignificant number of oppressor nations, the latter possessing colossal wealth and powerful armed forces."[55] In the oppressor countries, socialists had to support the demands of oppressed nations as a precondition to breaking the workers' movement from chauvinism and the nationalism of its own ruling class. "In the internationalist education of the workers of the oppressor countries, emphasis must necessarily be laid on their advocating freedom for the oppressed countries to secede and their fighting for it."[56]

Even if the movement for self-determination was led by a nascent bourgeoisie, Lenin argued, socialists supported their struggle against imperialism. "*Insofar as* the bourgeoisie of the oppressed nation fights the oppressor, we are always, in every case, and more strongly than anyone else, *in favor*, for we are the staunchest and the most consistent enemies of oppression."[57] He added, "The bourgeois nationalism of *any* oppressed nation has a general democratic content that is directed *against* oppression, and it is this content that we *unconditionally* support."[58]

Arguing against the idea that national struggles were a diversion from the class struggle, Lenin wrote:

> To imagine that a social revolution is *conceivable* without revolts by small nations in the colonies and in Europe, without revolutionary outbursts by a section of the petty bourgeoisie with *all its prejudices*, without a movement of the politically non-conscious proletarian and semi-proletarian masses against oppression by the landowners, the church, and the monarchy, against national oppression, etc.—to imagine all this is to *repudiate social revolution*.... The dialectics of history are such that small nations, powerless as an *independent* factor in the struggle against imperialism, play a part as one of the ferments, one of the bacilli, which help the *real* anti-imperialist force, the socialist proletariat, to make its appearance on the scene.[59]

But Lenin's emphasis on the importance of national struggles and his support for the right of self-determination did not involve any compromise with nationalist ideology.

Support for the right of self-determination was a means to achieve international working-class unity, not to encourage fragmentation. In the oppressor nations, socialists upheld the right of self-determination both to combat chauvinism and to demonstrate their solidarity with workers in the oppressed nation. In the oppressed nation, socialists needed to combine opposition to imperialism with clear support for international working-class unity. Socialists "of the oppressed nations must attach prime significance to the unity and the merging of the workers of the oppressed nations with those of the oppressor nations."[60] A sharp distinction had to be drawn between upholding the *right* to secession and actually advocating it. "The right of nations to freely secede must not be confused with the *advisability* of secession by a given nation at a given moment."[61]

Support for self-determination was thus a means to advance the struggle for socialism, not an end in itself. Moreover, support for national liberation should in no way compromise the political or organizational independence of the workers' movement. The Communist International declared:

A resolute struggle must be waged against the attempt to clothe the revolutionary liberation movements in the backward countries which are not genuinely communist in communist colors. The Communist International has the duty of supporting the revolutionary movement in the colonies and the backward countries only with the object of rallying the constituent elements of the future proletarian parties—which will be truly communist and not only in name—in all the backward countries and educating them to a consciousness of their special task, namely, that, of fighting against the bourgeois-democratic trend in their own nation. The Communist International should collaborate provisionally with the revolutionary movement of the colonies and backward countries, and even form an alliance with it, but it must not amalgamate with it; it must unconditionally maintain the independence of the proletarian movement, even if it is only in an embryonic stage.[62]

A number of Communists from the United States attended the Comintern's second congress. John Reed, author of *Ten Days That Shook the World*,[63] spoke on the status of U.S. Blacks in the session on the national question. Reed's standpoint on Black oppression in the speech is often compared to that of Debs. He argued that "the only proper policy for the American Communists to follow is to consider the Negro first of all as a laborer." Blacks, he said, "did not demand national independence" and "consider themselves first of all Americans and feel very at home in the United States."[64] Some writers have ridiculed Reed's assessment of Marcus Garvey's movement—which, he argued, "has met with little, if any success"—as evidence of the Communist Party's detachment from Black struggles and as proof that the party was fundamentally no different from the reformist Socialist Party, at least on this vital issue. But this is a flawed assessment. Leaving aside his assessment of the level of support for Garveyism, Reed's speech was unambiguous in its support of the Black struggle. He denounced segregation and disfranchisement, noting that the "clergy of Southern churches teach that there is also a heaven in which the Jim Crow system is in operation."[65] He criticized the Socialist Party for "never seriously" endeavoring to recruit Blacks, and condemned the existence of segregated sections of the party. Reed also condemned the lynchings and race riots that followed the First World War, and supported the right of Blacks to armed self-defense against racist attacks. Nor was Reed blind to the rise of "race consciousness," arguing that the Black struggle offered socialism a "twofold opportunity: first, a strong race and social movement; second, a strong proletarian labor movement."[66]

Reed's argument didn't take root until the Russian party intervened. "[T]he American Communists received a letter from Lenin some time in 1921," historian Theodore Draper noted, "expressing surprise that their reports to Moscow made no mention of party work among Negroes and urging that they should be recognized as a strategically important element in Communist activity."[67]

The Fourth Congress of the Comintern, held in 1922, adopted the National and Colonial Commission's "Theses on the Negro Question." The four theses stated:

(i) The fourth congress recognizes the necessity of supporting every form of the Negro movement which undermines or weakens capitalism, or hampers its further penetration.

(ii) The Communist International will fight for the equality of the white and Black races, for equal wages and equal political and social rights.

(iii) The Communist International will use every means at its disposal to force the trade unions to admit Black workers, or, where this right already exists on paper, to conduct special propaganda for the entry of Negroes into the unions. If this should prove impossible, the Communist International will organize the Negroes in trade unions of their own and use united front tactics to compel their admission.

(iv) The Communist International will take steps immediately to convene a world Negro congress or conference.[68]

Articles on Black struggles began to appear in the CP press, and the party established an organizer for its work among Blacks. The program adopted by the CP (then called the Workers' Party) at its 1922 convention was much stronger than the one adopted in 1919. It read in part:

The Negro workers of this country are exploited and oppressed more ruthlessly than any other group. The history of the Southern Negro is the history of brutal terrorism, of persecution and murder. During the war tens of thousands of Southern Negroes were brought to the industrial centers of the North to supply the needs of the employers for cheap labor. In the Northern industrial cities the Negro has found the same bitter discrimination as in the South. The attacks upon the Negroes of East St. Louis, Illinois, the riot in Chicago, are examples of the additional burden of oppression, which is the lot of the Negro worker. Although the influx of Negro workers in the Northern industrial centers has laid the foundations for a mass movement of Negroes who are industrial workers, the anti-Negro policy of organized labor has made it impossible to organize these industrial workers.... The Workers' Party will seek to end the policy of discrimination followed by the labor unions. It will endeavor to destroy altogether the barriers of race prejudice that have been used to keep apart the Black and white workers and weld them into a solid mass for the struggle against the Capitalists who exploit them.[69]

Despite the sentiment expressed in such resolutions, however, the Communist Party's initial efforts to recruit Blacks met with little success. In 1925, for example, the party launched the American Negro Labor Congress (ANLC) to organize Black workers excluded from the racist American Federation of Labor. As James Ford, one of the small handful of Blacks who joined the party via the ANLC, put it, "For the period of its existence it was almost completely isolated from the basic masses of the Negro people."[70] The ANLC was met with hostility by the AFL and the "small segment of the Black community that expressed prolabor views,"[71] including the most prominent Black trade unionist, A. Philip Randolph, president of the Sleeping Car Porters' union. Even Black observers sympathetic to the ANLC's aims found the "behavior of some of its organizers extraordinarily bizarre,"[72] best expressed by the evening entertainment at the ANLC's founding convention—a Russian ballet.

The CP did succeed, however, in recruiting a small number of Blacks who would later prove crucial in extending the party's influence. The most important success in this period was its recruitment of several leaders of the African Blood Brotherhood (ABB). The ABB was founded by Cyril V. Briggs in the fall of 1917 (there is some controversy over the exact date) as "a revolutionary secret order," and its platform called for the "absolute race equality" of Blacks and "fellowship...with the class-conscious revolutionary white workers." The ABB also called for armed resistance to lynching, unqualified franchise rights for Blacks in the South, a struggle for equal rights against all forms of discrimination, and the organization of Blacks into the existing trade unions.[73] In its first years, the ABB combined a radical Black nationalism with a strong sympathy to the ideas of the Bolshevik Revolution. Briggs became increasingly critical of Marcus Garvey's UNIA, and in 1921 joined the Communist Party. Most of the ABB's leadership followed Briggs into the party, forming its first generation of Black leaders.

By the end of the 1920s, the Communist Party's approach to Blacks underwent an important transformation. Unfortunately, the impetus for the change came not from an honest evaluation of party work in the United States, but from an international maneuver by the now Stalin-controlled Comintern. At its sixth congress in 1928, the Comintern declared that Southern Blacks in the United States constituted a nation and that the party should adopt the slogan of "Self-Determination in the Black Belt" for party work among Blacks. As Lee Sustar explains:

> The self-determination slogan was the American version of the Comintern's "new theory" that national liberation struggles had to go through distinct "stages"—first a bourgeois nationalist stage, and only after that the struggle for

socialism. The problem with this approach is that it means subordinating the needs of workers to those of the middle class—who upon victory, will turn their backs, or worse, on their former allies.... In the 1920s, followers of Marcus Garvey demanded not self-determination in the South, but rather an exodus to Africa—for which the CP attacked them. In the early 1930s, the CP denounced the Ethiopian Peace Movement, a back-to-Africa group, and the National Movement for the Establishment of a Forty-Ninth State, which advocated Black migration to sparsely settled areas in the United States. The CP favored Black self-determination only if it meant acceptance of the Black Belt theory.[74]

There is considerable controversy over the origins of the Black Belt theory, but it is clear that the party initially opposed the slogan and that the theory had little bearing on the actual conditions or aspirations of Blacks. Until 1910, it *might* have been possible to speak of Blacks as a separate oppressed nation, given that 90 percent of Blacks lived in the South, with a majority of those living in rural areas.[75] But any such basis was completely destroyed by the successive waves of Black migration northward, beginning with the First World War. Moreover, as Leon Trotsky was to argue, the slogan of "Self-Determination for the Black Belt" could easily be seen as a demand by whites for segregation![76]

No real forces other than the Communist Party advanced the Black Belt proposal. The theory was effectively marginalized within the CP's work, which was mainly focused in the Northern cities. But the slogan did have one positive effect. By raising the importance of fighting racism, it helped transform the Communist Party into a major force among Blacks.[77]

The Communist Party's campaign to free the Scottsboro Boys is the most famous example of the party's antiracist work in this period. The case involved nine young men falsely accused of gang rape and sentenced to death in 1931. The existing Black organizations shunned the case. The NAACP did not send a lawyer to help the men until after they were convicted in an Alabama court.[78] The party undertook an international campaign to free the Scottsboro Boys, and gained widespread respect among Blacks for its principled defense of the young men. A May 16, 1931, protest march in Harlem that began with a march of several hundred Communists, most of them white, ended with a mass rally involving more than three thousand Black Harlemites. At the rally, the throng heard from one of the Scottsboro mothers, and from Communist speakers who addressed the crowd in Finnish, Spanish, and Romanian.[79] The Scottsboro campaign carried on for years with events like this one, which succeeded in stopping the Scottsboro executions and ultimately freeing the men.

The 1930s struggle to build industrial unions drew in thousands of Black workers. In workplaces like the Chicago stockyards, or the steel mills of the Great Lakes states, Communist organizers often proved crucial to forging a link between the unions and Black workers. The number of Blacks in unions jumped from one hundred thousand in 1935 to just under five hundred thousand in 1940.[80] Black membership in the Communist Party also rose considerably, from slightly less than 1,000 at the beginning of the 1930s to 5,005 in 1939.[81] As a result of its activism around the Scottsboro case and the union movement, the CP's Black membership grew from two hundred members in 1930 (less than 3 percent of the total) to seven thousand in 1938 (over 9 percent). In some cities, the percentage of Black members was considerably higher. In Chicago in 1931, close to one-quarter of the city's 2,000 members was Black. As Blacks constituted 11 percent of the total U.S. population at the time, these figures represented a small but important step in building a multiracial movement. At a time when segregation was rampant—legally in the South, de facto in the North—the CP was virtually the only integrated organization in the country.

The success of the Communist Party alarmed middle-class Black organizations. For the first time in the United States, a significant layer of Blacks saw a socialist organization as a viable political alternative. W. E. B. Du Bois, at the time still a member of the NAACP (he didn't join the Communist Party until the early 1960s), wrote: "The task that I have recently been setting myself is to blunt the wedge that the Communist Party is driving into our group."[82]

Indeed, some in the NAACP thought they could use the fear of the Communist Party as a means to win support for their organization. "Evidently the NAACP leadership was really delighted by the Communist Party's activity in the South," Philip Foner noted.[83] In a letter dated June 6, 1933, Walter White assured James Weldon Johnson, secretary of the NAACP until 1931, "[E]verywhere I went in the South the white people are afraid of the effect of Communist propaganda on the Negro. As a result, *they are willing now more than ever before to consider the program of the NAACP and to make concessions to it*, if for no other reason than that in their opinion, it is the lesser of two evils."[84]

But if some whites in the South were drawn to the NAACP as a result of the CP's activities, Blacks perceived the CP differently. As Paul D'Amato has written:

> The CP initiated a multitude of struggles against racism through the Depression decade. CP members led struggles against poor housing and evictions, for unemployment relief, against police terror and lynching. They organized mass campaigns for the defense of victims of racist injustice; they petitioned against segregation in baseball; they organized interracial meetings and dances, demonstrations, and social gatherings both in the North and in the South; they initiated campaigns to root out manifestations of rac-

ism inside the party. When Communists traveled to Washington to demonstrate on behalf of the Scottsboro Boys, they stopped off on the way to sit down in restaurants that refused to serve Blacks—a tactic adopted by the civil rights movement in the 1960s. In these years, the CP was able to challenge traditional Black organizations like the NAACP and the Garveyites.[85]

The Communist Party demonstrated in practice the possibility of overcoming racism and the building of a multiracial political organization dedicated to transforming society. The problem is that, by the late 1920s, the Communist Party had begun the process of degeneration from revolutionary Marxism to Stalinism. This was to affect the entire work of the party, including its commitment to Black liberation. One marker of this problem was the already mentioned imposition of the "Black Belt" theory in 1928–29. Another example was the Comintern's 180-degree turn in the opposite direction in 1935 when it called for the building of a broad "people's front" against fascism. Motivated primarily by Stalin's effort to seek allies among the bourgeois governments of the West for the impending war against Hitler, the "Popular Front" ended the CP's sectarian lunacy of 1929–34 that equated reformists with fascists. But in moving away from sectarianism, the CP came to embrace as allies such figures as President Franklin Roosevelt.

With the formation of a "Popular Front" with bourgeois opponents to fascism, the party began to compromise its earlier commitment to combatting racism. It opposed a proposed march on Washington against segregation because, party officials argued, this would only disrupt the war effort. The Communist Party became the most ardent supporter of the Second World War, and subordinated everything to this aim, including the right of workers to strike and the struggle for Black civil rights. Not only did this make it easier for the government to witch-hunt the organization after the war, but it also laid the basis for the disillusionment of hundreds of Black workers who had joined the party during the 1930s.

The CP's accommodation to Roosevelt and the New Deal liberals meant supporting the Democratic Party, which refused to challenge segregation for fear of alienating its Southern "Dixiecrat" wing. Roosevelt even refused to support anti-lynching legislation at a time when dozens of mob lynchings were being committed against Blacks every year.

The Stalinist opportunism of the CP disillusioned many Black members who had been attracted to the CP's work against racism. Though the party continued to grow, its political zigzags, dictated by the bureaucracy in Russia, ultimately compromised and undermined its commitment to fighting racism. The CP's credibility was further eroded when in 1939, as a result of the Hitler-Stalin pact, the party again reversed its policy of united front work and began denouncing Roosevelt again. With Hitler's invasion of Russia, the party then became Roosevelt's biggest cheerleader, calling on Blacks to subordinate their demands for integrating the army and war production industries to the success of the war effort. The party even supported the internment of Americans of Japanese descent.

In spite of its Stalinism, the CP's work in the 1930s showed that building a fighting unity between Blacks and whites is possible in the United States. Had the CP been a genuine revolutionary party, one which combined a commitment to fighting racism with a willingness to unite with other forces not yet won to revolutionary ideas, it could have grown even more massively. It could have provided a clear alternative to New Deal liberalism, the NAACP, and the cul-de-sac of Black nationalism. Because it didn't provide this kind of alternative, an opportunity of historic proportions was lost.

Trotsky and Black Nationalism

Leaders of the Russian Revolution had successfully influenced American communists to change their approach to Black struggles in the 1920s. One of those leaders, Leon Trotsky, was to break with the Communist movement and lead an opposition to the bureaucratization and degeneration of the Russian Revolution. In 1933, Leon Trotsky had pushed his allies in the United States to address the issues of racism and Black oppression directly, challenging them to overcome their political passivity on these fundamental questions.

Trotsky admitted knowing little about the concrete situation of Blacks in the United States, and tried to learn what he could from organizers in the Socialist Workers Party. Unfortunately, they were not very familiar with conditions in the South either, and were unable to tell Trotsky whether or not Blacks in the South even spoke a different language.[86] Through his analysis, though, Trotsky was able to reach some important conclusions. He argued that the slogan of self-determination for Blacks should be supported:

> The Negroes are a race and not a nation. Nations grow out of racial material under definite conditions....
>
> We of course do not obligate the Negroes to become a nation; whether they are is a question of their consciousness, that is, what they desire and what they strive for. We say: if the Negroes want that then we must fight against imperialism to the last drop of blood, so that they gain the right, wherever and however they please, to separate a piece of land for themselves....
>
> If the situation was such that in America common actions took place involving white and Black workers, that class fraternization already was a fact, then perhaps our comrades' arguments would have a basis (I do not say that it would be correct); then perhaps we would divide the Black

workers from the white if we began to raise the slogan of "self-determination."

But today the white workers in relation to the Negroes are the oppressors, scoundrels, who persecute the Black and the yellow, hold them in contempt, and lynch them.[87]

"The argument that the slogan for self-determination leads away from the class point of view is an adaptation to the ideology of the white workers," he added. "The Negro can be developed to a class point of view only when the white worker is educated."[88]

The struggle for Black rights, Trotsky argued, should be viewed as part of the process of what he described in his theory of permanent revolution: "The [Black] petty bourgeoisie will take up the demand for equal rights and for self-determination but will prove absolutely incapable in the struggle; the Negro proletariat will march over the petty bourgeoisie in the direction toward the proletarian revolution."[89]

This dynamic, Trotsky went on to argue, can transform Black workers from an excluded and oppressed group within the working class to its most advanced. "The Russians were the European Negroes," he argued. "It is very possible that the Negroes will proceed through self-determination to the proletarian dictatorship in a couple of gigantic strides, ahead of the great bloc of white workers. They will then be the vanguard."[90]

Finally, Trotsky warned that racism and Black nationalism were fundamentally different. As such, he urged a "merciless struggle not against the supposed national prepossessions of the Negroes but against the colossal prejudices of the white workers and [which] makes no concession to them whatever."[91]

Trotsky further developed his views on Black nationalism in a historic dialogue with the Trinidadian Trotskyist C. L. R. James in Coyoacán, Mexico, in 1939. The discussions between James and Trotsky covered three points: the position to be adopted toward the slogan of "self-determination"; a proposal to launch an all-Black political organization, indep-en-dent of the Socialist Workers Party; and the structure, program, and activity of such an organization.

In the first set of discussions, Trotsky again argued in favor of Black self-determination. In preparation for the meeting, James had drafted a preliminary statement outlining his views on the question. On self-determination James wrote:

> The Negro must be won for socialism. There is no other way out for him in America or elsewhere. But he must be won on the basis of his own experience and his own activity. There is no other way for him to learn, nor for that matter, for any other group of toilers! *If he wanted self-determination,* then however reactionary it might be in every other respect, it would be the business of the revolutionary party to raise that slogan. If after the revolution he insisted on carrying out that slogan and forming his own Negro state, the revolutionary party would have to stand by its promises...patiently trust to economic development and education to achieve an integration. But the Negro, fortunately for socialism, does not want self-determination.[92]

James concluded his arguments against self-determination by arguing that the Black population in the United States lacked the "tradition of language, literature and history to add to the economic and political oppression."[93] In his first contribution in the discussion, James went on to state that:

> The danger of our advocating and injecting a policy of self-determination is that it is the surest way to divide and confuse the workers in the South. The white workers have centuries of prejudice to overcome, but at the present time many of them are working with the Negroes in the Southern sharecroppers' union, and with the rise of the struggle there is every possibility that they will be able to overcome their agelong prejudices. But for us to propose that the Negro

have this Black state for himself is asking too much from the white workers: especially when the Negro himself is not making the same demand.[94]

In response, Trotsky took up several points. Firstly, he found James' views on the question confusing. Was James arguing for the elimination of the slogan of self-determination from the SWP's program, or was he saying that the SWP would fight for self-determination if Blacks mobilized and fought around the demand? Secondly, Trotsky objected to the use of the term "reactionary" to describe the demand for self-determination. Thirdly, he argued that he was against making the demand the central slogan of the Trotskyists, but "only to proclaim our obligation to support the struggle" if Blacks themselves wanted it.[95] In a shift from his earlier position, Trotsky went on to explain, "[I]t seems to me that the CP's attitude of making an imperative slogan of it was false. It was a case of the whites saying to the Negroes, 'You must create a ghetto for yourselves.' It is tactless and false and can only serve to repulse the Negroes. Their only interpretation can be that the whites want to be separated from them."[96]

James concluded by expressing his complete agreement with Trotsky, and argued that he only used the term reactionary to describe self-determination if seen from the vantage point of a socialist solution. Trotsky argued that this view was abstract; self-determination by Blacks could only be the result of a massive struggle, which would be "a tremendous revolutionary step."[97]

The following day, discussion revolved around the possibility of the SWP helping to launch a Black organization. James put forward a number of proposals for such an organization. These included making plans for the study of the history of Blacks and the Black struggle, launching a weekly paper, and making *International African Opinion* the new organization's theoretical journal. The organization would be open to all Blacks, James proposed, and would be an activist organization, intervening in trade unions, against fascism and war, fielding candidates, and fighting discrimination. In anticipation of tactics used in the civil rights movement in the 1960s, James argued that Blacks should go to segregated restaurants, sit in, "ordering...for instance some coffee," and campaign around the issue of segregation.[98]

Differences between James and Trotsky emerged on two main points. First, Trotsky expressed some skepticism about the whole project of initiating a new organization. If a mass movement already existed, argued Trotsky, then of course he would be in favor of participation within it, but it was another question for the SWP to launch such an organization on its own. "But the question remains as to whether we can take upon ourselves the initiative of forming such an organization of Negroes as Negroes—not for the purpose of winning some elements to our party but for the purpose of doing systematic educational work in order to elevate them politically."[99] Were such an organization only to attract disillusioned Black intellectuals who had left the Communist Party, then it would not serve any purpose. "The real question," he continued, "is whether or not it is possible to organize a mass movement."[100]

The other argument involved James' initial proposal to have the organization's paper exclude socialist politics. Trotsky argued that it was one thing to acknowledge the heterogeneous character of the proposed organization, but it was quite another "to tie our hands in advance."[101]

The immediate result of these discussions was the SWP's adoption of a resolution largely based on these discussions at its convention in July 1939. The organization's journal, *New International,* also devoted an issue to a discussion of the

Black question in December of the same year.[102] All the other plans, however, were shelved. The outbreak of war in Europe and the ensuing split in the SWP over whether the USSR was still to be considered a socialist country, saw C. L. R. James leave the SWP. He left the SWP with the breakaway organization called the Workers' Party in 1940.

In 1947, James rejoined the SWP, and in 1948 he wrote its major resolution on the Black question. Entitled "The Revolutionary Answer to the Negro Problem in the U.S.A.," James described it as a "clear political program which summarized the political attitudes and ideas which I had placed before Trotsky in 1938." The core of the resolution argued that unlike previous socialists in the United States,

> We say, number one, that the Negro struggle, the inde-pen-dent Negro struggle, has a vitality and a validity of its own....
>
> We say, number two, that this independent Negro movement is able to intervene with terrific force upon the general social and political life of the nation, despite the fact that it is waged under the banner of democratic rights, and is not led necessarily either by the organized labor movement or the Marxist party.
>
> We say, number three, and this is the most important, that it is able to exercise a powerful influence upon the revolutionary proletariat, that is has got a great contribution to make to the development of the proletariat in the United States, and that it is in itself a constituent part of the struggle for socialism.[103]

The discussions between C. L. R. James and Leon Trotsky marked an important advance in the understanding of the dynamics of the Black struggle in the United States. They also contained important insights that would later be validated by the emergence of the civil rights and Black Power movements in the 1950s and 1960s. The backwardness of the labor movement on the one hand, and the weakness of the left on the other, combined in such a way that a Black struggle emerged independently of these forces in the civil rights struggle. The general thrust of the movement challenged the capitalist system and its institutions, even if its leadership did not aim to do this. Blacks, in massive numbers, went from being politically inactive to being in the forefront of the struggle. In this context, the SWP's understanding of the impetus to self-determination led the party to be generally sympathetic to the emergence of Black nationalism in the 1960s, as opposed to the Communist Party and the social democratic left, which denounced Malcolm X and the Black Panthers.

However, there were also several ambiguities and weaknesses in the James–Trotsky discussion, several of which can be identified in James' subsequent political development. Most striking is the enormous gulf that lay between the proposal for a Black organization and the forces actually available to the SWP. The need for revolutionary leadership was apparent, but the forces of the Trotskyist Fourth International were weak. "The discrepancy between our forces and our tasks," Trotsky wrote, meant that in practice the SWP could do little to implement the program he had suggested.[104] Worse, the lack of real forces would lead some of Trotsky's followers to exaggerate the importance of the "correct" program and set of demands in building real influence in the movement. Likewise, vying for control of the organization's apparatus among various forces on the left could easily become a substitute for attracting Black workers.

Trotsky was aware of the dangers involved, but overestimated the capacity of the SWP to launch a mass Black organization. "It is a question," Trotsky insisted "of awakening the Negro masses."[105] Considering the size and composition of the SWP, however, this was a utopian task.

One of Trotsky's principal concerns was the SWP's increasing adaptation to an "aristocratic" milieu and its continued isolation from the mass of workers, "of whom the Negroes are the most exploited."[106] But he hoped that the proper education of the core activists and organizers of the party would put them in a position to become the leadership of a new Black upsurge. "[T]he harsh and tragic dialectic of our epoch is working in our favor," he wrote in late 1938. "Brought to the extreme pitch of exasperation and indignation, the masses will find no other leadership than that offered by the Fourth International."[107]

Trotsky's overestimation of the opportunities and prospects for revolutionaries at least had the merit of keeping alive the banner of Bolshevism. By contrast, James' overestimation of immediate revolutionary prospects led him to embrace a theory of spontaneity. While Trotsky was wrong to expect the launching of an organization that would "awaken the Black masses," James made the mistake of identifying a revolutionary potential with present actuality. Thus, for example, during the Second World War, James argued that the formation of workers' soviets—that is, a worker's revolution in Europe—was on the immediate agenda for socialists.[108] And while Lenin was right to have built a revolutionary party in Russia before the October Revolution, James wrote, "The task is to abolish organization. The task today is to call for, to teach, to illustrate, to develop *spontaneity*—the free creative activity of the proletariat."[109]

While James was undoubtedly correct in emphasizing the material basis for an independent Black struggle in the United States and in stressing the impact it would have, he left a number of important questions unanswered. A Black movement did develop in the United States, but it was not independent of class forces. The civil rights movement, as we shall see later, was above all of benefit to the Black middle class. Related to this is the question of socialist intervention in such a movement. What should socialists argue within such a movement? How should they relate to Black popular struggles? James did not deal with these questions because, as we have seen, he came to reject the need to build a revolutionary party.

CHAPTER EIGHT

The Roots of the Civil Rights Movement

The roots of the civil rights movement of the 1950s and 1960s lie in the transformed conditions and experience of Blacks during the Second World War. Large numbers of jobs previously closed to Black workers were suddenly available. Black migration to the North reached an unprecedented scale. Until the eve of the First World War, 90 percent of Blacks lived in the South. As late as 1940, 77 percent of all Blacks resided in the former slave states—compared to 27 percent of whites.[1] By 1950, the figure had declined to 68 percent, a trend that would continue into the 1960s.[2] In 1910, 57 percent of all Black male workers and 52 percent of all Black female workers were farmers. Eight percent of men and 42 percent of women were employed as domestics or personal servants. Only one sixth of the Black population worked in manufacturing or industry. By 1940, 28 percent of Black workers were service workers, and farm employment had dropped to 32 percent. By 1960, 38 percent of Blacks were industrial workers, 32 percent service workers, and only 8 percent of all Blacks employed worked on farms.[3] The urbanization of the Black population transformed its character—and as we will explore in this chapter, heightened the confidence of Blacks in both the North and the South to challenge racism. By 1946, Black employment in manufacturing had increased 135 percent over its 1940 proportion, and under the auspices of the CIO, Black workers joined industrial unions by the tens of thousands. One hundred thousand Black workers joined the aircraft industry organized by the United Auto Workers (UAW), 5,000 Blacks joined the National Maritime Union, and in one Baltimore local of the Industrial Union of Marine and Shipbuilding Workers of America, Black employment went from 5 percent of the workforce in 1941 to 20 percent by 1943, and even elected a Black shop steward.[4]

The role played by Blacks during the war proved to be decisive. Thousands of Blacks were drafted into the army. More than three million Black men registered for the service, of whom 500,000 were stationed abroad.[5] Having fought for "democracy" abroad, Blacks returning from the war believed they ought to have some rights at home—and they intended to fight for those rights.

It was against this backdrop that several legal challenges to segregation, largely initiated by the NAACP, were to prove successful. The most famous of these was the 1954 Supreme Court ruling in *Brown v Board of Education of Topeka,* which ordered the desegregation of public schools and struck down the "separate but equal" doctrine that was at the core of segregation in the South. Many civil rights historians assert that *Brown v Board of Education of Topeka* and similar court decisions raised the confidence and combativeness of Blacks. While this is undoubtedly the case, the focus on the 1954 Supreme Court ruling tends to overlook how several factors *retarded* the emergence of the civil rights movement for almost a decade. The *Brown* decision, in fact, only confirmed the basic thrust of the Court's rulings since the 1940s. A May 1946 Supreme Court decision, for example, ruled that laws requiring segregation on interstate buses were unconstitutional. In April 1944 the Court ended, by an eight to one majority, the use of all-white primary elections.[6] As Manning Marable points out:

> By the spring of 1946, there were 75,000 Black registered voters in Texas and 100,000 Black voters in Georgia. Yet the sit-ins, the non-violent street demonstrations, did not yet occur; the facade of white supremacy was crumbling, yet for almost ten years there was no overt and mass movement which challenged racism in the streets.[7]

This ten-year delay can be attributed to two factors: the decimation of the left (most crucially the Communist Party) in the McCarthyite witch-hunts that accompanied the Cold War, and the complicity of the trade union leadership and liberal Black politicians in the witch-hunts. Arguably the most prominent Black leader and trade unionist of the period, A. Philip Randolph, fully supported the anti-Communist purge of the unions—even though it "was the principal reason for the decline in the AFL-CIO's commitment to the struggle against racial segregation."[8]

The NAACP and other middle-class Black organizations likewise joined in the witch-hunt, eager to prove their patriotism. The NAACP refused to assist Black Communist Party members who were subpoenaed by the House Un-American Activities Committee. The NAACP even abandoned one of its founding members, W. E. B. Du Bois, when he was indicted as "an agent of a foreign principal" in 1951.[9] Du Bois was not a Communist Party member or a Marxist, but he understood that the Black middle classes had a stake in the system:

> The reaction of Negroes [to the case] revealed a distinct cleavage not hitherto clear in American Negro opinion. The intelligentsia, the successful business and professional men, were...either silent or actually antagonistic. The reasons were clear; many believed that the government had actual

proof of subversive activities on our part; until the very end they awaited their disclosure. [These Blacks] had become American in their acceptance of exploitation as defensible, and in their imitation of American "conspicuous expenditure."... They proposed to make money and spend it as pleased them. They had beautiful homes, large and expensive cars and fur coats. They hated "communism" and "socialism" as much as any white American.[10]

The Lynching of Emmett Till

These factors delayed the emergence of the civil rights movement, but there could be no return to old ways. When war production was ended and Black workers lost their new jobs, estimates are that they were "affected two and one-half times as severely as white workers."[11] Jobs that had become available to Black workers because of the labor shortage were once again subject to a color bar. Nevertheless, Blacks had become a permanent, and growing, segment of the workforce.

In the South, segregation still reigned unchallenged, and Blacks were still stripped of the most basic rights. Writes a biographer of Martin Luther King, Jr., "This was a violent time in Alabama—an era when a judge and jury sentenced a Negro man to death for stealing $1.95 from a white woman (commuted later by Governor Folsom) and when police officers often meted out harsher justice informally, beyond the meager restraints of a court."[12]

In response to the signs of challenge to Jim Crow, white supremacists began organizing a renewed campaign of terror. Yet, rather than deflating the "new mood" among Blacks, resistance to change only deepened the resolve of thousands to fight back. "Toward the end of 1955," wrote one observer, "the spirit of rebellion and resistance was spreading among Black people in every corner of the South."[13]

In Mississippi the lynching of Emmett Till, a fourteen-year-old Black boy from Chicago, was also a catalyst that helped to turn a mood of anger into a mood of action. The following editorial, from a small-circulation journal, the *American Socialist*, captured the significance of the Till case:

> Much violence has calloused our sensibilities in this day and age. Yet there is something about the murder of Emmett Louis Till to touch even the coldest heart. The thought that in this America, full-grown and brawny men would abduct a grade-school child, and beat in his helplessness until all his teeth were out, his head caved in, his body mutilated with horrible wounds, put a bullet into his brain and drop him into a river—truly, even the most emotionally impervious cannot fail to be aroused.
>
> In a decaying social order, man's inhumanity to man includes man's inhumanity to children. And the children, even in their years of hope and light-heartedness, are forced to taste the bitter fruits of knowledge. During the Second World War, one of those public school essay contests in which children are asked to write answers to usually fatuous questions was held, the question being: "How would you punish Hitler for his crimes?" On one paper written by a little Black girl, the answer was startling: "I would put him in a Black skin and force him to spend the rest of this life in the United States." Here was a pathetic early wisdom. And Emmett Louis Till also, in his final hour, knew more about our Southland and the desperate forces at work in it than any college of sociologists. May we be granted the power to build a world in which our children will be spared such lessons![14]

But "the coldest hearts," it turned out, were not "touched." The brutal murder of Emmett Till was compounded by the impunity with which his accused murderers behaved, and by the complete disinterest and inaction of local, state, and federal authorities.

In 1955, those accused of Till's murder were acquitted by an all-white, all-male jury in sixty-seven minutes. One of the jurors said the deliberation was actually extended to make it look better: he later explained to the press: "If we hadn't stopped to drink pop, it wouldn't have taken that long."[15]

In 1955, the response of the federal government was to simply ignore the case. But Till's mother sought to get her government to bring the truth to light. On September 2, 1956, she sent a telegram to President Dwight D. Eisenhower:

> The President
> The White House
> I the mother of Emmett Louis Till am pleading that you personally see that justice is meted out to all persons involved in the beastly lynching of my son in Money, Miss. Awaiting a direct reply from you.
> Mamie E. Bradley[16]

In spite of FBI records and news reports at the time citing specific individuals directly involved in Till's murder, President Eisenhower didn't take any action. Responding to advice from the Justice Department and FBI, he did not even bother to reply to Bradley's telegram. In a memo dated October 23, 1956, Max Rabb, Eisenhower's Secretary of the Cabinet, explained to James C. Hagerty, White House Press Secretary:

> While it cannot be said openly, the FBI had definite knowledge that Mrs. Bradley permitted herself to be the instrument of the Communist Party, which seized upon the case as a cause celebre and upon her as the means of making the race question a burning issue. Mrs. Bradley was taken around the United States by Communists as a prize exhibit and they pulled all the stops in their exploitation. While the facts in the case reflected discredit upon those who perpetrated the crime, Lou Nichols [Assistant Director of the FBI] labeled Mrs. Bradley herself as a "phoney." Any recognition

of her would have been used to further Communist causes in this country. Subsequently, Mrs. Bradley was discredited for using her son's death as a means of making a living. The boy's father, incidentally, was executed by the Army in Italy on a sex charge.

For these reasons, it was felt inadvisable to make a courteous reply. Such a response would have been distorted to build up the Communist claim that this was another Willie McGee or Rosenberg case.[17]

At the time, FBI Director J. Edgar Hoover wrote a memo declaring that there was no legal basis for federal involvement in Till's case: "There has been no allegation made that the victim [Emmett Till] has been subjected to the deprivation of any right or privilege which is secured and protected by the Constitution and the laws of the United States."[18] Like Rabb, Hoover's main concern was that the Communist Party would use the case to further its aims.

Mississippi's *Jackson Daily News* published an editorial on September 25, 1955, that read, "Practically all the evidence against the defendants was circumstantial evidence. It is best for all concerned that the Bryant-Milam [the defendants'] case be forgotten as quickly as possible. It has received far more publicity than it should have been given."[19]

It was in these conditions that the civil rights movement exploded onto the scene, a harbinger of which was the fifty thousand people who turned out to Till's funeral in Chicago.

The Montgomery Bus Boycott

The growth of militancy among Southern Blacks produced its own leadership and organization, since virtually no political organization existed that stood for the interests of the mass of Southern Blacks. The two main political parties in the United States maintained segregation. The existing

Black organizations—the NAACP and the Urban League—
were organizations of middle-class professionals, aiming
to end segregation through legal means and not through a
mass struggle. The politics and leadership that would come
to dominate this upsurge first emerged in the 1955 Montgomery Bus Boycott in Montgomery, Alabama.

The bus boycott was sparked by the refusal of Rosa Parks
to give up her seat on a bus to a white passenger, on December 1, 1955. Parks was a seamstress and secretary of the local
NAACP chapter. The driver called the police, who promptly
arrested Mrs. Parks. She was charged with violating the city's
segregation ordinance. The very next day a meeting at Martin Luther King, Jr.'s church called for a one-day boycott of all
Montgomery's buses on Monday, December 5. On that day the
Montgomery Improvement Association (MIA) elected its first
president, Martin Luther King, Jr. The boycott lasted 381 days,
elevating the struggle—and King—to national prominence.

The initial demands of the Montgomery movement were
quite moderate, and did not aim to challenge the system of
segregation as such. The MIA asked for courteous treatment
of Black passengers, seating on a first-come, first-served
basis, with Blacks seated in the rear and employment of Black
drivers on the predominantly Black routes. The local chapter
of the NAACP had discussed a boycott for the last year, but
had failed to act. Resistance by Montgomery officials and the
virtually unanimous support for the boycott by Montgomery's
Black population changed the character of the struggle. King
said later:

> Feeling that our demands were moderate, I had assumed
> that they would be granted with little question; I had be-
> lieved that the privileged would give up their privileges on
> request. This experience, however, taught me a lesson.
> I came to see that no one gives up his privileges without

strong resistance. I saw further that the underlying purpose
of segregation was to oppress and exploit the segregated,
not simply to keep them apart.[20]

The new leaders, like King, were not radicals. But King
was not only an expression of the "new mood," he was also influenced by it. The civil rights leaders believed that theirs was
a moral struggle and that the "nation" suffered from the blight
of racism. "It is...a moral issue...which may well determine the
destiny of our nation in the ideological struggle with communism," argued King.

King and other leaders of the movement played down any
suggestion that the bus boycott was designed to challenge
the existing order of things. As King put it in 1955: "We are
not asking for an end to segregation." Instead, Blacks sought
the right to sit, not stand, in seats that were not occupied by
whites, because, King said, "we don't like the idea of Negroes
having to stand up when there are vacant seats."[21]

Their basic strategy would revolve around nonviolent
mass action to pressure the authorities into negotiations,
leading, it was hoped, to concessions. As such, it was not a
struggle of Black against white: "We are out to defeat injustice and not white persons who may be unjust."[22] King was
well aware that the movement's demands would be met with
concerted resistance, but this only elevated the moral character of struggle itself:

> We will match your capacity to inflict suffering with our ca-
> pacity to endure suffering.... We will soon wear you down by
> our capacity to suffer.[23]
>
> Rivers of blood may have to flow before we gain our free-
> dom, but it must be our blood.[24]

The non-violent approach does not immediately change
the heart of the oppressor. It first does something to the
hearts and souls of those committed to it. It gives them new

self-respect; it calls up resources of strength and courage that they did not know they had.[25]

SCLC, SNCC, and CORE: The Movement Radicalizes

After the success of the Montgomery boycott a number of the leading participants—many of them, like King, preachers—saw the need to form a new organization to give the movement direction. In 1957 the Southern Christian Leadership Conference (SCLC) was established. It aimed to use nonviolent direct action to press for its demands, and fight for the right to vote. It is easy to see the limitation of such tactics today, but it is important to stress that the commitment to mass action was real, even if the aim of such action was to pressure Southern or federal authorities. The movement thus developed a momentum and vitality that began to go beyond the intentions of its founders.

The SCLC also found itself in conflict with established Black organizations like the NAACP that saw a mass movement as a threat to their lobbying and legal efforts. Within a few years, however, the movement had begun to enter a new phase, beyond the control of the traditional organizations and even King himself.

After the civil rights movement's initial successes in 1956 and 1957, Southern racists counter-attacked. White Citizens' Councils were organized around the South. Once again terror was unleashed in an effort to defeat the movement.

C. Vann Woodward describes this period as a time when "all over the South the lights of reason and tolerance and moderation began to go out." He writes:

A fever of rebellion and malaise and fear spread over the region. Books were banned, libraries were purged, newspapers were slanted, magazines disappeared from stands, television programs were withheld, films were excluded. Teachers, preachers, and college professors were questioned, and many were driven out of the South.... Words began to shift their significance and lose their common meaning. A "moderate" became a man who dared open his mouth, an "extremist" one who favored eventual compliance with the law, and "compliance" took on the connotations of treason. Politicians who had once spoken for moderation began to vie with each other in defiance of the government.[26]

King and his associates looked to the federal government for assistance, but none was forthcoming. In a 1958 meeting between SCLC leaders and Eisenhower, the president would not commit himself to doing anything, concluding the meeting by informing King: "Reverend, there are so many problems... Lebanon...Algeria."[27] Many of the liberal establishment who had supported the Montgomery boycott began to distance themselves from the movement, arguing that the demands were excessive and that Blacks couldn't expect change to come overnight. The earlier victories began to look increasingly empty. The much-heralded 1954 *Brown* desegregation decision, for example, had left Southern education virtually unchanged. The Supreme Court's decision left implementation of the desegregation order to each state, to be carried out "with all deliberate speed."[28] But the judges and school boards were committed to segregation. As late as 1962 not a single Black student attended white schools or colleges in Mississippi, Alabama, or South Carolina.[29] By 1964, ten years after the original *Brown* ruling, only 2.3 percent of Southern Blacks were enrolled in desegregated schools. Justice Black, a member of the Court, was forced to admit in 1964, "There has been entirely too much deliberation and not enough speed" in complying with the ruling.[30]

But the South could not turn back the clock as it had done after Reconstruction. On February 1, 1960, four Black students from North Carolina Agricultural and Technical College sat in the "whites only" section of a drugstore lunch counter and asked for some coffee. They were not served, but they refused to move until the store was closed. The next day thirty students joined the protest, which became known as the sit-in. On February 3, over fifty Black students and three white students joined in the protest. News of the protest spread like wildfire, as did the tactic employed. "By April 1960," writes historian Harvard Sitkoff, "the tactic had spread to seventy-eight Southern and border communities; some two thousand students had been arrested. By August 1961, according to the Southern Regional Council, more than 70,000 Blacks and whites had participated in sit-ins and three thousand had been jailed. It was a watershed."[31]

In April 1960, a new student organization was formed to coordinate future actions. The founding conference of the Student Nonviolent Coordinating Committee (SNCC) was called by Ella Baker, executive director of SCLC, and addressed by King. The conference was attended by 120 student activists representing 56 colleges and high schools in 12 Southern states and the District of Columbia.[32] The students largely accepted King's strategy and overall politics, "were afflicted with an anti-leftist political bias,"[33] and therefore had little interest in working-class struggles. An early SNCC member describes SNCC's members as motivated "by a determination to secure the means for their own economic and social mobility, which in the circumstances clearly necessitated a direct assault on the tradition and law which limited them absolutely."[34]

SNCC, however, was not to become a mere appendage or youth organization of SCLC. Like Students for a Democratic Society (SDS)—which sent observers to SNCC's founding meeting—the organization radicalized very quickly, became the left wing of the civil rights movement, and gave birth to the Black Power movement. Inexperienced, loosely organized, and without clear direction, SNCC floundered for several months after its founding convention. But it began to attract national attention [along with the Congress of Racial Equality (CORE)] in 1961 with its "Freedom Rides" campaign. As Lee Sustar put it:

> The fledgling organization sent two representatives to the first "Freedom Ride," in early 1961 to protest against segregated facilities on Greyhound and Trailways' Southern bus line. When a racist mob forced the initial thirteen riders to give up, SNCC mobilized dozens more Black students for "jail-ins" in Jackson and other cities.
>
> The Freedom Rides brought SNCC and other civil rights groups into their first major conflict with the Kennedy administration. Robert F. Kennedy, then attorney general, faced a dilemma. If he provided protection to the Freedom Riders, he risked alienating the "Dixiecrats" [Southern Democrats] who held the balance of power in the Democratic Party.
>
> But if Kennedy allowed the rides to continue unprotected, the racist beatings and possible lynchings would become an international embarrassment and give the lie to the "progressive" image the new administration was presenting to the newly independent countries of Africa and Asia.[35]

Kennedy offered SNCC and other civil rights activists a deal: stop the Freedom Rides and instead concentrate on voter registration in Mississippi with a guarantee that organizers would be protected by the federal government. Kennedy minced no words in explaining his proposed Voter Education Project. "If you cut out this freedom rider and sitting-in stuff and concentrate on voter registration," he told representatives of the student organizations, "I'll get you a tax exemption."[36]

Kennedy's proposal was greeted with skepticism by some SNCC activists, but the majority saw it as an opportunity to build the movement and enhance SNCC's reputation. SNCC accepted Kennedy's offer, received foundation grants to finance the campaign, and established its headquarters in McComb, Mississippi. It soon became clear, however, that SNCC's faith in the Kennedy administration was misplaced. They were met with harassment, violence, and arrests—and received no protection from the federal government. "Before year's end, the McComb police had jailed virtually the entire SNCC staff. The events in McComb were only the beginning of the pattern that would force SNCC to re-examine and eventually reject its liberalism and reliance on the Democrats."[37]

Fed up with the Kennedy administration's foot-dragging, SNCC activists redoubled their efforts. Martin Luther King's decision to try to desegregate Birmingham, Alabama, and a planned march on Washington galvanized the civil rights movement. Birmingham—described as "America's Johannesburg"— was the perfect white supremacist Southern city. Its chief of police, Eugene "Bull" Connor, was intransigent in his defense of Jim Crow. Alabama's newly elected governor, George Wallace, was to become the symbol of racist reaction in the 1960s. He declared, "I draw the line in the dust and toss the gauntlet before the feet of tyranny and I say segregation now, segregation tomorrow, segregation forever."[38] The sit-ins and marches begun in April 1963 were met with ferocious violence, as Bull Connor unleashed police dogs, and used firehoses and clubs to disperse demonstrators, arresting hundreds in the process. Televised footage of the struggle in Birmingham sparked protests around the country and led thousands more to join the civil rights struggle. Under mounting pressure the Kennedy administration intervened and negotiated an agreement with Birmingham's corporate bosses and elected officials. The agreement, as historians Meier and Rudwick argue, brought not "freedom now" but token concessions that later were not carried out."[39] But it forced Kennedy to announce his intention to introduce civil rights legislation. Birmingham also forced Kennedy to identify himself more strongly with the civil rights movement—and to attempt to co-opt and control its activities. The 1963 March on Washington provided the perfect opportunity.

Modeled after the 1941 March on Washington movement launched by A. Philip Randolph, the 1963 March on Washington was seen by SNCC and CORE militants as a mass protest that would paralyze Washington to express a growing militancy and impatience among Blacks. Under the control of more conservative elements in the civil rights movement— among them King and Randolph—it was to be a celebration and endorsement of Kennedy's civil rights bill. In the end the march drew 250,000 to Washington and was seen by organizers and the Kennedy administration as a great success. But the march only convinced militants that King's strategy had to be rejected, and many shared Malcolm X's description of the event as "the farce on Washington." Even SNCC activist John Lewis, by no means a left-winger, had planned to criticize the Kennedy administration. "In good conscience we cannot support the administration's civil rights bill, for it is too little, too late," he had planned to say. "There's not one thing in the bill that will protect our people from police brutality.... What is in the bill that will protect the homeless and starving people of this nation? What is there in this bill to ensure the equality of a maid who earns $5.00 a week in the home of a family whose income is $100,000 a year?"[40] He never made those remarks, agreeing to remove them when pressured by march organizers. But even his censored speech raised thorny questions: "Where is our party? Where is the party that will make it unnecessary for us to march on Washington? Where is the political party that will make it unnecessary to march in the streets of Birmingham?"[41]

By the end of 1964 many SNCC members would answer Lewis' question by eliminating the Democratic Party from consideration. The strains between SNCC and civil rights leaders like King reached a breaking point, as SNCC consciously identified itself with more radical ideas. "By 1965 SNCC had become, in the eyes of supporters and critics, not simply a civil rights organization but a part of the New Left."[42] White violence, the government's refusal to act, the moderation of civil rights leaders, and the slow speed of change had led SNCC militants to reject the politics they accepted in 1960. The 1964 voter registration campaign SNCC undertook in Mississippi pushed it even more to the left.

The Mississippi Summer Project

Mississippi was, even by Southern standards, largely rural, poor, and very resistant to change. Fully two-thirds of the state's Black population lived in rural areas, compared with 39 percent for the rest of the South.[43] Only 6.7 percent of Mississippi's eligible Black voters were registered. SNCC activists knew they would be met with violent resistance and couldn't count on the government for protection. But they knew the involvement of large numbers of whites would get media attention and even force federal intervention. SNCC's call for volunteers was taken up—1,000 volunteers headed for Mississippi. Hardly was the campaign under way when on June 21 three civil rights workers, James Chaney, Andrew Goodman, and Michael Schwerner, disappeared. They had been murdered. Their bodies were only found after a massive manhunt two months later. Activists were met with violence at every turn during the six-week campaign. By the end, six Blacks had been murdered, one thousand arrested, thirty buildings bombed, and three dozen Black churches gutted by fire.[44] SNCC activists previously committed to nonviolence now argued for armed self-defense. As SNCC member James Forman explained: "The Mississippi Summer Project...confirmed the absolute necessity for armed self-defense—a necessity that existed before the project but which became overwhelmingly clear to SNCC people during and after it."[45]

To counter Mississippi's racist Democratic Party, SNCC formed a nonsegregated party, the Mississippi Freedom Democratic Party (MFDP). The MFDP signed up 80,000 voters and elected a delegation to the Democratic Party convention in Atlantic City. Arguing that it was the only party in Mississippi in which all could vote, the MFDP planned a fight to be seated instead of the segregationist Mississippi delegation. But the Democrats, liberal and conservative alike, would have none of it. Lyndon Johnson turned to Democratic liberals like Hubert Humphrey, United Auto Workers President Walter Reuther, and MFDP lawyer Joseph Rauh to urge the MFDP to give up its demands.[46] Leaders of the civil rights movement, including King, also put pressure on the MFDP to abandon their demands, urging them to accept Johnson's compromise offer to seat two MFDP delegates. The MFDP refused to give in, calling the compromise "a back of the bus" agreement. Instead, they staged a protest in the hall—taking the Mississippi delegation's seats—until party officials called on the police to remove them from the hall. The Democratic Party's treatment of the MFDP was the last straw for many activists. "Things would never be the same," wrote SNCC's Cleveland Sellers. "Never again would we be lulled into believing that our task was exposing injustices so that the 'good' people of America would eliminate them."[47]

SNCC began to look to the ideas of Malcolm X, Black nationalism, and the African liberation movements for guidance. On a trip to several newly independent African states, SNCC leaders met and established a relationship with Malcolm X. The organization started to develop links with the organized left and called for the abolition of HUAC. By July 1965 SNCC had adopted an anti-Vietnam War resolution that argued that Blacks should not "fight in Vietnam for the white man's freedom, until all the Negro people are free in Mississippi."[48] Stokely Carmichael's election to head SNCC in 1966 and his advocacy of "Black Power" symbolized the change in SNCC's politics. The growing challenge to King's leadership was not limited to SNCC or the South. The mood had definitely shifted from the politics of reform to those of militancy. The ideas of Malcolm X began to exert considerable influence within the movement.

CHAPTER NINE

The Politics of Malcolm X

Racial segregation was not the law in the North, but it was the reality. In virtually all aspects of life, Northern Blacks encountered racism and segregation. Blacks who left the South found themselves forced to live in huge urban ghettos. Black schools were inferior and segregated. The jobs that Blacks had moved north to find proved to be the worst and the lowest-paid. Skilled or professional jobs were reserved for whites. Blacks were constantly subject to "white" authority, especially police harassment. "When our Black fathers go to work in the mornings, they hear the muttered insults of their white neighbors," the novelist and poet Richard Wright wrote in *Twelve Million Black Voices,* describing the experience of Southern Blacks encountering racism in the North for the first time. "Bricks are hurled through the windows of our homes; garbage is tossed at our Black children when they go to school; and finally bombs explode against our front doors."[1]

A study conducted in Los Angeles after the 1965 Watts rebellion showed that large percentages of Blacks had either suffered or witnessed harassment by police: almost a quarter said they had been mistreated by the police, and 40 percent said they had seen others abused.[2] Any illusions held by

Southern Blacks about the liberal North were not shared by the majority of Blacks living in Northern ghettos. And while Northern Blacks were inspired by the struggles in the South, their conditions made them receptive to a movement independent of—and quite different from—the one led by Martin Luther King, Jr.'s Southern Christian Leadership Council. In the first years of the explosion of the civil rights movement, the most significant organizational expression of this new movement was the Nation of Islam (NOI).

The Nation of Islam had its roots in the demise of the Garvey movement, which had collapsed in the late 1920s but still could claim some supporters in various areas. Disoriented and without any organization or leadership, some of Garvey's followers attempted to maintain a semblance of organization. In Detroit, some of these Garveyites joined the newly formed Nation of Islam, whose members were popularly known as the Black Muslims. By the late 1950s, the group's membership reached an estimated 100,000, with Malcolm X its most prominent member. [3]

Malcolm X was born Malcolm Little in Omaha, Nebraska, in 1925. His father was a Baptist minister and a former member of Garvey's UNIA. When Malcolm X was four, his family's home was burned down by Ku Klux Klan members. After living in various state institutions, Malcolm moved to Boston and from there to New York City. He became involved in petty criminal activity on the East Coast, was convicted for larceny in Boston, and sentenced to an eight- to ten-year jail term in 1946. While in prison, he became involved with the NOI, and on his release in 1952, he quickly rose to prominence in the organization, playing a crucial role in increasing its size and influence.

In formal terms, the ideas of the Nation of Islam were profoundly conservative. The organization combined elements of orthodox Islam with ideas of its own making, claiming that the "Original Man" was Black and that whites were a degenerate and inferior offshoot, destined to rule the world for 6,000 years, after which they would be destroyed. That 6,000-year period was coming to a close, and Blacks could only save themselves by withdrawing into their own society and separating from whites. The only salvation lay in following Elijah Muhammad, Allah's messenger on earth. The Black Muslims preached a doctrine of hard work, thrift, obedience, and humility. The Nation's militia, the Fruit of Islam, strictly enforced an ultra-puritanical sexual morality.

Seeing economic independence from white society as crucial, the organization also encouraged its members to "buy Black." The Nation of Islam established dozens of businesses, owned farmland, and built mosques in most major Northern cities. The NOI did not condemn capitalism, only whites. Indeed, the Black Muslims believed in copying white capitalists: "Everywhere, the Negro is exploited by the white man; now, the Black Man must learn to protect his own, using the white man's techniques."[4]

Like Garvey, Elijah Muhammad called for establishing an independent Black state—in the United States or elsewhere. "The best thing the white man can do is give us justice and stop giving us hell. I'm asking for justice. If they won't give us justice, then let us separate ourselves from them and live in four or five states in America, or leave the country altogether."[5]

Beyond pressing for demands or defending their interests, the organization was hostile to political involvement. That such an inward-looking religious sect was capable of substantial growth is a testimony to the widespread bitterness of large numbers of urban Blacks. To hundreds of young recruits, the Nation of Islam represented self-respect, self-reliance, and Black pride. The group's unabashed condemnation of white America, as well as its rejection of integration and nonviolence, rang true, and especially appealed to Malcolm X.

The bold and articulate Malcolm X quickly became a pull for more militants to join the Nation of Islam. A 1959 television documentary called *The Hate That Hate Produced,* which featured an interview with Malcolm X by Mike Wallace, brought the Muslims much greater national attention, and fuelled their growth.[6] The NOI's message was not designed to appease whites. In the televised interview, Malcolm X bluntly stated, "I charge the white man with being the greatest liar on earth.... I charge the white man with being the greatest robber on earth. I charge the white man with being the greatest deceiver on earth. I charge the white man with being the greatest troublemaker on earth."[7] And in response to the charge that the Nation was racist, he said, unapologetically, "If we react to white racism with a violent reaction, to me that's not Black racism. If you come to put a rope around my neck and I hang you for it, to me that's not racism. Yours is racism, but my reaction has nothing to do with racism."[8]

Malcolm X rejected the view that integration into American society was either possible or desirable.

> When someone sticks a knife into my back nine inches and then pulls it out six inches they haven't done me any favor. They should not have stabbed me in the first place.... During slavery they inflicted the most extreme form of brutality against us to break our spirit, to break our will...after they did all of this to us for three hundred and ten years, then they come up with some so-called Emancipation Proclamation.... And today the white man actually runs around here thinking he is doing Black people a favor.[9]

According to Malcolm X, the federal government and the Democratic Party were no allies, but part of the problem.

> Roosevelt promised, Truman promised, Eisenhower promised. Negroes are still knocking on the door begging for

civil rights. Do you mean to tell me that in a powerful country like this, a so-called Christian country, that a handful of men from the South can prevent the North, the West, the Central States and the East from giving Negroes the rights the Constitution says they already have? No! I don't believe that and neither do you. *No white man really wants the Black man to have his rights, or he'd have them!* The United States does everything else it wants to do.[10]

Malcolm X was sharply critical of liberals who talked about racism in the South, but had nothing to say about conditions in the North.

[T]hey front-paged what I felt about Northern white and Black Freedom Riders going *South* to "demonstrate." I called it "ridiculous"; their own Northern ghettos, right at home, had enough rats and roaches to kill to keep all of the Freedom Riders busy.... The Northern Freedom Riders could light some fires under Northern city halls, unions, and major industries to give more jobs to Negroes.... Yes, I will pull off that liberal's halo that he spends such efforts cultivating! The North's liberals have been so long pointing accusing fingers at the South and getting away with it that they have fits when they are exposed as the world's worst hypocrites.[11]

He was also sharply critical of the civil rights movement's leaders, comparing them to house slaves in the slave South. Far from leading the struggle, their role was to contain it.

Just as the slavemaster of that day used Tom, the house Negro, to keep the field Negroes in check, the same old slavemaster today has Negroes who are nothing but moderate Uncle Toms, twentieth century Uncle Toms, to keep you and me in check, to keep us under control, keep us passive and peaceful and nonviolent. That's Tom making you nonviolent. It's like when you go to the dentist, and the man's going to take your tooth. You're going to fight him when he starts pulling. So he squirts some stuff in your jaw called novocaine, to make you think they're not doing anything to you. So you sit there and because you've got all of that novocaine in your jaw, you suffer—peacefully. Blood running all down your jaw, and you don't know what's happening. Because someone has taught you to suffer—peacefully.[12]

Malcolm went on to attack the whole premise of nonviolence that underlay the Southern desegregation movement. Instead, he argued for Black self-defense: "Be peaceful, be courteous, obey the law, respect everyone; but if someone puts a hand on you, send him to the cemetery. That's a good religion. In fact, that's the old-time religion.... Preserve your life, it's the best thing you've got. And if you've got to give it up, let it be even-steven."[13]

Technically, Malcolm X was only amplifying the teachings of Elijah Muhammad, and indeed always prefaced any of his speeches with the phrase "Elijah Muhammad teaches...." But Malcolm X had turned these ideas into an indictment of the system, increasingly breaking out of the straitjacket of the NOI. While Muhammad shunned politics, Malcolm was becoming more political. One Muslim complained, "It was Malcolm who injected the political concept of 'Black nationalism' into the Black Muslim movement, which...was essentially religious in nature."[14] Aware that the growing politicization of the movement was having an effect on the NOI, including its leading spokesperson, Elijah Muhammad had taken measures to reassert his control. A police attack on the Nation in Los Angeles in 1962 drove home the bankruptcy of the NOI's politics. In April 1962, a Black Muslim had been killed and several wounded by the Los Angeles police department. The NOI preached self-defense, and the police murder entailed taking retaliatory action. Malcolm X immediately flew out to Los Angeles to direct the Nation of Islam's response. "A campaign in defense of the Los Angeles victims and around

the issue of police brutality could, if skillfully and boldly conducted, forge bonds of solidarity and unity between Muslims
and non-Muslim Negroes strong enough to discourage or
deter government prosecution of the Nation of Islam," argued George Breitman, editor of several books of Malcolm
X's speeches.[15] But this went against the whole approach that
Elijah Muhammad advocated, and he "stayed the Black Muslims' hand."[16] Verbal radicalism, often extreme in its denunciations of whites, was acceptable in an earlier period when
members of the NOI were establishing their reputation as
opponents of the system. But the explosion of anger among
Blacks demanded more than words; it demanded action, and
that was one thing Elijah Muhammad would not countenance.

Politics Force a Break with the NOI

Malcolm X's break with the Nation of Islam finally came in
December 1963. Responding to a question from the audience
at a meeting in New York City, Malcolm attributed John F.
Kennedy's assassination to the hate and violence produced
by a society that whites themselves had created. The "chickens have come home to roost," Malcolm said. "Being an old
farm boy myself, chickens coming home to roost never did
make me sad; they've always made me glad." The statement
was consistent with the hostility to the U.S. administration
that Black Muslim ministers had expressed in the past. Elijah
Muhammad did not see it that way, informing Malcolm that
"the country loved this man," and that he would be suspended
for ninety days so that "Muslims everywhere can be disasso-
ciated from the blunder."[17] Malcolm accepted the suspension
without protest, but it soon became clear that the suspension
was in fact an expulsion.

Malcolm's initial assessment of his break with Elijah Muhammad is interesting because it underscored the fact that he was not yet fully conscious that he had come to express a profoundly different political viewpoint from the Nation of Islam. Malcolm still considered himself a loyal member until late February 1964. He initially explained the split by saying, "Mr. Muhammad and I are not together today only because of envy and jealousy."[18] But while this is certainly true, it was only symptomatic of the fundamentally different relationship that he was developing to the Black struggle. As he put it:

> If I harbored any personal disappointment whatsoever, it was that privately I was convinced that our Nation of Islam could be an even greater force in the American Black man's overall struggle—if we engaged in more *action*. By that, I mean that I thought privately that we should have amended, or relaxed, our general non-engagement policy. I felt that, wherever Black people committed themselves, in the Little Rocks and the Birminghams and other places, militantly disciplined Muslims should also be there—for all the world to see, and respect, and discuss.
>
> It could be heard increasingly in the Negro communities: "Those Muslims *talk* tough, but they never *do* anything, unless somebody bothers Muslims." I moved around among outsiders more than most other Muslim officials. I felt the very real potentiality that, considering the mercurial moods of the Black masses, this labeling of the Muslims as "talk only" could see us, powerful as we were, one day suddenly separated from the Negroes' frontline struggle.[19]

On March 8, 1964, Malcolm X formally announced his break with the Nation of Islam. The Black Muslim movement, he said, "had gone as far as it can because it was too sectarian and too inhibited."[20]

> I am prepared to co-operate in local civil rights actions in the South and elsewhere and shall do so because every campaign for specific objectives can only heighten the political

consciousness of the Negroes and intensify their identification against white society....

There is no use deceiving ourselves. Good education,
housing and jobs are imperatives for Negroes, and I shall
support them in their fight to win these objectives, but I
shall tell the Negroes that while these are necessary, they
cannot solve the main Negro problem.[21]

Malcolm went on to criticize the leadership of the civil rights
movement:

I shall also tell them that what has been called the "Negro
revolution" in the United States is a deception practiced
upon them, because they have only to examine the failure
of this so-called revolution to produce any positive results in
the past year.

I shall tell them what a real revolution means—the
French Revolution, the American Revolution, Algeria, to
name a few. There can be no revolution without bloodshed,
and it is nonsense to describe the civil rights movement in
America as a revolution.[22]

In order to become involved in the civil rights movement,
Malcolm drew the conclusion that he needed to separate politics and religion. The first organization he founded was religious, the Muslim Mosque, Inc. But its aim was to provide a
bridge for his supporters in the Black Muslims. In April he
explained:

It's true we're Muslims and our religion is Islam, but we don't
mix our religion with our politics and our economics and
our social and civil activities—not any more. We keep our
religion in our mosque. After our religious services are over,
then as Muslims we become involved in political action, economic action and social and civic action. We become involved
with anybody, anywhere, anytime and in any manner that's
designed to eliminate the evils, the political, economic and
social evils that are afflicting the people in our community.[23]

In the same speech he described himself as an adherent of Black nationalism, which he defined in these terms: "[W]e should control the economy of our community. Why should white people be running all the stores in our community? Why should white people be running the banks in our community? Why should the economy of our community be in the hands of the white man?"[24] He added, "The social philosophy of Black nationalism only means that we have to get together and remove the evils, the vices, alcoholism, drug addiction, and other evils that are destroying the moral fiber of our community."[25]

From Black Nationalism to Third Worldism

Soon after this speech Malcolm was to take the first of two trips to Africa. These trips had an important impact on his ideas. He met with several important African heads of state—including Kwame Nkrumah of Ghana and Gamal Abdul Nasser of Egypt—and was influenced by the ideas of "third worldism." In general terms, "third worldism" was the view that the world was dominated by two superpowers—the USA and the USSR—and that the developing countries of the world represented an independent alternative. A defining moment for third worldism was the conference of non-aligned nations held in Bandung, Indonesia, in 1955. When Malcolm X returned to New York, he announced the formation of the Organization of Afro-American Unity (OAAU), modeled after the Organization of African Unity (OAU), which brought together the different African heads of state. The OAAU was a Black nationalist organization that sought to build community organizations, schools, Black enterprises, and voter registration campaigns to ensure community control of Black politicians.

After his visit to Africa, Malcolm began to argue that the

Black struggle in the United States was part of an international struggle, one that he connected to the struggle against capitalism and imperialism. "It is impossible for capitalism to survive, primarily because the system of capitalism needs some blood to suck. Capitalism used to be like an eagle, but now it's more like a vulture," he argued.[26] He also began to argue in favor of socialism. Referring to the African states, he argued:

[A]ll of the countries that are emerging today from under the shackles of colonialism are turning towards socialism. I don't think it's an accident. Most of the countries that were colonial powers were capitalist countries, and the last bulwark of capitalism today is America. It's impossible for a white person to believe in capitalism and not believe in racism. You can't have capitalism without racism. And if you find one and you happen to get that person into a conversation and they have a philosophy that makes you sure they don't have this racism in their outlook, usually they're socialists or their political philosophy is socialism.[27]

In connecting the struggle against racism with capitalism and imperialism, Malcolm abandoned his previous attitude toward whites: "In the past, yes, I have made sweeping indictments of *all* white people. I never will be guilty of that again—as I know now that some white people *are* truly sincere, that some truly are capable of being brotherly toward a Black man."[28] On another occasion he said:

We will work with anyone, with any group, no matter what their color is, as long as they are genuinely interested in taking the type of steps necessary to bring an end to the injustices that Black people in this country are afflicted by. No matter what their color is, no matter what their political, economic or social philosophy is, as long as their aims and objectives are in the direction of destroying the vulturous system that has been sucking the blood of Black people in this country, they're all right with us.[29]

He no longer defined the struggle for Black liberation as a racial conflict. "We are living in an era of revolution, and the revolt of the American Negro is part of the rebellion against the oppression and colonialism which has characterized this era," he said. "It is incorrect to classify the revolt of the Negro as simply a racial conflict of Black against white, or as purely an American problem. Rather, we are today seeing a global rebellion of the oppressed against the oppressor, the exploited against the exploiters."[30]

While Malcolm no longer believed all whites were the enemy, he maintained the need for separate all-Black organization: "Whites can help us, but they can't join us. There can be no Black-white unity until there is first some Black unity. There can be no workers' solidarity until there is first some racial solidarity. We cannot think of uniting with others, until we have first united ourselves."[31] But Malcolm's new conception of the struggle also led him to question his previous understanding of Black nationalism. In January 1965, Malcolm answered the question, "How do you define Black nationalism?" in the following terms:

> I used to define Black nationalism as the idea that the Black man should control the economy of his community, the politics of his community, and so forth.
>
> But when I was in Africa in May, in Ghana, I was speaking with the Algerian ambassador who is extremely militant and is a revolutionary in the true sense of the word.... When I told him that my political, social and economic philosophy was Black nationalism, he asked me very frankly, well, where did that leave him? Because he was white. He was an African, but he was Algerian, and to all appearances he was a white man. And he said if I define my objective as the victory of Black nationalism, where does that leave him? Where does that leave revolutionaries in Morocco, Egypt, Iraq, and Mauritania? So he showed me where I was alienat-

ing people who were true revolutionaries, dedicated to overthrowing the system of exploitation that exists on this earth
by any means necessary.

So, I had to do a lot of thinking and reappraising of my
definition of Black nationalism. Can we sum up the solution
to the problems confronting our people as Black nationalism? And if you notice, I haven't been using the expression
for several months. But I still would be hard pressed to give
a specific definition of the overall philosophy, which I think is
necessary for the liberation of Black people in this country.[32]

Political Trajectory

During this period Malcolm's political ideas were evolving
rapidly—a development cut short by his death. Malcolm X
was assassinated before he could fully develop his views on
a series of political topics. Some socialists, such as George
Breitman (then a member of the Socialist Workers Party), argued that Malcolm was moving toward revolutionary socialism at the time of his death. This idea, however, was more a
reflection of the SWP's understanding of the relation between
Black nationalism and socialism than of Malcolm's own ideas.
According to Breitman, Malcolm was

> a Black nationalist plus a social revolutionist, or in the pro-
> cess of becoming one.
>
> Socialists should be the last to be surprised at such a de-
> velopment. We have for some time been stressing the ten-
> dency of nationalism to grow over into and become merged
> with socialism; we have seen just that transformation occur
> in Cuba with Castro and his movement, which began as na-
> tionalist. We have argued against many opponents that the
> logical outcome of Black nationalism in a country like ours
> is to reach the most advanced, most radical social and politi-
> cal conclusions.[33]

Leaving aside the relationship between Black nationalism

and socialism, which I will discuss later, Breitman's assessment of Malcolm X is too one-sided. While it is clear that Malcolm's political ideas were on the whole moving to the left, there is little evidence that he was adopting revolutionary socialist politics. His idea of socialism did not involve working-class self-emancipation and workers' power, but rather saw socialism as synonymous with national independence and economic development. His uncritical stance toward the newly independent African regimes actually blunted the edge of some of his earlier formulations. The complete absence of any concept of class in his assessment of the African regimes was mirrored in his advocacy of cross-class alliances among Blacks in the United States. His willingness to engage in electoral politics and his advocacy of "community control" were by no means, as later developments would prove, necessarily a challenge to the system.

The absence of class politics in Malcolm's ideas meant that while he understood the need for "allies," he did not look to Black—or white—workers as the agency for change. He therefore never saw the need to build a revolutionary organization that would attempt to overcome racial divisions, instead advocating building a broad-based all-Black organization.

In answer to the question "Can there be any revolutionary change in America while the hostility between Black and white working classes exists? Can Negroes do it alone?" Malcolm answered:

> Yes. They'll never do it with working-class whites. The history of America is that working-class whites have been just as much against not only working Negroes, but *all* Negroes, period, because all Negroes are working-class within the caste system. The richest Negro is treated like a working-class Negro. There never has been any good relationship between the working-class Negro and the working-class whites...[and] there can be no worker solidarity until there's

first some Black solidarity. There can be no white/Black solidarity until there's first some Black solidarity. We have got to get our problems solved first and then if there's anything left to work on the white man's problems, good, but I think one of the mistakes Negroes make is this worker solidarity thing. There's no such thing—it didn't even work in Russia.[34]

It is impossible to predict how Malcolm's politics would have developed had he lived. In the end, he was still a Black nationalist, but had developed ideas that put him squarely on the left of the Black nationalist movement. His hostility to the system and the twin capitalist parties, his commitment to end racism, his identification with anti-imperialism, and his call to struggle "by any means necessary" represented an enormous advance in the ideas of the time. Gunned down as he was about to address a meeting at the Audubon Ballroom in Washington Heights, New York, Malcolm X had become one of the most important radical Black figures in the United States, and his influence was growing, especially among younger Blacks. His death was therefore welcomed by defenders of the system, both Black and white. The *New York Times* editorial for February 22 read:

Malcolm X had the ingredients for leadership, but his ruthless and fanatical belief in violence not only set him apart from the responsible leaders of the civil rights movement and the overwhelming majority of Negroes. It also marked him for notoriety, and for a violent end....

Malcolm X's life was strangely and pitifully wasted. But this was because he did not seek to fit into society or into the life of his own people. He could not even come to terms with his fellow Black extremists. The world he saw through those horn-rimmed glasses of his was distorted and dark. But he made it darker still with his exaltation of fanaticism.

Yesterday someone came out of that darkness that he spawned, and killed him.[35]

The *Times* assessment was shared by Black opponents of Malcolm X. Elijah Muhammad, leader of the Nation of Islam, told the press, "He seems to have taken weapons as his god. Therefore we couldn't tolerate a man like that. He preached war. We preach peace."[36] Carl T. Rowan, a syndicated Black columnist, described him as "an ex-convict, ex-dope peddler who became a racial fanatic.... A Black who preached segregation and race hatred."[37] The social democrat Bayard Rustin, associate of Martin Luther King, Jr., added to this chorus in March 1965, "Now that he is dead, we must resist the temptation to idealize Malcolm X, to elevate charisma to greatness." Later, he added, "Malcolm is not a hero of the movement, he is a tragic victim of the ghetto."[38]

The real tragedy, of course, is that Malcolm X was gunned down just as he was beginning to "think for himself," as he put it, and to express a radical program for Black liberation. His premature death and the subsequent suppression and decline of the Black movement have made it easier for second-rate reformists to claim Malcolm as theirs. But anyone who listens to Malcolm's speeches or reads any of his writings can be in no doubt as to his trajectory, which is summarized well in his famous "Ballot or the Bullet" speech, given April 3, 1964, in Cleveland:

> I'm not a politician, not even a student of politics; in fact, I'm not a student of much of anything. I'm not a Democrat, I'm not a Republican, and I don't even consider myself an American....
>
> Well, I am one who doesn't believe in deluding myself. I'm not going to sit at your table and watch you eat, with nothing on my plate, and call myself a diner. Sitting at the table doesn't make you a diner, unless you eat some of what's on that plate. Being here in America doesn't make you an American. Being born here in American doesn't make you an American. Why, if birth made you American, you wouldn't need any legislation, you wouldn't need any

amendments to the Constitution, you wouldn't be faced with civil-rights filibustering in Washington, D.C., right now....

No, I'm not an American. I'm one of the twenty-two million Black people who are the victims of Americanism. One of the twenty-two million Black people who are the victims of democracy, nothing but disguised hypocrisy. So, I'm not standing here speaking to you as an American, or a patriot, or a flag-saluter, or a flag-waver—no, not I. I'm speaking as a victim of this American system. And I see America through the eyes of the victim. I don't see any American dream; I see an American nightmare.[39]

CHAPTER TEN

Black Power

1965 marked an important turning point for the Black liberation movement. The hegemony exercised by the "old guard" leaders like Martin Luther King, Jr., was finally broken. The movement had succeeded in defeating Jim Crow in the South, and the government passed civil rights and voting rights legislation. The center of the movement would shift to the Northern cities—where the majority of Blacks lived in 1965. Northern Blacks were inspired by and supported the civil rights struggles in the South, but the end of Jim Crow legislation did not directly affect them. Jobs, poor housing, discrimination, police violence, and substandard education remained fundamental problems.

These conditions would lead to an explosion of anger, just as Malcolm X had predicted in February 1965. "Nineteen sixty-five will probably be the *longest, hottest, bloodiest* summer that has yet been seen in the United States since the beginning of the Black Revolution, primarily because the same causes that existed in the winter of 1964 still exist in January, in February, of 1965. Now, these are causes of inferior housing, inferior employment, inferior education. All of the evils of a bankrupt system still exist where Black Americans are concerned."[1] The spring and summer months witnessed massive riots in every major city in the United States from 1964 to 1968. The immediate causes of the riots differed from city to city, but they shared a common characteristic. A white policeman shooting a fifteen-year-old triggered Harlem's 1964 rebellion.[2] A traffic arrest of a twenty-one-year-old Black man two blocks from his home sparked the Watts rebellion in 1965.[3] The riot lasted six days and spread over forty-six square miles of Los Angeles. Property damage was estimated at $40 million. Thirty-four people, twenty-eight of them Black, were killed; more than one thousand were injured; and the police arrested some four thousand people.[4]

The Detroit rebellion the following summer was even larger. Forty-three people were killed; almost two thousand were injured. The federal government ordered fifteen thousand state police and National Guard members to quell the rebellion. Black anger was not aimed at random whites, but rather at symbols of authority and property. Blacks widely viewed the riots as a legitimate form of protest; some also viewed them as a rejection of the politics of nonviolence. When Martin Luther King, Jr., toured the riot area in Watts, a young man told him, "We won...because we made them pay attention to us."[5] In a survey of Watts, 58 percent of residents and 57 percent of those arrested thought the effects of the riot would be favorable, with only 18 and 27 percent, respectively, anticipating unfavorable results.[6] Thirty-eight percent of residents and 54 percent of those arrested believed the riot "helped the Negro's cause."[7]

The riots also had a tremendous impact on activists. As SNCC member Cleveland Sellers recalled, "We were all very conscious of the fact that the axis of the struggle appeared to be shifting away from the rural South to the cities in the North. The totally unexpected rebellions in Harlem, Watts,

Chicago and Philadelphia made a big impact on our thinking."[8] The riots also greatly influenced the thinking of the Johnson administration and the U.S. ruling class generally.

For those who had wished the problem away, they forcefully reasserted the importance of racism in U.S. society and drove home three key points: first, that the question of racism and civil rights could no longer be dismissed as purely a problem of the backward Southern states. Indeed, the riots helped spur the civil rights legislation usually credited exclusively to the work of Congress and the president.

In the wake of the riots, the federal government set up the President's National Advisory Commission on Civil Disorders—known as the Kerner Commission after its chair, Illinois Governor Otto Kerner—to study the root causes of the urban rebellions. In 1968, the commission issued a report, which concluded that the United States was "moving toward two societies, one Black, one white—separate and unequal."[9]

"Segregation and poverty have created in the racial ghetto a destructive environment totally unknown to most white Americans," the report stated. "What white Americans have never fully understood—but what the Negro can never forget—is that white society is deeply implicated in the ghetto. White institutions created it, white institutions maintain it, and white society condones it."[10]

The impacts of the civil rights movement and of the riots across Northern cities can be measured in part by examining the changed rhetoric adopted by government officials when talking about poverty and racial oppression. "The only genuine, long-range solution for what has happened lies in an attack—mounted at every level—upon the conditions that breed despair and violence," President Lyndon Johnson said in a nationwide address on July 27, 1967, when he announced the appointment of the Kerner Commission. "All of us know what those conditions are: ignorance, discrimination, slums, poverty, disease, not enough jobs. We should attack these conditions—not because we are frightened by conflict, but because we are fired by conscience. We should attack them because there is no other way to achieve a decent and orderly society in America."[11]

But the liberal acknowledgement of the problems of racism, of urban ghettos, and of Black poverty and unemployment only went so far. Because, at heart, liberalism believes that the American society and economy is *not* fundamentally unjust or unequal. Rather, it believes "social problems" like poverty and racism can be ameliorated with social programs that aim to fix problems on the margins of the system. So on the one hand, this led to a proliferation of programs intended to address discrete elements of inequality in education, housing, and health care. On the other hand, this led to a series of theories seeking to blame Blacks themselves, rather than the government or structural racism, for their conditions. Academics and politicians began to attribute the problems of Black life to a "culture of poverty."[12] Among the most prominent of these blame-the-victim views was the idea that the root of the problem could be found in the breakdown of the Black family.

While paying lip service to the questions of poverty, lack of jobs, and housing, for example, President Johnson said,

> Perhaps most important—its influence radiating to every part of life—is the breakdown of the Negro family structure....
>
> It flows from centuries of oppression and persecution of the Negro man. It flows from the long years of degradation and discrimination, which have attacked his dignity and assaulted his ability to produce for his family....
>
> The family is the cornerstone of our society.... And when the family collapses it is the children that are usually damaged. When it happens on a massive scale the community

itself is crippled.

So, unless we work to strengthen the family, to create the conditions under which most parents will stay together—all the rest: schools, and playgrounds, and public assistance, and private concern will never be enough to cut completely the circle of despair and deprivation.[13]

The authors of Johnson's speech were Assistant Secretary of Labor Daniel Patrick Moynihan and presidential assistant Richard N. Goodwin. The speech was largely based on a report, written by Moynihan, entitled *The Negro Family: The Case for National Action*. The central contention of Moynihan's report was that Black men had an aversion to work and to taking responsibility for their families. In addition, the alleged criminality of Black men, which featured prominently in the report, further compounded the problems of the ghetto. "It is probable that at present, a majority of the crimes against the person, such as rape, murder, and aggravated assault are committed by Negroes," the report reads, while then going on to acknowledge, "There is, of course, no absolute evidence."[14] These racist theories of the "culture of poverty" became one of the underpinnings of the conservative assault on the social safety net after 1980.

As much as the riots shook up the Northern liberals, they also represented the mobilization of new forces in the civil rights struggle and the crystallization of a new political mood, best summed up by the slogan "Black Power." Stokely Carmichael launched the slogan during a 1966 civil rights march through Mississippi. "This is the twenty-seventh time I have been arrested—and I ain't going to jail no more!" Carmichael told a rally of supporters. "The only way we gonna stop them white men from whuppin' us is to take over. We been saying freedom for six years and we ain't got nothin'. What we gonna start saying now is Black Power!" As the crowd chanted back

"Black Power," Carmichael continued, "That's right, that's what we want. Now, from now on, when they ask you what you want, you know what to tell them. What do you want?" "Black Power!" "What do you want? Say it again!" "Black power, Black power, BLACK POWER!"[15]

The slogan became widely popular among radicals, but was sharply denounced by the conservative leaders of the civil rights movement. Speaking before the NAACP convention in July 1966, Roy Wilkins, the organization's executive secretary, proclaimed, "No matter how endlessly they try to explain it, the term 'Black Power' means anti-white power.... It is a reverse Mississippi, a reverse Hitler, a reverse Ku Klux Klan." A "quick, uncritical and highly emotional" slogan, he said, it would only lead to "Black death."[16] King tried to defuse the split between left and right, calling the slogan an "unwise choice of words."[17] Still trying to maintain some connection with the radicals, King acknowledged that Black Power "had ready appeal," but "beneath all the satisfaction of a gratifying slogan, Black Power is a nihilistic philosophy born out of the conviction that the Negro can't win."[18]

Not all civil rights leaders rejected the phrase Black Power. Floyd McKissick of the Congress of Racial Equality (CORE), an organization founded by University of Chicago students George Houser and James Farmer in 1942, adopted the slogan, arguing, "1966 shall be remembered as the year we left our imposed status of Negroes and became Black men...1966 is the year of the concept of Black Power."[19] CORE's 1966 convention adopted a resolution stating that CORE was no longer in favor of integration. CORE further announced that nonviolent direct action was "a dying philosophy," and told whites they were no longer welcome as members of the organization.[20] In 1966, Stokely Carmichael took over the leadership of SNCC, and the organization likewise adopted Black separatism, and expelled its white members.

The rise of Black nationalist politics represented a further radicalization of the movement. But the idea of Black Power, while popular, was also very vague. Who would exercise this power and to what ends? Initially an expression of revolt, Black Power meant different things to different people. Stokely Carmichael and political scientist Charles V. Hamilton, authors of the book *Black Power*, gave this definition:

> The concept of Black power...is a call for Black people in this country to unite, to recognize their heritage, to build a sense of community. It is a call for Black people to begin to define their own goals, to lead their own organizations and to support those organizations. It is a call to reject racist institutions and values of this society.
>
> The concept of Black power rests on a fundamental premise: *Before a group can enter the open society, it must first close ranks.* By this we mean that group solidarity is necessary before a group can operate effectively from a bargaining position of strength in a pluralistic society.[21]

But while Carmichael drew radical Black nationalist conclusions, others would interpret the idea quite differently. The Black Power slogan became the springboard for both a move to the left and a move to the right. Four interconnected interpretations of Black Power emerged: (i) as Black capitalism, (ii) as Black electoral power, (iii) as cultural nationalism, and (iv) as radical Black nationalism.

The adoption of Black Power as an expression of Black capitalism grew very quickly. A key organizer and chairperson of the first major Black Power conference, held in July 1967, in Newark, New Jersey, was lifelong Republican Nathan Wright, Jr. Wright supported Nixon's election—and later in life was an ardent supporter of Ronald Reagan. The conference concluded that Black Power was really about getting a "fair share" of the pie, that is, U.S. capitalism. The next conference was formally cosponsored by a white-owned corporation, the Clairol Company. Clairol's president addressed the meeting and endorsed Black Power. The phrase, he declared, meant Black "ownership of apartments, ownership of homes, ownership of businesses, as well as equitable treatment for all people."[22]

The ambiguity of the phrase Black Power even allowed the enemies of the Black struggle, such as President Richard Nixon, to use it. In a 1968 speech, Nixon defined Black Power as "the power that people should have over their own destinies, the power to affect their own communities, the power that comes from participation in the political processes of society."[23] In a later speech, he said:

> [M]uch of the Black militant talk these days is actually in terms far closer to the doctrines of free enterprise than to those of the welfarist thirties—terms of "pride," "ownership," "private enterprise," "capital," "self-assurance," "self-respect."... What most of the militants are asking is not separation, but to be included in—not as supplicants, but as owners, as entrepreneurs—to have a share of the wealth and a piece of the action. And this is precisely what the Federal central target of the new approach ought to be. It ought to be oriented toward more Black ownership, for from this can flow the rest—Black pride, Black jobs, Black opportunity and yes, Black power....[24]

Along with encouraging Black capitalism, the concept of Black Power was also connected to electoral power. But far from challenging the system, these efforts were intended to help contain Black anger. The politics of CORE's director, Floyd McKissick, and his successor, Roy Innis, typified this trend. McKissick had vocally supported Carmichael's use of the Black Power slogan, and the organization officially declared itself "Black nationalist." But its Black nationalism did not include refusing financial support in the form of government or corporate grants.

In July 1967, the Ford Foundation announced that it was giving $175,000 to the Cleveland CORE chapter to support voter registration efforts, exploration of economic development programs, youth and adult community worker training, and attempts to improve program planning among civil rights groups.[25] The Ford Foundation's seeming generosity was an indication that one section of the ruling class was eager to see the incorporation of middle-class Blacks in order to isolate and reduce the influence of the militant wing of the movement. CORE was chosen to receive the grant because it was considered to be a militant organization that had a hearing among Blacks who rejected the conservatism of the NAACP and the Urban League. CORE combined very militant rhetoric with an equally conservative practice.

CORE's voter registration drive in Cleveland was especially important to the Ford Foundation because it hoped to channel Black anger into an electoral campaign. A Black urban rebellion had rocked Cleveland in 1966. "It was predictions of new violence in the city that led to our first staff visits there in March," explained Ford Foundation director McGeorge Bundy.[26] In November 1967, Carl Stokes was elected mayor of Cleveland, the first Black mayor of a major American city. The Ford Foundation and CORE had been successful in their efforts. While his election was seen as the dawning of a new day for Cleveland's Blacks, Stokes established a pattern that has become the norm in subsequent elections of Black mayors. As Lee Sustar describes it:

> Black Clevelanders soon found out that the new mayor was more interested in making a deal with the Democratic machine than with the progress of the movement. Only two of

Stokes' first ten appointments went to Blacks.

The new mayor hired sixty-seven-year-old right-winger Michael Blackwell as police chief—a shock to Blacks who had endured days of police terror in the [1966] Hough rebellion.... Stokes' commitment to "law and order" won him the renewed backing of local business and the media and national Democrats in his re-election campaign of 1969.[27]

The other important current to emerge in the Black Power movement was that of the cultural nationalists. Unlike other Black nationalists, the cultural nationalists rejected political struggle, instead stressing the importance of a distinct "African" culture. This trend was best represented by Ron Karenga, organizer of a group called (ironically enough) US. "We must free ourselves culturally before we can succeed politically," argued Karenga.[28] This didn't prevent him from launching a ferocious, and often violent, campaign against the Black Panther Party, which he opposed bitterly. His upholding of African tradition was likewise utterly reactionary. "To go back to tradition is the first step forward," argued Karenga, paraphrasing an African proverb. But for women especially, Karenga's "tradition" was certainly a step backward. According to Karenga,

What makes woman appealing is femininity but she can't be feminine without being submissive.

The role of the woman is to inspire her man, educate their children and participate in social development.

Equality is false; it's the devil's concept. Our concept is complementary. Complementary means you complete or make perfect that which is imperfect.

The man has any right that does not destroy the collective needs of his family.[29]

Karenga and US even opposed birth control, sparking a protest from a group of poor Black women whose campaign specifically targeted the middle-class politics of the cultural nationalists.[30] Karenga didn't so much want to transform U.S. society as to carve a niche in it. The *Wall Street Journal* astutely observed that Karenga was "typical of many militants who talk looting and burning but actually are eager to gather influence for quiet bargaining with the predominantly white power structure."[31]

The electoralists and cultural nationalists were able to adapt the Black Power slogan to their own ends in part because of the complete confusion displayed by the radical proponents of the slogan, including Stokely Carmichael himself. At times, Carmichael appeared to be moving away from a purely racial analysis of U.S. society only to sharply move back in that direction. Thus, for example, at a meeting in Cuba in 1967, Carmichael said, "We greet you as comrades because it becomes increasingly clear to us each day that we share with you a common struggle; we have a common enemy. Our enemy is white Western imperialist society."[32] Within a few months of this speech, Carmichael dropped any mention of capitalism and imperialism, stressing instead, "We are talking about a certain type of superiority complex that exists in the white man wherever he is.... The major enemy is the honky and his institutions of racism."[33]

The Black movement had reached an impasse. It was no longer possible to use the slogans of 1965–67 to advance the struggle in 1968 and beyond. Much of what had been accepted as truth by a majority of activists was now either being questioned or rejected. The sense of forward advance felt by hundreds of thousands of participants in the civil rights movement had been replaced by anger, frustration, and doubt about the prevailing strategies being advanced by the movement's leadership. The coalition that Martin Luther King, Jr. had relied on for the desegregation struggles in the South had come unstuck as the battle moved to the North. Leaders of the civil rights and Black Power movements began to see through the hypocrisy of many of their liberal allies who had supported the Southern desegregation struggles, but refused to support the struggles in the North.[34]

MLK's Response

Martin Luther King, Jr., in particular, began to reassess a number of his previous assumptions and started to criticize the character of U.S. society itself. In his address to the 1967 SCLC convention, King declared:

> We must honestly face the fact that the Movement must address itself to the question of restructuring the whole of American society. There are 40 million poor people here. And one day we must ask the question, "Why are there 40 million poor people in America?" And when you begin to ask that question, you are raising questions about the economic system, about a broader distribution of wealth. When you ask that question, you begin to question the capitalistic economy. And to ask questions about the whole society. We are called upon to help the discouraged beggars in life's market place. But one day we must come to see that an edifice which produces beggars needs restructuring. It means that questions must be raised. You see, my friends, when you deal with this, you begin to ask the question, "Who owns the oil?" You begin to ask the question, "Who owns the iron ore?" You begin to ask the question, "Why is it that people have to pay water bills in a world that is two-thirds water?" These are questions that must be asked....
>
> When I say question the whole society, it means ultimately coming to see that the problem of racism, the problem of economic exploitation, and the problem of war are tied together.... A nation that will keep people in slavery for 244 years will "thingify" them, make them things. Therefore they will exploit them, and poor people generally economi-

cally. And a nation that will exploit economically will have to
have foreign investments...and will have to use its military
might to protect them. All of these problems are tied together. What I am saying today is that we must go from this
convention and say, "America, you must be born again!"[35]

King's questioning of the character of U.S. society led him
to more and more radical positions. On November 11, 1967,
King flew to Chicago to address an antiwar group. In a private
discussion with Reverend D. E. King, he said, "D. E., I haven't
discussed this with the Board [of SCLC], but I have found out
that all that I have been doing in trying to correct this system
here in America has been in vain." He added, "I am trying to
get to the roots of it to see just what ought to be done.... The
whole thing will have to be done away with."[36]

King recognized that formal equality under the law was
not the same as real equality. Speaking of the "golden age" of
the civil rights movement, 1954 to 1965, King said, "This period did not accomplish everything. Even though we gained
legislative and judicial victories...these legislative and judicial
victories did very little to improve the lot of millions of Negroes in the teeming ghettos of the North."[37] In fact, he said,
"The changes that came about during this period were at best
surface changes; they were not really substantive changes."[38]

Summarizing the change in King, Michael Eric Dyson
writes:

[D]uring the last three years of his life, King questioned
his own understanding of race relations. As King told journalist David Halberstam, "For years I labored with the idea
of reforming the existing institutions of the society, a little
change here, a little change there. Now I feel quite differently. I think you've got to have a reconstruction of the
entire society, a revolution of values." King also told Halberstam something that he argued in his last book, *Trumpet of*

Conscience: that "most Americans are unconscious racists." For King, this recognition was not a source of bitterness but a reason to revise his strategy. If one believed that whites basically desired to do the right thing, then a little moral persuasion was sufficient. But if one believed that whites had to be made to behave in the right way, one had to employ substantially more than moral reasoning.[39] King also showed frustration, questioning his methods and assumptions. "I'm tired of marching for something that should have been mine at birth," he said in Chicago, openly wondering if the U.S. had given up on trying to confront its social ills.[40]

Importantly, King also publicly spoke out against the U.S. war in Vietnam, rejecting the idea that civil rights leaders should only speak on questions of domestic injustice and discrimination:

> They applauded us in the sit-in movement when we nonviolently decided to sit in at lunch counters. They applauded us on the freedom rides when we accepted blows without retaliation. They praised us in...Birmingham and Selma, Alabama. Oh, the press was so noble in its applause and praise when I would say "Be nonviolent toward Bull Connor.... Be nonviolent toward Jim Clark." There is something strangely inconsistent about a nation and a press that would praise you when you say, "Be nonviolent toward Jim Clark," but will curse you and damn you when you say, "Be nonviolent toward little brown Vietnamese children."[41]

King began to see the connections much more clearly between racism at home and racism abroad, in particular between the economic inequities at home and the war budget. King also started to rethink his understanding of violence. He was keenly aware that the growing urban unrest in the North was an expression of the frustration and impatience that existed among Blacks—and a corresponding sympathy and openness to more radical solutions. After the Watts riots,

King declared, "It was a class revolt of the under-privileged against the privileged."[42] In 1967, he concluded, "after Selma and the voting rights bill we moved into an era which must be an era of revolution.... The whole structure of American life must be changed."[43]

King now made clear that there was a great deal of difference between the violence of the U.S. state and the violence of those rioting in urban centers across the country, and he began to use a different vocabulary to describe his tactics, referring to "massive nonviolence," "aggressive nonviolence," and even "nonviolent sabotage."[44]

Trying to overcome the collapse of the coalition he built to challenge Southern segregation, the apparent failure of the movement in the North, and the growing impatience among Black activists and Blacks more generally, King formulated a new strategy:

> Nonviolence must be adapted to urban conditions and urban moods. Non-violent protest must now mature to a new level, to correspond to heightened Black impatience and stiffened white resistance. This high level is *mass civil disobedience*. There must be more than a statement to the larger society, there must be a force that interrupts its functioning at some key point.... To dislocate the functioning of a city without destroying it can be more effective than a riot because it can be longer lasting, costly to the larger society, but not wantonly destructive. It is a device of social action that is more difficult for a government to quell by superior force.... It is militant and defiant, not destructive.[45]

King's most powerful indictment of the war came on April 4, 1967, exactly one year before he was murdered. In a speech at New York City's Riverside Church, aptly titled "A Time to Break Silence: Declaration of Independence from the War in Vietnam," King declared:

Since I am a preacher by calling, I suppose it is not surprising that I have seven major reasons for bringing Vietnam into the field of my moral vision. There is at the outset a very obvious and almost facile connection between the war in Vietnam and the struggle I and others have been waging in America. A few years ago there was a shining moment in that struggle. It seemed as if there was a real promise of hope for the poor, both Black and white, through the poverty program. There were experiments, hopes, new beginnings. Then came the buildup in Vietnam, and I watched this program broken and eviscerated as if it were some idle political plaything of a society gone mad on war. And I knew that America would never invest the necessary funds or energies in rehabilitation of its poor so long as adventures like Vietnam continued to draw men and skills and money like some demonic, destructive suction tube. So I was increasingly compelled to see the war as an enemy of the poor and to attack it as such.

Perhaps a more tragic recognition of reality took place when it became clear to me that the war was doing far more than devastating the hopes of the poor at home. It was sending their sons and their brothers and their husbands to fight and to die in extraordinarily high proportions relative to the rest of the population. We were taking the Black young men who had been crippled by our society and sending them eight thousand miles away to guarantee liberties in Southeast Asia which they had not found in southwest Georgia and East Harlem. So we have been repeatedly faced with the cruel irony of watching Negro and white boys on TV screens as they kill and die together for a nation that has been unable to seat them together in the same schools. So we watch them in brutal solidarity burning the huts of a poor village, but we realize that they would hardly live on the same block in Chicago. I could not be silent in the face of such cruel manipulation of the poor.

My third reason moves to an even deeper level of awareness, for it grows out of my experience in the ghettos of the North over the last three years, especially the last three summers. As I have walked among the desperate, rejected, and angry young men, I have told them that Molotov cocktails and rifles would not solve their problems. I have tried to offer them my deepest compassion while maintaining my conviction that social change comes most meaningfully through nonviolent action. But they asked, and rightly so, "What about Vietnam?" They asked if our own nation wasn't using massive doses of violence to solve its problems, to bring about the changes it wanted. Their questions hit home, and I knew that I could never again raise my voice against the violence of the oppressed in the ghettos without having first spoken clearly to the greatest purveyor of violence in the world today: my own government. For the sake of those boys, for the sake of this government, for the sake of the hundreds of thousands trembling under our violence, I cannot be silent.[46]

These kinds of views were not welcomed by many of the liberals who had previously praised King in the struggle to end Jim Crow. As Dyson observes,

King's assault on America as the "greatest purveyor of violence in the world today" elicited a predictably furious reaction from the White House. The news media was even harsher.... Richard Lentz notes that *Time* magazine had, early in King's opposition to the war, characterized him as a "drawling bumpkin, so ignorant that he had not read a newspaper in years, who had wandered out of his native haunts and away from his natural calling." *Newsweek* columnist Kenneth Crawford attacked King for his "demagoguery" and "reckless distortions of the facts." The *Washington Post* said that King's Riverside speech was a "grave injury" to the civil rights struggle and that King had "diminished his usefulness to his cause, to his country, and to his people." The *New York Times* editorialized that King's speech was a "fusing of two public problems that are distinct and separate" and that King had done a "disservice to both."[47]

Soon thereafter, Martin Luther King, Jr. was assassinated in Memphis, Tennessee, where he had gone to support a sanitation workers' strike.

Martin and Malcolm

Martin Luther King, Jr.'s, assassination signaled the end of an era. For many, his assassination graphically showed that there was little hope of achieving real change in the United States by pursuing a strategy of "loving thy enemy" and turning the other cheek.

It was also painfully obvious that the two most capable leaders of the Black freedom struggle—Malcolm X and Martin Luther King, Jr.—had been cut down, just as they were beginning to challenge the very roots of economic and racial inequality built into U.S. society.

Malcolm X and Martin Luther King, Jr. started from very different political positions. Their politics in the early 1960s were sharply at odds. But in the months before they were each murdered, they drew very similar conclusions about the character of the system, the limitations of reforms under capitalism, and, crucially, that the United States needed a profound structural transformation if racism and Black oppression were to be overcome.

Of course, there remained considerable political differences between them. Malcolm X became the inspiration for a new generation of Black activists—indeed, a whole new generation of revolutionaries. King, by contrast, was seen as too accommodating to liberalism and his politics of nonviolent civil disobedience had proved unable (as King himself admitted) to transform the North—that is, a non-Jim Crow capitalist society.

But whatever their differences, they both, in distinct ways, stand out as principled fighters for Black liberation. They certainly stand head and shoulders above anyone who succeeded them. And they also shared a common fate in the attempt to blunt and sanitize their politics. Malcolm X, who was denounced as a fanatic by the *New York Times* at the time of his death, has become an accepted figure—even among some liberals. King is the toast of right-wing Democrats and Republicans who stand diametrically opposed to what he stood for.

This is not because of some failing by either King or Malcolm X. As the Russian revolutionary Vladimir Lenin wrote in 1917 about the fate of Karl Marx in his book *State and Revolution,*

> What is now happening to Marx's doctrine has, in the course of history, often happened to the doctrines of other revolutionary thinkers and leaders of oppressed classes struggling for emancipation. During the lifetime of great revolutionaries, the oppressing classes have visited relentless persecution on them and received their teaching with the most savage hostility, the most furious hatred, the most ruthless campaign of lies and slanders. After their death, attempts are made to turn them into harmless icons, canonize them, and surround their *names* with a certain halo for the "consolation" of the oppressed classes and with the object of duping them, while at the same time emasculating and vulgarizing the *real essence* of their revolutionary theories and blunting their revolutionary edge. At the present time, the bourgeoisie and the opportunists within the labor movement are co-operating in this work of adulterating Marxism. They omit, obliterate, and distort the revolutionary side of its teaching, its revolutionary soul.[48]

CHAPTER ELEVEN

The Black Panthers and DRUM

The radicalization of the Black struggle in the late 1960s was mirrored by a similar growth of opposition throughout U.S. society. The civil rights movement inspired a generation of young people—Black and white—to become active politically. The overall character of U.S. society and particularly the war in Vietnam pushed a section of students and youth in the United States to move sharply to the left. At the same time, the radicalization was not confined to students. In fact, the Black struggle found its most radical manifestations in the ghettos of the North and in the auto plants of Detroit and other manufacturing centers. The two organizations that most embodied this radicalization were the Black Panther Party for Self-Defense (BPP) and the Dodge Revolutionary Union Movement (DRUM).

These organizations captured the best of Black radical and nationalist ideas of the late 1960s and, for a brief period, influenced many thousands of activists. Thousands more knew of them. Marxism also influenced the BPP and DRUM since both saw the need for a radical reconstruction of capitalist society. Though each looked to different social forces and argued for different strategies on how to change the world, they reflected the maturation and evolution of the struggle that had lasted for more than a decade when they emerged.

Huey P. Newton and Bobby Seale formed the Black Panther Party in 1966. Seale and Newton had met while they were students in a community college in Oakland, California. The Panthers were to gain notoriety a year later because of their activities in countering police brutality in Oakland by organizing patrols to monitor the police.[1] Their monitoring activities included carrying unconcealed weapons and observing police arrests, which was perfectly legal—but needless to say, it was not well received by the police department. Soon, the California legislature took steps to adopt legislation to outlaw the Panthers' armed patrols. On May 2, 1967, the Panthers responded by organizing a delegation of armed members to march into the state capitol building, proceed to the visitors' gallery of the legislative chambers, and read out a statement.[2] This action catapulted the Panthers into the national limelight. Overnight, the Black Panther Party became a national phenomenon.

The Panthers were not just a police brutality monitoring organization. The ten-point program the party adopted consisted of a set of demands and political positions. These demands combined a set of immediate demands as well as some reforms that questioned the whole basis of the system:

1. *We want freedom. We want power to determine the destiny of our Black Community.*

We believe that Black people will not be free until we are able to determine our destiny.

2. *We want full employment for our people.*

We believe that the federal government is responsible and obligated to give every man employment or a guaranteed income. We believe that if the white American businessmen will not give full employment, then the means of production should be taken from the businessmen and placed in the community so that the people of the community can organize and employ all of its people and give a high standard of living.

3. *We want an end to the robbery by the white man of our Black Community.*

We believe that this racist government has robbed us and now we are demanding the overdue debt of forty acres and two mules. Forty acres and two mules was promised 100 years ago as restitution for slave labor and mass murder of Black people. We will accept the payment in currency which will be distributed to our many communities. The Germans are now aiding the Jews in Israel for the genocide of the Jewish people. The Germans murdered six million Jews. The American racist has taken part in the slaughter of over fifty million Black people; therefore, we feel that this is a modest demand that we make.

4. *We want decent housing, fit for shelter of human beings.*

We believe that if the white landlords will not give decent housing to our Black Community, then the housing and the land should be made into cooperatives so that our community, with government aid, can build and make decent housing for its people.

5. *We want education for our people that exposes the true nature of this decadent American society.*

We want education that teaches us our true history and our role in the present-day society.

We believe in an educational system that will give to our people a knowledge of self. If a man does not have knowledge of himself and his position in society and the world, then he has little chance to relate to anything else.

6. *We want all Black men to be exempt from military service.*

We believe that Black people should not be forced to fight in the military service to defend a racist government that does not protect us. We will not fight and kill other people of color in the world who, like Black people, are being victimized by the white racist government of America. We will protect ourselves from the force and violence of the racist police and the racist military, by whatever means necessary.

7. *We want an immediate end to POLICE BRUTALITY and MURDER of Black people.*

We believe we can end police brutality in our Black Community by organizing Black self-defense groups that are dedicated to defending our Black community from racist police oppression and brutality. The Second Amendment to the Constitution of the United States gives a right to bear arms. We therefore believe that all Black people should arm themselves for self defense.

8. *We want freedom for all Black men held in federal, state, county and city prisons and jails.*

We believe that all Black people should be released from the many jails and prisons because they have not received a fair and impartial trial.

9. *We want all Black people when brought to trial to be tried in court by a jury of their peer group or people from their Black communities, as defined by the Constitution of the United States.*

We believe that the courts should follow the United States Constitution so that Black people will receive fair trials. The 14th Amendment of the U.S. Constitution gives a man a right to be tried by his peer group. A peer is a person from a similar economic, social, religious, geographical, environmental, historical and racial background. To do this the court will be forced to select a jury from the Black Community from which the Black defendant came. We have been, and are being tried by all-white juries that have no understanding of the "average reasoning man" of the Black Community.

10. *We want land, bread, housing, education, clothing, justice and peace.*

And as our major political objective, a United Nations-supervised plebiscite to be held throughout the Black colony in which only Black colonial subjects will be allowed to participate for the purpose of determining the will of Black people as to their national destiny.

> When in the course of human events, it becomes neces-
> sary for one people to dissolve the political bonds which have
> connected them with another, and to assume, among the
> powers of the earth, the separate and equal station to which
> the laws of nature and nature's God entitle them, a decent re-
> spect to the opinions of mankind requires that they should
> declare the causes which impel them to the separation.[3]

The Black Panther Party became the most influential of
the radical Black formations of the late 1960s. The politics of
the BPP were a mixture of radical Black nationalism, Third
World Marxism, and community service politics. The most
successful of the community service programs the Panthers
developed was their free breakfast program for school children, organized by Bobby Seale. In October 1968 the party
newspaper placed an ad for volunteers to help serve the
breakfasts. Within a year, at the end of 1969, the free breakfast program was operational in nineteen cities. Nationally, an
estimated 20,000 children received a free breakfast through
the Panther program before going to school.[4]

The Panthers saw themselves as revolutionaries and believed that the capitalist system needed to be overthrown.
They sought to make alliances with those whom they perceived shared a common interest, including whites. They were
also quite hostile to those forces in the Black movement who,
they believed, claimed to stand for Black freedom, but in reality wound up supporting the continued existence of capitalism.
So, for example, while labeling themselves Black nationalists,
they were sharply critical of the cultural nationalists. Huey P.
Newton summarized the views of the BPP:

> There are two kinds of nationalism, revolutionary national-
> ism and reactionary nationalism. Revolutionary nationalism
> is first dependent upon a people's revolution with the end
> goal being the people in power. Therefore to be a revolution-

ary nationalist you would by necessity have to be a socialist. If you are a reactionary nationalist you are not a socialist and your end goal is the oppression of the people.

Cultural nationalism, or pork chop nationalism, as I sometimes call it, is basically a problem of having the wrong political perspective. It seems to be a reaction instead of responding to political oppression. The cultural nationalists are concerned with returning to the old African culture and thereby regaining their identity and freedom. In other words, they feel that the African culture will automatically bring political freedom. Many times cultural nationalists fall into line as reactionary nationalists.[5]

Newton linked the fight against racism to the fight against capitalism: "The Black Panther Party is a revolutionary Nationalist group and we see a major contradiction between capitalism in this country and our interests. We realize that this country became very rich upon slavery and that slavery is capitalism in the extreme. We have two evils to fight, capitalism and racism. We must destroy both racism and capitalism."[6]

After a brief merger between the Panthers and SNCC, Stokely Carmichael, who was appointed Prime Minister of the Black Panther Party, resigned from the organization. In responding to his resignation, Eldridge Cleaver, BPP minister of information, wrote:

The enemies of Black people have learned something from history even if you haven't, and they are discovering new ways to divide us faster than we are discovering new ways to unite. One thing they know, and we know, that seems to escape you, is that there is not going to be any revolution or Black liberation in the United States as long as revolutionary Blacks, whites, Mexicans, Puerto Ricans, Indians, Chinese and Eskimos are unwilling or unable to unite into some functional machinery that can cope with the situation. Your talk and fears about premature coalition are absurd, because no coalition against oppression by forces possessing revolutionary integrity can ever be premature. If anything, it is too late, because the forces of counterrevolution are sweeping the world, and this is happening precisely because in the past people have been united on a basis that perpetuates disunity among races and ignores basic revolutionary principles and analyses.[7]

Destroying capitalism was a task beyond the grasp of the 11 percent of the population that the Black population represented. Therefore, the Panthers recognized the need to ally with the oppressed and exploited of all racial and ethnic groups to fight against a common enemy. Or as Bobby Seale put it: "Working class people of all colors must unite against the exploitative, oppressive ruling class. Let me emphasize again— we believe our fight is a class struggle not a race struggle."[8]

Although they pledged support to the ideas of Marxism, a distorted form of Marxism—Maoism—influenced many of the Panthers. Maoism was especially prevalent among radicals in the United States because it had a number of characteristics that made it attractive to a younger generation. Maoism, the ruling ideology of the "communist" People's Republic of China, gained ground for two main reasons: first, it offered a general identification with Third World liberation movements, like the one in Vietnam; and second, it fit with the lack of confidence in indigenous working-class forces as the catalyst for change in the U.S. that many radicals felt. A perceptive analysis of this process explained it this way: "[T]he unevenness of the radicalization process in its effect on the various sectors of the American population has faced the radical movement...with a growing sense of isolation. In the context of this sense of isolation from the bulk of the American people, under the impact of a great hunger for political identity, the affinity felt by most SDSers [Students for a Democratic Society] for revolutionary leaderships in the Third World was increasingly transformed into a primary identification."[9] Many radicals even tried to imitate the style and practice of what they perceived to be the practice of Chinese radicals. During its most radical period, that of the "Cultural Revolution" in China, the Maoists built up a grotesque personality cult around their leader, Chairman Mao Zedong. Mao's hagiographers turned him into a virtual god. Transferring this to the BPP in the United States, Huey Newton asserted that: "A revolutionary must realize that if he is sincere, death is imminent due to the fact that the things he is saying and doing are extremely dangerous. Without this realization, it is impossible to proceed as a revolutionary. The masses are constantly looking for a guide, a Messiah, to liberate them from the hands of the oppressor. The vanguard party must exemplify the characteristics of worthy leadership."[10] This was a far cry from Karl Marx's warning that "the educators must be educated," a point he made in arguing against elitist forms of socialism delivered by a savior.

Yet, there was no denying the massive sympathy (if not outright support) that existed in Black communities for the Black Panthers. A January 13, 1970, *Wall Street Journal* front page story was headlined: "Panther Supporters" and the subhead read: "Many Black Americans Voice Strong Backing for Defiant Militants." The reporters concluded that the Panthers had a large base of support. In fact, they wrote, "a clear majority of Blacks [in San Francisco, New York, Cleveland, and Chicago] support both the goals and methods of the Black Panthers. An even larger percentage believes, moreover, that police officials are determined to crush the party by arresting or killing its key officials."[11]

The success and growth of the Black Panther Party was a great cause for concern for the U.S. government. Beginning in 1967, the FBI launched COINTELPRO—a massive covert program of disruption and repression against the movement.

An FBI memorandum expanding the program described COINTELPRO's goals as:

1. Prevent the <u>coalition</u> of militant Black nationalist groups....

2. Prevent the <u>rise of a "messiah"</u> who could unify and electrify the militant nationalist movement...Martin Luther King, Stokely Carmichael and Elijah Muhammad all aspire to this position....

3. Prevent <u>violence</u> on the part of Black nationalist groups....

4. Prevent militant Black nationalist groups and leaders from gaining <u>respectability</u> by discrediting them....

5. ...prevent the long-range <u>growth</u> of militant Black nationalist organizations, especially among youth.[12]

The Black Panther Party was not among the original "Black Nationalist" targets as defined by the FBI in 1967. By September 1968, however, FBI Director J. Edgar Hoover described the Panthers as "the greatest threat to the internal security of the country." The BPP, claimed Hoover, is "schooled in the Marxist-Leninist ideology and the teaching of Chinese Communist leader Mao Tse-tung" and it spreads "their gospel of hate and violence not only to ghetto residents, but to students in colleges, universities and high schools as well."[13]

By July 1969, the Black Panthers had become the primary focus of the program, and were ultimately the target of 233 of the total authorized "Black Nationalist" COINTELPRO actions. The Church Commission report states unambiguously:

Although the claimed purpose of the Bureau's COINTEL-PRO tactics was to prevent violence, some of the FBI's tactics against the BPP were clearly intended to foster violence, and many others could reasonably have been expected to cause violence.[14]

The FBI's program to destroy the Black Panther Party

included a concerted effort to muzzle Black Panther publications—to prevent Panther members and persons sympathetic to their aims from expressing their views, and to encourage the mass media to report stories unfavorable to the Panthers. These tactics also involved disseminating inflammatory or false information, promoting dissent within the BPP and between the BPP and other organizations.

In May 1970, FBI headquarters ordered the Chicago, Los Angeles, Miami, Newark, New Haven, New York, San Diego, and San Francisco field offices to advance proposals for crippling the BPP newspaper, the *Black Panther*. Immediate action was deemed necessary because: "The Black Panther Party newspaper is one of the most effective propaganda operations of the BPP.... Distribution of this newspaper is increasing at a regular rate thereby influencing a greater number of individuals in the United States along the Black extremist lines."[15]

The degree of government repression against the Black Panthers or its effects in sending a chilling message to all activists should not be underestimated. And this repression was not limited to the BPP. COINTELPRO was applied to any groups or movements that were seen as a threat—whether real or imagined. But the BPP and the radical wing of the Black liberation movement were not only stopped by government violence and infiltration. There were also limitations in the politics, strategy, and tactics of the Panthers that contributed to their decline. One of the most important among those weaknesses was their acceptance of a semi-militaristic notion of politics (following Mao Zedong's slogan, "power flows from the barrel of a gun"). Furthermore, they believed that the source of revolutionary change and social power lay in the dispossessed and marginalized—the urban "lumpen proletariat"—rather than the mass of workers. The emphasis on "picking up the gun" was more exaggerated by some Panther leaders than others, but it was firmly part of the culture of the party.

The Panthers' focus on organizing the lumpen proletariat flowed from their understanding of the dynamics of the class structure in the U.S. Blacks formed an internal colony, they argued, and, therefore, they were fighting a struggle for national liberation likened to the guerrilla movements in Algeria, Cuba, or Vietnam. The emphasis on organizing the most dispossessed and marginalized—analogous to the peasantry from which Third World guerrillas drew their support—made the Panther organization unstable. It meant that the organization found it difficult to establish consistent routines, a problem exacerbated by the influx of thousands of raw recruits into the party in the late 1960s. This instability made the party more easily infiltrated. The emphasis, more with some members than others, on the "gun" allowed the U.S. government to isolate and "outgun" the BPP. A concerted campaign of government repression along with the party's own internal weaknesses led to its effective demise as a coherent force by the early 1970s.[16]

Unfortunately, although large numbers of working-class Blacks (and others) identified with the Panthers, the Panthers' focus on the lumpen proletariat led them away from their potentially most powerful allies, radicalized workers. Eldridge Cleaver, who could argue against Stokely Carmichael on the need to have a non-racial outlook, could at the same time describe the working class in the United States in the following terms: "In reality, it is accurate to say that the Working Class, particularly the American Working Class, is a parasite upon the heritage of mankind, of which the Lumpen has been totally robbed by the rigged system of Capitalism which in turn, has thrown the majority of mankind upon the junkheap while it buys off a percentage with jobs and security."[17]

The Dodge Revolutionary Union Movement, on the other

hand, was an organization that based itself on Black industrial workers. The organization grew out of a 1968 wildcat strike in Detroit's automobile factories. The significance of DRUM lay in the simple fact that the movement had gone from organizing in the streets, in communities, and was now organizing at workplaces—at the very heart of capitalism. As Dan Georgakas and Marvin Surkin point out in their history of DRUM, *Detroit: I Do Mind Dying:*

> No less an authority than the *Wall Street Journal* took them very seriously from the day of the first wildcat, for the *Wall Street Journal* understood something that most of the white student radicals did not yet understand: the Black movement of the sixties had finally arrived at one of the most vulnerable links of the American economic system—the point of mass production, the assembly line.[18]

Unlike the Black Panthers, the leaders of DRUM believed that Black workers, not the urban unemployed, were the decisive and potentially most powerful social group to organize. DRUM believed that because of their vital role in some of the United States' most important industries, Black workers had a key role to play in changing society.

DRUM assigned to Black workers the role of being the vanguard of the working class. White workers in the United States could not be considered a reliable ally in a united working-class struggle. As Mike Hamlin, one of DRUM's leaders, put it: "Whites in America don't act like workers. They don't act like proletariat. They act like racists. And that's why I think Blacks have to continue to have Black organizations independent of whites."[19]

DRUM not only organized against the auto companies, but also targeted the United Automobile Workers (UAW) because of its complicity with management, its failure to represent its Black members, and the virtual absence of Blacks within the leadership of the union. Within months of the formation of DRUM, other Revolutionary Union Movements, "RUM"s, were formed in other Detroit workplaces, notably at Ford and General Motors plants, and at United Parcel Service.

The RUMs were to come together to form the League of Revolutionary Black Workers in 1969. The leadership of DRUM aimed to coordinate the various workplace organizations under a central leadership, and to reach out to the Black community in Detroit as well as nationally. As Georgakas summarizes the significance of DRUM and the League:

> That the League was built around workers and not students or street people or welfare mothers or other sectors of society was not accidental. The people who created the League were Marxists. They believed that you organized workers, not because of some mythical notion of workers' nobility, but because workers have real power. Workers are the nexus of the means of production. When they take action, everyone is affected. If workers exert political power, anything is possible. It does not follow that students are not important, that welfare mothers should not be organized, that some street people may not indeed become more than fickle lumpen proletarians. The League simply pointed out that no other class formation was strong enough to lead a mass movement. Moreover, workers have families. Thus, you automatically plug into education, health, and housing issues.

At that time, Detroit was the most industrialized city in the United States, and one out of six American jobs were linked, directly or indirectly, to the auto industry. The League soon received calls, telegrams, and visitors from all over the country wanting to create similar groups. There was contact with an ongoing movement at the Ford plant in Mahwah, New Jersey, and with a GMC plant in Fremont, California. Other queries came from steelworkers in Birmingham, Alabama, and autoworkers in Baltimore, Maryland. The League realized that these and similar groups could be fused into a Black Workers Congress (BWC) that would operate nationally to unite workers. So, the *Wall Street Journal* was right to be worried.[20]

The League rode the wave of radicalization that swept across U.S. society. Like the Panthers, the organization initially grew in leaps and bounds, capturing the mood of the time and filling an enormous vacuum created by the unwillingness of the unions or the traditional Black organizations to meet their concerns and needs. But the very success of the League would raise political and strategic questions that its leadership could not answer. Eventually, these questions would lead them to part ways. It was one thing, for example, to lead a successful wildcat—and quite another to build an organization capable of withstanding victimization, repression, and cooptation.

Like the Black Panther Party, the League was a Black-only organization, and saw white workers as part of the problem, rather than potential allies. This, of course, was understandable given the historical context and should not be an argument to detract from the accomplishments of the League. But it is one thing to understand and support the political necessity of organizing an excluded and oppressed minority, and another to conclude that this method of organizing is the only way of achieving liberation. As significant a percentage as Black workers represented in the auto plants—indeed, in Detroit as a whole—there was no way to organize a successful opposition to the auto companies (let alone to overthrow capitalism) without finding a way to win over white workers. This is not to say that DRUM should not have organized; or that one of its main tasks was to recruit white workers to the cause of Black liberation. But if Marxism was their inspiration, a multiracial class strategy should have followed.

Moreover, the question of power, that is, how to transform the whole of society, had to take up questions outside the auto plants. The League split in 1971 over differences of how to move forward. The split is often described as one between the nationalists, who wanted to orient to the Black ghettos of Detroit, and the "Marxists," who wanted to expand the League outside Detroit and to bring it into alliance with other forces. In truth, the political lines of the split were not so clear-cut. Both sides accepted ideas of Black nationalism and never broke out of that frame of reference. DRUM collapsed "for all the reasons all the organizations of that period ultimately failed. These included the inevitable personality problems, financial pressures, sheer fatigue, and the counter-thrust from the other side"[21] as the auto companies moved to victimize DRUM activists in the plants. More specifically, DRUM activists, who had succeeded in forming the organization after years of work together, found it hard to adjust to a new situation:

> The situation arose that one group wanted to continue in the manner that had brought success in the past, with an emphasis on local resources, while the other wanted to continue in the manner that had brought success in the past but with activists that included politically tested non-Detroiters. Each essentially was relying on a strategy that had previously succeeded without paying sufficient attention to the new details of the developing political dynamic.[22]

In DRUM and the Black Panther Party, the Black movement had produced some of the most effective revolutionaries and socialists in two generations. These leaders had real mass influence. But in the end the movement was stymied. The system proved to have more flexibility and room for reform than the revolutionaries believed was possible. In part, this was because the system fought so hard against any concessions. But faced with the choice of a real challenge to its power and granting some reforms, those in power chose the latter. While jailing, harassing, exiling, and assassinating the Black Power movement's more radical sections (like the Black Panthers), the Democratic Party machine set out to co-opt the mainstream section of the movement, with considerable success.

The 1967 urban rebellions and the prospects of more militant activity prodded the Democratic Party machines, particularly in Northern urban centers, to make concessions to Black sentiment. Radical commentator Robert L. Allen explained in 1969, "from the liberal point of view, some concessions must be made if future disruptions such as the 1967 riot are to be avoided." The election of Black politicians would not change the conditions of Black people's lives in their jurisdictions, yet "[B]lack people were supposed to get the impression that progress was being made, that they were finally being admitted through the front door.... The intent is to create the impression of real movement while actual movement is too limited to be significant."[23]

Thousands of Black radicals realized the need to break from the Democrats in this period, identifying their political outlook with radical groups like the Black Panther Party and DRUM. But powerful forces worked against them. As the 1970s wore on, the postwar economic boom slowed. It crashed into recession in 1974–75. This made reforms harder to win as the government looked to cut back on spending. As the movement saw its opportunities to win concrete gains contract, its goals contracted as well. Thus, the goal of transforming society from below gave way to electoralism in the Democratic Party.

CHAPTER TWELVE

Making Race a Central Wedge Issue

The mid-1970s were a time of recession, inflation, and economic uncertainty that symbolized the end of the postwar boom across the capitalist world. In the U.S., this economic crisis led to the first widespread layoffs and cutbacks in government spending in two decades. As a result, the radical movements of the 1970s ran into much more determined opposition to the social change they sought. The U.S. ruling class defeated the challenges to its rule posed by the radicalization of the 1960s and 1970s with a strategy that combined repression with reform. The previous chapter outlined the repressive measures the government took against the radical wing of the movement. Meanwhile, the reform option took shape in the creation of a space in the Democratic Party for a layer of Black officials with a stake in the system.

It has been more than forty years since the first Black mayor was elected in a major city. Since that time, it has become clear that Democratic officials elected through strong Black voter turnout answer to the same moneyed interests as the white officials who preceded them. In hundreds of instances, Black politicians' actions toward the poor and working-class Blacks who constitute their base range from neglect at best to outright attack at worst. Atlanta Mayor Maynard Jackson, for example, viciously defeated a strike of Black sanitation workers in 1977— to the delight of the predominantly white businessmen who made up the city's Chamber of Commerce.[1] Coleman Young, mayor of Detroit, was so determined to break a municipal workers' strike in 1986 that he threatened to call out the National Guard. And perhaps most disracefully, Philadelphia Mayor Wilson Goode engineered the firebombing of the Black countercultural group MOVE, which advocated armed self-defense against police brutality, in 1985. Eleven people were killed in the attack—including six children—and more than sixty-one homes were destroyed.[2]

The approach of creating political space for Black Democratic candidates reached its zenith with Jesse Jackson's 1984 and 1988 presidential campaigns, organized through his National Rainbow Coalition (NRC). In 1984, Jackson was able to win 21 percent of the total votes cast in the Democratic primaries—and he won a number of important Southern states outright. But thanks to party rules limiting the number of delegates he could claim at the party's convention, Jackson was able to gain the backing of only 11 percent of the delegates. So Jackson was thrown into the position of having to endorse Walter Mondale as the Democratic candidate, even though Mondale went on, predictably, to nix every element of the NRC's platform proposals. In the end, the platform itself barely touched on issues of importance to Black America.[3]

Jackson enjoyed broader support in 1988, when he ran a decidedly more mainstream race. Keeping his campaign message relatively conservative, he was able to consolidate the support of the Black Democratic establishment. In a shift from 1984, when they had opposed his candidacy, officials such as Mayor Andrew Young in Atlanta and U.S. Rep. Mickey Leland

(D-Texas) this time backed Jackson—or at least didn't endorse his opponents. They were no doubt swayed by the support Jackson won among their constituencies in the 1984 race.

Jackson's attempts to consolidate his position within the Democratic Party were in line with the overall trajectory of his career, since he had been on the right wing of the civil rights movement from the beginning. He had made a name for himself within the SCLC through his outstanding abilities as a fundraiser, but politically he was firmly within the conservative wing of the group. As part of this wing, he opposed Martin Luther King, Jr.'s launch of the Poor People's Campaign in 1968, for example. And Jackson disagreed with the direction of King's politics toward the end of his life—where King attempted to connect civil rights with workers' rights and demands for greater social spending.[4]

Jackson would go on to announce his independence from SCLC in 1971 with the formation of his Chicago-based Operation PUSH. But Jackson made this move on a right-wing basis that revolved around calls for "Black capitalism" (something even Richard Nixon publicly supported). Operation PUSH emphasized support for Black businesses, self-reliance, and the development of conservative mores within the Black community.

Cheering capitalism is something Jackson has done enthusiastically throughout his career. In a letter to *Business Week* in 1987, Jackson wrote:

> A strong, healthy private economy is essential to our national well-being and our hopes for social progress. The future of the business Establishment and of the nation itself are dependent upon attention to the long-range effects of current American business polices. The long term interests of American business and the American people are mutual and inseparable.[5]

This stance has gone hand in hand with devoted efforts

on Jackson's part to prevent Black militants from building political alternatives to the two-party system. When more than
8,000 Blacks from widely varied political backgrounds gathered in Gary, Indiana, for the National Black Political Convention in 1972, Jackson was instumental in shutting down the
efforts of radicals there to create an all-Black left-wing party.[6]
The convention endorsed a Black Political Agenda that criticized the American system as a whole, and condemned both
the Democrats and the Republicans for their failure to address
the needs of Black people. Jackson came out strongly against
the Agenda, and claimed it was only a draft to delegates from
Michigan—the majority of whom were conservative and
firmly within the Democratic Party. Jackson argued that any
delegates who opposed the electoral strategies put forward by
the convention's leadership were destroying Black unity.

Jackson's hostility to independent politics was made yet
clearer when he threw his support behind George McGovern's
presidential bid in 1972. He also backed Jimmy Carter in 1976.
And in 1980, after Carter had outraged many Black voters with
his surprisingly conservative policies, Jackson argued that
Blacks "had the responsibility" to consider the candidacies of
Republicans as well as Democrats, in effect arguing that Ronald
Reagan may have had more to offer Black people than Carter.[7]

Many on the left have chosen to ignore Jackson's actual record when it comes to the relationship between the Rainbow
Coalition and the Democrats—arguing that it provided a "mass
base" from which an independent third party could be built.
But Jackson has shown his commitment to staying within the
Democratic fold, no matter how badly the party treated him
and his supporters at times. As he argued in 1984, "The poor
have too much invested in the Democratic Party to pick up
our marbles and go home."[8] From its founding, the NRC func-
tioned much more as a progressive caucus within the Demo-

cratic Party—one that was quickly pulled rightward. Jackson's success in shoring up the support of the Black Democratic establishment in his 1988 campaign did not then set him up to advance the needs and concerns of Black people within the party. At best, it consolidated his role as the leader of the Democratic Party's liberal wing, which would then go on to make apologies for the right-wing leadership of the party.

Despite Jackson's success, it became commonplace for politicians of both main parties to use what has become known as the "race card" to their advantage. Appealing to the basest of fears and prejudices, politicians of both parties have used racism to mobilize voters and to stigmatize government programs for the poor. For these reasons, the issue of race has been central to the move rightward by both parties. In 1964, Lyndon Baines Johnson appeared miles to the left of the arch-conservative Republican Barry Goldwater. Democrats and much of the left strongly urged a vote for Johnson as the only salvation from Armageddon. Goldwater, setting himself up as an opponent of civil rights legislation in Congress, won only the most hard-core segregationist states of the Deep South.[9] The Goldwater campaign provided a road map for future Republican campaigns. But by 1996, even Goldwater declared that he believed the Republican Party had gone too far to the right under the influence of Christian fundamentalism.[10]

The rightward shift of both parties can be traced back to the 1968 presidential election. The third-party campaign by Alabama governor George Wallace became a model for future presidential campaigns by both Democratic and Republican hopefuls. Wallace ran as a "law-and-order" candidate and a diehard segregationist. He appealed to Democratic Party voters who were opposed to granting any concessions to the Black movement. To the surprise of many pundits, Wallace received just under 14 percent of the vote.[11]

Many of the issues that Wallace campaigned around became the core of the New Right's agenda in the 1980s. Using populist rhetoric to denounce "big government," Wallace also called for the "defense of traditional values," as well as a renewed patriotism and militarism. At the center of his campaign, however, was racial politics. Wallace had first gained national attention as an ardent white supremacist. As noted in Chapter Eight, in his 1963 Alabama gubernatorial inaugural address, Wallace proclaimed, "I say segregation now, segregation tomorrow, segregation forever."[12] For the presidential election campaign, he largely avoided direct race-baiting, instead masking his racist message with various code words. The real meaning of his message was unmistakable. He called for an increased use of force to suppress the Black urban uprisings, derided the Black movement and the War on Poverty, and launched a McCarthyite attack on liberal politicians and intellectuals.

Wallace's success at the polls did not go unnoticed. Then-Republican Party strategist Kevin Phillips, an aide to Attorney General John Mitchell, submitted a lengthy analysis of U.S. voting trends to President Nixon, arguing that a Republican victory and a long-term realignment could be achieved by using race as a "wedge issue." Phillips summarized his argument in a 1969 book, *The Emerging Republican Majority*. The book's main argument was that a turn to the right and the use of veiled anti-Black rhetoric could be the basis for Republican electoral success in the South. The Wallace campaign, according to Phillips, signaled the growing alienation of Southern racists with the Democratic Party: the "principal force which broke up the Democratic Coalition [was the] Negro socioeconomic revolution and liberal Democratic ideological inability to cope with it."[13]

He added:

> Until the national Democratic Party embraced the Negro socioeconomic and civil rights revolution of the nineteen-sixties, the Deep South upcountry shunned the economic conservatism of both the Republicans and Dixiecrats.... Although the civil rights revolution was straining Democratic loyalties all over the South, the poor white hill counties saw Goldwater as the Dixiecrat-style economic conservative whose commitment to New Deal farm, home loan, rural electrification, Social Security and other programs was minimal.... Liberalism lost its support base in the upcountry by shifting its principal concern from populist economics to government participation in social and racial upheaval.[14]

In the words of Thomas and Mary Edsall, authors of *Chain Reaction: The Impact of Race, Rights and Taxes on American Politics*, "Race and taxes...functioned to force the attention of the public on the costs of federal policies and programs. Those costs were often first experienced in terms of loss— the loss of control over school services, union apprenticeship programs, hiring, promotions, neighborhoods, public safety, and even over sexual morals and a stable social order." In addition, "Opposition to busing, to affirmative action, to quotas, and to housing integration have given a segment of the traditionally Democratic white electorate ideological common ground with business and the affluent in shared opposition to the federal regulatory apparatus."[15]

This strategy, dubbed the Southern strategy, became the cornerstone of the Republican Party's post-1972 presidential election efforts. Nixon went out of his way to appeal to the racist vote in the South. After Supreme Court judge Abe Fortas resigned in April 1969, Nixon nominated Judge Clement Haynsworth, Jr., who was a segregationist from South Carolina. The Senate rejected his nomination in a vote of 55–45. Unbowed, Nixon nominated another segregationist Southerner, G.

Harold Carswell in 1970. Carswell was seen as unqualified and was also rejected. These defeats represented a blow to Nixon, but he used them to appeal to racist Southerners.

> I understand the bitter feelings of millions of Americans who live in the South about the act of regional discrimination that took place in the Senate yesterday [April 8, 1970]. They have my assurance that the day will come when men like Judges Carswell and Haynsworth can and will sit on the high Court.[16]

Nixon reached out to Southern right-wingers, such as Senator Strom Thurmond, in order to ensure Southern support, foreshadowing many of the themes that later became part of Ronald Reagan's campaign arsenal. Nixon urged Congress to impose a moratorium on court-ordered busing, nominated conservatives to the Supreme Court, pleaded with the Court for postponement of Mississippi's desegregation plan, and lobbied Congress to defeat the fair-housing enforcement program and the extension of the Voting Rights Act of 1965.

The issues of "reverse discrimination," ending affirmative action, busing, and government programs for the poor all became rallying points of this "New Right." Ronald Reagan's presidency represented a continuation—albeit with greater gusto—of the assault on the gains of the civil rights movement of the 1960s. Ronald Reagan opposed every major piece of civil rights legislation that came before Congress, as did his vice president, George Bush, including the Civil Rights Act of 1964, which he denounced as a "bad piece of legislation."[17] On the campaign trail in August 1980, Reagan declared himself a champion of "state's rights"—a phrase understood by many Southern whites as an endorsement of white supremacy. Reagan's message was all the more obvious since he launched his presidential campaign in the town of Philadelphia, Mississippi, where three civil rights workers—James Chaney, Andrew Goodman, and Michael Schwerner—were murdered by members of the Klan in 1964. (In 1984, Reagan again returned to Philadelphia and asserted that "The South Shall Rise Again.")[18]

Reagan questioned the very idea that Blacks faced racist discrimination in the United States. "Sometimes I wonder if they really want what they say they want," Reagan remarked, "because some of those leaders are doing very well leading organizations based on keeping alive the feeling that they're victims of prejudice."[19] In a speech to the National Black Republican Council on September 15, 1982, Reagan argued that Blacks "would be appreciably better off today" if the Great Society programs of Lyndon Johnson had not been passed: "The big taxers and big spenders in Congress had started a binge that would slowly change the nature of our society, and even worse, it threatened the character of our people."[20]

According to the Reagan administration, the problem lay with the victims of racism, not the racists—or the system itself. In fact, *antiracists* were the problem. As Reagan's U.S. Civil Rights Commission Chairman, Clarence Pendleton, Jr., put it: "The new racists, many of them Black, exhibit the classical behavior system of racism. They treat Blacks differently than whites because of their race."[21]

President George Bush I followed in Reagan's footsteps. Central to Bush's election were the scurrilous "Willie Horton" ads that accused his Democratic opponent, Massachusetts governor Michael Dukakis, of being "soft on crime." The ads faulted Dukakis for the fact that Horton, a Black prisoner released on a Massachusetts prison furlough program, raped and murdered a white woman. More than a decade of race-baiting also created space in mainstream politics for many who were previously considered right-wing crackpots and fringe elements—such as Nazi and Klan member David Duke. At a packed December 4, 1991, news conference in Washington, D.C., the former grand wizard of the Ku Klux Klan announced that he was entering the race for the Republican Party's presidential nomination. He denounced George Bush for selling out the party's principles by signing a 1991 civil rights bill, by raising taxes, and by failing to protect the American worker from foreign competition. Bush denounced Duke as a "charlatan," and tried to distance himself from the self-avowed Nazi, but the link between Bush and Duke was clear. The conservative business magazine the *Economist* commented that Bush's condemnation of Duke would carry

> more conviction had Mr. Bush not won his election to the presidency in 1988 on the back of television advertisements attacking his opponent for supposed leniency towards a murderer, Willie Horton. Mr. Horton just happened to be Black. Nothing should be read into that, protested the Republicans at the time, nor into much of the advertising that some Republicans have since taken to using in campaigns elsewhere in America. Yet the language used in those campaigns is the same coded language used by "the reformed" Mr. Duke, as the voters, Black and white, well understand.[22]

The Democrats and the Democratic Leadership Council

The shift to the right in U.S. politics was not wholly due to the Republican Party. A crucial component to the Republicans' success over the last thirty years has been the role played by its alter ego, the Democratic Party. The collaboration of the Democratic Party was an indispensable precondition for Reaganism coming to dominate mainstream politics. As Kevin Phillips (the earlier mentioned architect of the GOP's successful Southern strategy) wrote in his book *The Politics of Rich and Poor,* "part of the reason that U.S. 'survival of the fittest' periods of economic restructuring are so relentless rests on the performance of the Democrats as history's second most enthusiastic capitalist party. They do not interfere much with capitalist momentum, but wait for excesses and the inevitable populist reactions."[23]

Phillips rightly argues that the policies associated with Reaganism were first introduced by Jimmy Carter. "The case can be made that even Jimmy Carter provided more assistance to economic change than Nixon did, in part by extending bipartisan support for economic deregulation and tight money during the late 1970s."[24] During the 1976 presidential campaign, Carter declared, "he saw nothing wrong with communities 'trying to maintain the ethnic purity of their neighborhoods,' and that he would not promote the power of the govenment to force 'the intrusion of alien groups' into a neighborhood."[25] Carter again embarrassed his Black supporters just before the election when he refused to resign from his Plains, Georgia, Baptist church, when, citing a 1965 resolution banning "niggers and civil rights agitators," church deacons banned four Black men from Sunday service.[26] These statements should have come as no surprise to anyone who had followed Carter's career. In his 1970 gubernatorial campaign, he attacked his Republican opponent in the general election by reminding voters what role the Republican Party played during the Civil War: "The last time the Republicans were in Atlanta was 100 years ago. They burned it down."[27]

Once in office, Carter appointed Dixiecrat Griffin Bell to the position of U.S. attorney general. As a federal judge in the 1960s, Bell had upheld a Georgia court ruling that banned Black state assemblyman Julian Bond from taking his seat, and had supported President Nixon's nomination of the openly racist G. Harold Carswell to the Supreme Court. As attorney general, Bell refused to enforce federal rights legislation.[28] This produced a crisis among Black Democrats who had campaigned for Carter's election. Gary, Indiana, Mayor Richard Hatcher admitted, "[I]t's difficult for any Black leader who pushed the election of Jimmy Carter to face the people he campaigned with."[29]

Despite its image today as being the party of racial minorities, for most of its history the Democratic Party was the party of white supremacy. Southern Democrats—the Dixiecrats—always had enormous influence inside the party. But the civil rights movement challenged the alliance between Northern capitalists and Southern racists at the heart of the party. And, importantly, the Black vote was no longer marginal. Black votes were necessary to elect John F. Kennedy in 1960 and Jimmy Carter in 1976. With the Republican adoption of the "Southern strategy," the Democrats lost an increasing number of votes to the Republicans.[30]

In the aftermath of the 1980 elections, Democratic Party bosses began in earnest to try to shed their image as the party of "civil rights." After Reagan's reelection in 1984, Democratic pollster William Hamilton warned the party's leaders that they "can't very well lose the white male vote by 2 to 1 and expect to be serious players in a two-party system."[31] In February 1985, newly elected Democratic National Committee (DNC) chair Paul Kirk announced that caucuses within the DNC (representing such groups as Blacks, Hispanics, Asian/ Pacific Islanders, women, gays and lesbians) were "political nonsense," and promised to abolish them. Former DNC chair Robert Strauss summed up the new consensus among party leaders on "special interest groups." "The defeat will mean nothing to them. The hunger of these groups will be greater. Women, Blacks, teachers, Hispanics. They have more power, more money than ever before. Do you think these groups are going to turn the party loose? Do you think labor is going to turn the party loose? Jesse Jackson? The others? Forget it."[32]

The Democratic Party's move to the right was spurred by the creation of the Democratic Leadership Council (DLC) in February 1985. Initiated by several prominent Democrats, the council's aim was to move the party back to the middle by shedding its liberal, antibusiness, soft-on-defense image.[33] According to one Democratic strategist, "The fear of a lot of people is that this group wants to take the cream of the party's leadership and leave [DNC Paul] Kirk with Jesse Jackson and the single-issue interest groups."[34] The liberal wing of the party was in agreement with the turn. According to Ted Kennedy in 1985: "There is a difference between being a party that cares about women and being the women's party. And we can and must be a party that cares about minorities without becoming a minority party."[35]

The DLC strategy carried the day in the Democratic Party, and its partisans viewed themselves as vindicated when the DLC ticket of white Southerners Bill Clinton and Al Gore won the 1992 and 1996 presidential elections. At best, the Clinton-Gore administration promoted a "race-neutral" approach to social policy that simply tried to avoid issues of racial discrimination. At worst, it pandered to racism by scapegoating Black welfare recipients or Latino immigrants. This was no accident, because abandoning any notion of government action to correct racial injustice has been central to New Democrat politics from the start. Clinton abandoned Lani Guinier, his original choice to head the Justice Department's Civil Rights Division, in the face of a hysterical right-wing campaign branding Guinier a "quota queen."[36] While claiming a posture of wanting to "mend" rather than "end" affirmative action, Clinton ordered the end of dozens of federal affirmative action "set-aside" programs. "I've done more to eliminate programs—affirmative action programs—I didn't think were fair," Clinton boasted in one of the 1996 presidential debates, "and to tighten others up than my predecessors have since affirmative action's been around."[37] The administration pressed the Congressional Black Caucus to drop from the 1994 crime bill a "Racial Justice Act" that required assurances that the death penalty wouldn't be administered in a racially discriminatory way.[38] And the administration refused to change federal drug sentencing laws on crack cocaine that overwhelmingly discriminate against Black offenders.[39]

Just how much the Clinton-Gore administration took Black support for granted became evident in the aftermath of George W. Bush's stolen presidential election in 2000. Democrat Gore received near-monolithic support from Blacks in spite of doing little to deserve it. And despite well-documented cases of Black disenfranchisment in Florida, candidate Gore demobilized protests in the interests of "stability."[40] An aggressive Republican campaign and a corrupt Supreme Court decision pushed Bush into the White House, even though Gore had won more than half a million more votes than Bush. In some ways, the imposition of Bush in 2000 seemed the latest revenge of the Confederacy. The Electoral College, an institution established at the behest of slaveholders to protect their interests, foisted on the country a president who received fewer popular votes than his opponent. The historic legacy of racism and inequality, built into the constitutional system, reared its head again on the cusp of the twenty-first century.

Black Liberation and Socialism

In the wake of the scandalous government neglect of the impoverished African-American residents of the Gulf Coast when Hurricane Katrina struck in August 2005, one can all too easily come to the conclusion that nothing at all has changed for Blacks in the United States since the 1960s. But this is incorrect. Although many of the gains that were achieved have been rolled back, the United States today is not what it was in the days of Jim Crow. Legal segregation has been dismantled. In the realm of mainstream politics, it is no longer acceptable to advance openly racist policies. Despite the reality of massive social change in the conditions of Black Americans in the post-Second World War era, it is also the case that the benefits of the 1960s have been unevenly shared. As the movement and mass mobilizations subsided and recession deepened in the mid-1970s, the principal beneficiaries of the 1960s struggles proved to be the Black middle classes.[1] As one study of the economic position of U.S. Blacks concludes:

> Between 1939 and the early 1970s, a Black male worker pushed his average earnings from 42 to 67 percent of a white male worker's earnings. Black women did even better, almost reaching parity with white women by the end of the 1970s, despite the fact that Black women on average were

still more poorly educated than white women.

Yet this long period of Black progress was very uneven. Blacks' income relative to whites' leveled off for a crucial decade during the Eisenhower 1950s. This was true for both men and women. The slowdown in the 1950s was important for three reasons. First, it signaled the end of very rapid gains in the 1940s—gains that came from a major incorporation of Blacks into the industrial working class. Second, it represented the politically pregnant pause that preceded the next round of gains in the late 1960s and 1970s—gains that came mainly from Black access to white universities and partial incorporation into white-collar professions. Third, it helps us understand why Black incomes went up—it tells us that, far from being "evolutionary," Blacks' relative economic improvement was concentrated in special political periods: the 1940s, and the dozen years between the early 1960s and 1975. *And once those gains were won, they could be taken back.*[2]

One of the most conspicuous aspects of the advances of the Black middle class is the success of a group of Black politicians who have attained high government positions. Ironically, the conservative Republican administration of George W. Bush appointed Blacks to the highest governmental positions they have achieved—secretary of state and national security adviser. But Colin Powell and Condoleezza Rice are the exceptions to the general pattern that has concentrated Black gains among the ranks of elected officials, most of them Democrats. In 1964 there were only 100 Black elected officials. By 1990 this number had grown to 7,000. In 2001, the Joint Center for Political and Economic Studies reported that there were 9,101 Black elected officials in office that year.[3] Black mayors have been elected to office in nearly every major American city in the last three decades.

This Black middle class necessarily has a contradictory relation to the Black struggle. On the one hand, they will support certain kinds of struggle so long as it advances their interests. Thus, one businessman explained his attitude to the Black radicals of the 1960s:

> When you ask about the Black militant, I have to say I appreciate the changes he helped bring about in the last ten years. Unless there were people running around the streets throwing bricks, I wouldn't be where I am. It wasn't until the riots that we got legislation in the Johnson administration.
>
> It took a Rap Brown and a Stokely to make [white] business look around and talk to Whitney Young. If they weren't burning down cities and having riots, the business environment wouldn't have asked "who can we talk to?"[4]

But this appreciation of Black militancy is sharply curtailed if it threatens the Black businessman or businesswoman's own position *or the system itself.* Historically, the Black middle class has supported certain extensions of Black rights, but is sure not to pursue policies contradictory to its class interests. Under Reconstruction, for example, none of the elected Black officials did anything to obtain land for newly freed slaves. One Black official actually proposed a policy for a "permanent halt to the confiscation of land and disfranchisement for political offense" of the Southern bourgeoisie.[5] Likewise, in the 1970s and 1980s, it has often been the Black mayors and the Black middle classes who have opposed the aspirations of Black workers. But because of the relatively weak position of this class vis-à-vis the overall U.S. ruling class—and because of the pervasive character of racism in the United States—this layer of Blacks will both fight to increase their wealth and influence within the system, even as they voice some opposition to it. This is what the Jesse Jackson presidential campaigns represented for the Black middle class.

The integration of the Black middle class within the Democratic Party and other institutions of capitalism (like major corporations, the media, the military, and so on) is unlikely to be reversed, despite the racism within the Democratic Party and society at large. This, however, does not represent a victory for the mass of Blacks, but is rather the bittersweet result of the struggles of the 1960s. The creation of a Black political machine in cities across the country (and within the Democratic Party) is a victory over segregation to be sure. But the spoils of this victory are few and not spread throughout the Black population as a whole. Jesse Jackson's campaign did not help build an alternative to capitalism or galvanize large numbers of Blacks into action. Rather, it succeeded in channeling Black discontent in a safe direction.[6] Jackson himself has always been clear about his ambitions, and his political orientation. He aims to be the spokesperson for Black people in the United States, and in order to maintain his credibility he will, of course, lend support to or even lead important struggles that challenge aspects of the system. In so doing, he will at times use radical slogans and rhetoric. But Jackson has been remarkably consistent in his political career—he is an unabashed proponent of the market and capitalism and is also an advocate for the Democratic Party. In the neoliberal 1990s, Jackson started touting his Wall Street Project, an effort to drum up Wall Street investment in Black business as the "fourth movement in the freedom symphony," following the struggles to overthrow slavery, establishing the right to vote, and winning civil rights. He added that "We need to become shareholders instead of sharecroppers."[7] This notion may sound preposterous, but it goes to show just how much even a "progressive" like Jackson has become a fixture in the system. Writes Chicago-based journalist Salim Muwakkil:

> In a world where, as a friend quips, "the IMF and all the other MFs control the global economy," there seems to be little alternative but to learn the rules of capitalism. In the

introduction to his new book, Jackson writes, "Failing to understand the role of money in a capitalist system is like being a fish that doesn't know how to navigate water."[8]

In a capitalist system that built itself first on Black slave labor and then proceeded to ensure that Black Americans are discriminated against, poorer, and paid less than others, it makes little sense to preach the virtues of money management. Even if Jackson's advice helped a few individuals here and there to succeed in the business world, it would do nothing to transform a system that thrives on racial inequality.

Capitalism, Racism, and Oppression

Capitalism not only gave rise to racism and racial oppression, but it *continues to depend on them*. The ruling class consciously cultivated racism to justify the enslavement of Africans. After the Civil War, racism became the cornerstone of the ruling class defense of its rule. The emergence of the United States as a world imperialist power only deepened—and vastly extended—the ideology of racism. At the turn of the nineteenth century U.S. racial ideology was integrated into a worldview—the "white man's burden"—which, though less explicitly "racial," is still an important part of the ideological arsenal that justifies U.S. domination internationally.

The acceptance of racist ideas was, of course, not limited to the ruling class, but it was the principal agent in racism's development and propagation. As the dominant class in society, it also shaped its ideas. As Marx put it, "[t]he ideas of the ruling class are in every epoch the ruling ideas."[9]

Acceptance of racist ideas by white workers should not be confused with their having a material interest in perpetuating racial oppression. The history of racism in the United States is not only a history of Black oppression, but also of the ability of the ruling class to use racism to maintain its power and wealth. From the poor whites of the South under slavery to the racist workers of today, adherence to racism ensures *their own* subordination. Black nationalists, and many socialists today, reject such a view. They point to the depths of racism among white workers historically as evidence that racism benefits all whites equally. Indeed, some argue that white *workers* have been the principal agent for the perpetuation of racism. Thus Herbert Hill writes: "If non-whites found it difficult to improve their condition, it was because institutions like organized labor prevented them from doing so."[10] The most obvious problem with such a line of argument is that it vastly overestimates the power of trade unions in controlling hiring practices and exonerates employers. Moreover, such an argument presents racism as a purely ideological question, ignoring the fact that racism and segregation were institutionalized and legal until the 1960s.

The conclusions from such an argument are also profoundly reactionary, since they close off any possibility of overcoming racism. As Manning Marable argues, adherents of such arguments are "basically idealists and not materialists. They say that the fundamental force that drives the motor of Black oppression...is race alone. They argue that all whites benefit materially and ideologically from racism which, in my view, looking at the data, looking at the facts and experiences of white people, is a disastrous misinterpretation of American and Black social history."[11]

Such views have become more widely prevalent in academia, and there is a "commonsense" acceptance of these arguments—in contradistinction to Marxism's alleged "economic reductionism." But most of these arguments against Marxism are largely based on a distortion or misunderstanding of Marxism. As Gregory Meyerson wrote in a critique of the important Cedric Robinson book, *Black Marxism*:

The "relative autonomy" of "race" has been enabled by a reduction and distortion of class analysis. The essence of the reduction and distortion involves equating class analysis with some version of economic determinism. The key move in the critique of economic determinist Marxism depends upon the view that the economic is the base, the cultural/political/ideological the superstructure.

Meyerson goes on:

Marxism properly interpreted emphasizes the primacy of class in a number of senses. One, of course, is the primacy of the working class as a revolutionary agent—a primacy which does not, as often thought, render women and people of color "secondary." Such an equation of white male and working class, as well as a corresponding division between a "white" male working class identity and all the others, whose identity is thereby viewed as either primarily one of gender and race or hybrid, is a view this essay contests all along the way. The primacy of class means that building a multiracial, multi-gendered international working-class organization or organizations should be the goal of any revolutionary movement: the primacy of class puts the fight against racism and sexism at the center. The intelligibility of this position is rooted in the *explanatory* primacy of class analysis for understanding the *structural determinants* of race, gender and class oppression. Oppression is multiple and intersecting but its causes are not.[12]

But even those who reject the argument that white workers are the principal agents of racist oppression still accept that white workers materially benefit from racism. Robert Allen is typical of this approach. He even uses Lenin's writings on imperialism as the basis for his argument.

Lenin warned that imperialism thereby tends to "create privileged sections...among the workers, and to detach them from the broad masses of the proletariat."... Thus, the resulting racism and chauvinism among white workers were much more than mere diversionary tactics introduced by conniving capitalists to divide the world working class; on the contrary, these ideological manifestations were firmly grounded in the dynamics of imperialist development.[13]

...Communist writers insisted upon regarding the white working class as the bearer of true enlightenment and fraternity; at the very minimum they contended that if only the workers would accept Marxism-Leninism *then* racial antagonisms would fade away. These contentions ignored the ideological impact of the very real advantages that have accrued to white workers as a result of racial discrimination at home and racist imperialism abroad.[14]

This is not the place to fully discuss Lenin's theory of the "aristocracy of labor."[15] Suffice it to say that Lenin argued that the benefits of imperialism would accrue to an "infinitesimal minority"[16] of the labor movement, not the mass of workers in advanced capitalist countries. Moreover, the argument that white workers benefit does not stand up to examination. As Martin Glaberman argues:

[T]he existence of a segregated Black workforce with inferior status limited, rather than enhanced, the ability of white workers to improve their wages and working conditions. In fact, employers were often willing to use, or threatened to use, Black workers as strikebreakers or simply replacements, to keep white workers in line...[otherwise] it would be difficult to understand why employers followed racist hiring patterns if it enhanced the power of the overwhelming majority of the working class.[17]

Statistical evidence confirms this argument. In a study of major metropolitan areas, Michael Reich found a correlation between the degree of income inequality between whites and Blacks and the degree of income inequality between whites. In those areas where the white/Black income differential was greatest, the percentage share of white income received by the top 1 percent of whites was greatest.[18] The legacy in the South and the lower unionization rate of both Black and white Southern workers reveals that, far from benefiting from racism, white workers lose out. As one author writes:

> But what is most dramatic—in each of these blue-collar groups, the southern white workers earned less than northern Black workers. Despite the continued gross discrimination against Black skilled craftsmen in the North, the "privileged" southern whites earned 4% less than they did. Southern male white operatives averaged...18% less than northern Black male operatives. And southern white service workers earned...14% less than northern Black male service workers.[19]

But if racism is not in the interests of white workers, why do they act *against* their material interests? First, both the ideas and institutions of capitalist society have been permeated by racism, influencing all aspects of society. But racism is not simply the result of the dominance of ruling-class ideology in the government, media, and schools. There is a material basis for racism built into capitalist competition. When Marx argued that capitalism created its own gravedigger, with the capacity and common interest to overthrow capitalist rule—the working class—he understood that capitalism also created obstacles to this process. Most crucially, capitalist competition is a barrier to working class unity.

> Competition separates individuals from one another, not only the bourgeois but still more the workers, in spite of the fact that it brings them together. Hence it is a long time before these individuals can unite.... Hence every organized power standing over and against these isolated individuals... can only be overcome after long struggles. To demand the opposite would be tantamount to demanding that competi-

tion should not exist in this definite epoch of history, or that the individuals should banish from their minds conditions over which in their isolation they have no control.[20]

The Irishman sees in the Negro a dangerous competitor. The sturdy farmers of Indiana and Ohio hate the Negro in second place after the slaveholder. To them he is a symbol of slavery and debasement of the working class, and the Democratic press daily threatens them with an inundation of their territories by the "nigger."[21]

This "common sense" can only be challenged on a mass scale through a process of struggle:

Both for the production on a mass scale of this communist consciousness, and for the success of the cause itself, the alteration of men on a mass scale is necessary, an alteration which can only take place in a practical movement, a *revolution*; the *revolution* is necessary, therefore, not only because the *ruling* class cannot be overthrown in any other way, but also because the class *overthrowing* it can only in a revolution succeed in ridding itself of all the old crap and become fitted to found society anew.[22]

Thus, in the process of challenging capitalist society, workers can begin to challenge the dominant ideas in society. So while the history of the American working-class movement includes a history of racism, it also contains heroic chapters of struggle that effectively confronted racism. The relative paucity of such struggles is not simply a reflection of the depths of racism, but more crucially, it is a reflection of the all-out efforts by the rich and powerful to undermine any threat to their rule. In addition, the domination of the trade union movement by a pro-capitalist bureaucracy and the correspondingly low level of political class consciousness among American workers are important factors to take into account. Unlike the caricature of Marxism most critics accept, economic struggles do not automatically in and of themselves lead to antiracist consciousness. This is why revolutionary socialists, especially Lenin, stressed the importance of political ideas. There is a constant theme in Lenin's writings about the need for those who aim to change the world to support all genuine resistance to all forms of exploitation and oppression.

> [Lenin reaffirmed] the need for the revolutionary socialist to support every movement against oppression, not only economic, but also political and cultural, and not only of workers, but of any downtrodden section of society.... [As Lenin wrote] "Working-class consciousness cannot be genuine political consciousness unless the workers are trained to respond to all cases of tyranny, oppression, violence, and abuse, no matter what class is affected—unless they are trained, moreover, to respond from a Social Democratic point of view and no other."[23]

Lenin's political approach reinforces the point of Meyerson above. Taking up the cause of the oppressed is not something separate from the class struggle. It is essential to the class struggle and the struggle for socialism.

The Limits of Black Nationalism

One of the legacies of the 1960s is the idea that the key political split in the history of Black resistance is that between "integrationists" like Martin Luther King, Jr., and "separatists" like Malcolm X or Stokely Carmichael. The integrationists are usually identified with accommodation and reformism, and the separatist current with resistance and radicalism. But this view is largely based on a one-sided reading of the 1960s struggles. The actual history of Black separatism is quite different. As a political current, Black nationalism is extremely heterogeneous, including advocates of Black capitalism, cultural nationalists, reformist politicians, and revolutionaries who oppose the system. What *all* varieties of Black separatism share is inconsistency and vacillation. This is necessarily built into *all* varieties of Black separatism, because neither the analysis nor strategy locate the one agent capable of transforming capitalist society—the working class. So while a separatist strategy can often tap the alienation felt by Blacks, it cannot provide a solution to the problems that face the mass of Black workers. At times, Black nationalist ideas can be radical in their critique of capitalism, as the Panthers' were. But they can also be much more conservative and pro-capitalist, stressing the need for "racial unity" as the basis for Black capitalism.

On the left it is often argued that Black nationalism is the inevitable and necessary expression of the Black struggle. Again, this is based on the assumption that future struggles will adopt the same character as those of the 1960s. But there is little reason to accept this view. Historically, Black separatism has become a mass current under certain specific circumstances. Most crucially, the growth of Black separatism—in the 1850s, 1920s, and 1960s—was the result of two interrelated factors: the existence of systematic, legal segregation and state resistance to Black demands for reform; a racist backlash and an inability to unite with whites because of their acceptance of racism. But in other periods, most crucially the period of mass upheaval in the 1930s, Black nationalism was a negligible force. The reason is not difficult to find. The Congress of Industrial Organizations' (CIO) commitment to unionize Black workers and the existence of a mass Communist Party undercut the appeal of separatism. The absence of such a workers' movement in the 1960s was an important factor in the growth of Black nationalism. But, as formal segregation came to an end and as class differentiation became more pronounced within the Black community, the appeal of Black nationalist politics waned. As the economic gains achieved by a minority of Blacks since the 1960s became more pronounced, the claim that *all* Blacks share the same interests could clearly be seen to be false.

This does not mean, however, that Black nationalism will disappear as a political current, because there is a material basis for its development. The persistence of racism, both ideological and institutional, in the United States lays the basis for organizing along racial lines—even if the basis for doing so across *class lines* is less and less tenable.

The idea that there is such a thing as a "Black community" that has common interests across class lines was more easily defended before the defeat of Jim Crow. The idea put forward by some, including the Communist Party in the 1930s, that Blacks constituted a nation and that the demand for separation was a necessary expression of the Black struggle, seems utterly anachronistic today. As Leon Trotsky argued against the views of the CP, Blacks are not a nation, but a national minority. As he put it, "An abstract criterion is not decisive in this question; far more decisive is the historical consciousness of a group, their [Blacks'] feelings, and their impulses."[24] Above all, the main factor that gives rise to Black nationalism is white racism. The dynamic of the Black struggle has not historically been toward becoming a nation, but white racism has helped give rise to Black nationalist consciousness. Historically, then, Black nationalism is a *defensive* reaction by Blacks.

Adopting C. L. R. James' formulations, some argue that the Black struggle is necessarily revolutionary and must also be organized separately from whites (even if some need for future "alliances" with other forces is acknowledged). A similar approach is shared by socialists who attempt to combine Black nationalism and Marxism. George Breitman, for example, defines Black nationalism as the tendency for Black people in the United States to unite as a group, as a people, into a movement of their own to fight for freedom, justice, and equality. Animated by the desire of an oppressed minority to decide its own destiny, this tendency holds Black people must control their own movement and the political and economic institutions of the Black community. Its characteristic attributes include racial pride, group consciousness, hatred of white supremacy, a striving for independence from white control, and identification with Black and non-white oppressed groups in other parts of the world.[25]

Breitman goes on to argue that Black nationalism in the United States differs from classic nationalism and African nationalism in that it does not share (or does not yet share) a commitment to a struggle for a separate Black nation. "So you can be a Black nationalist without being a separatist, although all separatists are Black nationalists."[26]

But such an understanding of Black nationalism confuses two elements: the appeal of a fight against white racism and the political program of Black nationalism. As Chris Harman writes: "Like all political ideologies, Black separatism exists at two levels—on the one hand as widespread, often not fully articulated currents of popular attitudes; on the other as more or less coherent analysis of the world and programs of action propounded by formal political organizations."[27]

It is important to understand this distinction to fathom the contradictory nature of the Black separatist appeal. Often the appeal of Black nationalism is its espousal of Black consciousness and pride rather than the formal program or ideas of its leaders. This distinction also lies at the heart of a Marxist approach to Black nationalism. As Lenin and Trotsky argued, the nationalism of an oppressed group cannot be equated with the nationalism of an oppressor group. Thus revolutionary socialists fully identify with the struggle of the oppressed, even if it expresses itself through a nationalist prism. But Marxists are not nationalists and supporting the struggles of the oppressed does not mean endorsing the politics that dominate that movement. The same is true when it comes to the question of independent or separate organization of the oppressed. Socialists defend the *right* of Blacks to organize separately in reaction to the racism of the dominant society. However, there is an enormous difference between defending the right to organize separately and advocating it or making it a matter of principle as the most effective means of organization. So, for example, revolutionary socialists should have defended the right of the Black Panther Party or the League of Revolutionary Black Workers to organize all-Black organizations—even if they believed that multiracial working-class organization is necessary to wage a successful struggle against capitalism. This is not some "concession" by socialists or an assertion that Black organizations need approval from anyone. Rather, it is a means of expressing solidarity with the struggle for Black freedom in the face of attacks from those who denounced the formation of all-Black organizations as simply a form of "reverse racism."

But it must also be said that such organizations alone cannot defeat the forces that oppress Blacks. Too many socialists confuse the defense of this right and its advocacy, turning what was a historical necessity into a virtue. As Lenin put it when arguing for the right of nations to self-determination, socialists are for the right to divorce (at the time this was not seen as acceptable for women), but advocating this right did not mean advocating that all married couples divorce.[28]

Marxism and Black Liberation

The relative weakness of the North American workers' movement (and, more generally, among workers in the advanced capitalist countries) has led many on the left to abandon any notion of working-class struggle, replacing it with the politics of "movementism." In brief, proponents of this argument stress the importance of "autonomy" for movements of the oppressed in order to achieve their liberation. They universally accept the idea that Marxism has ignored and/or downplayed questions of gender and race.[29]

The problem with such an approach is twofold. First, there is no necessary or immediate unity between groups of the oppressed. Second, movements of the oppressed have no real social power to fundamentally transform the system unless they become transformed into a movement of the *exploited* and oppressed, that is, unless they are allied or become part of the workers' movement that can champion the demands of *all* workers. Like the politics of Black separatism, a politics based on the "social movements" is bound to lurch from left to right because it has no material force by which to achieve its aims. Moreover, it is not true that these movements in and of themselves raise the issues and struggles of the oppressed because even the so-called autonomous movements are not autonomous of political forces and ideas. There is no guarantee that self-organization of the oppressed will produce the best political strategies for liberation. All too often the interests of middle-class elements have become dominant in the "autonomous" movements, as the history of the women's movement in the United States clearly shows.[30]

Indeed, despite the generally accepted denigration of the contribution of North American socialists to the struggle for Black liberation, the socialist movement also has *a consistent record of struggle against racism*. This is not to gloss over the often serious limitations of the movement including, as we have seen in the case of the Socialist Party, the involvement of open racists in the ranks of socialists. But this has to be understood not only as a failing of the Socialist Party on the Black question, but also as a more general indication of the SP's adherence to reformist politics on a whole number of questions. Moreover, the summary dismissal of the socialist movement by many writers today fails to ask such questions as whether in 1912 one would stand with the IWW that opposed entry in the First World War or with W. E. B. Du Bois. While Du Bois was a leading spokesperson for Black freedom, his backing of Woodrow Wilson, and his later endorsement of the First World War did nothing to advance the interests of Blacks. Likewise it is commonly asserted that the CP "placed the Soviet Union's survival above the battle for Black equality."[31] But while this is certainly true, it is also the case that the CP abandoned the *class struggle itself.* In short, the limitations of the socialist tradition with regard to Black liberation are, in part, an expression of the scarcity in the United States of the traditions and politics of genuine *revolutionary* Marxism. This should not be a reason to abandon Marxism. On the contrary, it is the single most convincing argument in favor of reestablishing the tradition and organization of revolutionary Marxism in the United States.

Notes

Introduction

1. Chertoff stated that "the critical thing was to get people out of there before the disaster.... Some people chose not to obey that order. That was a mistake on their part." CNN, *American Morning*, September 1, 2005.
2. Mike Marqusee, *Redemption Song: Muhammad Ali and the Spirit of the Sixties* (New York: Verso, 1999), 162.
3. Some Ali historians dispute that he coined this phrase, but it has become ensconced in Ali legend and is cited in numerous sources.
4. "Executive Summary," *State of Black America 2005,* National Urban League April 6, 2005, http://www.nul.org/stateofblackamerica.html.
5. Manning Marable, "The Contradictory Contours of Black Political Culture," in Mike Davis et al. eds., *The Year Left 2* (New York: Verso, 1987), 7.
6. Manning Marable, *Black American Politics: From the Washington Marches to Jesse Jackson* (New York: Verso, 1985), 247.
7. Frederick Douglass, "The Significance of Emancipation in the West Indies," in John W. Blassingame, ed., *The Frederick Douglass Papers,* Series One: *Speeches, Debates, and Interviews,* Volume 3: *1855–63* (New Haven: Yale University Press, 1985), 204.
8. See Robin D. G. Kelley, *Hammer and Hoe* (Chapel Hill: University of North Carolina Press, 1990) and Mark Naison, *Communists in Harlem During the Depression* (New York: Grove Press, 1983).

9. According to an October 2005 NBC/*Wall Street Journal* poll, Bush's job approval ratings among African Americans have dropped to 2 percent. Dan Froomkin, "A Polling Free-Fall among Blacks," *Washington Post*, October 13, 2005.

Chapter One: Slavery in the United States

1. Karl Marx and Frederick Engels, *Collected Works*, vol. 38 (London: Lawrence & Wishart, 1982), 101–2.

2. Quoted in James Axtell, *White Indians of Colonial America* (Fairfield, Washington: Ye Galleon Press, 1979), 8.

3. Frank M. Snowden, Jr., *Before Color Prejudice: The Ancient View of Blacks* (1983; repr., Cambridge, MA: Harvard University Press, 1991), 63.

4. Eric Williams, *From Columbus to Castro: The History of the Caribbean 1492–1967* (London: Andre Deutsch, 1970), 30.

5. C. H. Haring, *The Spanish Empire in Europe* (1947; repr., New York: Harbinger, 1963), 41.

6. Williams, *From Columbus*, 33.

7. Eric Williams, *Capitalism and Slavery* (1944; repr., London: Andre Deutsch, 1964), 19–20.

8. Marc Egnal, "The Economic Development of the Thirteen Continental Colonies, 1720 to 1775," *The William and Mary Quarterly*, 3rd Ser., vol. 32, no. 2. (April 1975): 201–2.

9. Theodore W. Allen, *The Invention of the White Race: The Origin of Racial Oppression in Anglo-America* (New York: Verso, 1997), 119.

10. David W. Galenson, "White Servitude and the Growth of Black Slavery in Colonial America," in "The Tasks of Economic History," special issue, *Journal of Economic History* 41, no. 1 (March 1981): 40.

11. Alexander Keyssar, *The Right to Vote* (New York: Basic Books, 2000), 6.

12. Betty Wood, *The Origins of American Slavery* (New York: Hill and Wang, 1997), 82.

13. Allen, *The Invention of the White Race*, 119.

14. Robin Blackburn, *The Making of New World Slavery* (New York: Verso, 1997), 328.

15. Figures quoted in Howard Zinn, *A People's History of the United States* (1980; repr., New York: HarperCollins, 1999), 29.

16. "Alden T. Vaughn, in an article in the *Virginia Magazine of History and Biography* on the origins of slavery and racism, wrote 'It may be more useful to see Anglo-American racism as a necessary precondition for a system of slavery based on ancestry and pigmentation,' which does nothing to explain the rise of racism as anything other than an ahistorical predetermination." Barbara Jeanne Fields, "Slavery, Race and Ideology in the United States of America," *New Left Review* 181 (May–June 1990): 100.

17. "It may be taken as a given that there would have been no enslavement without economic need, that is, without persistent demand for labor in underpopulated colonies.... [This] will not explain the enslavement of Indians and Negroes. The pressing exigency in America was labor, and Irish and English servants were available.... [I]t seems likely that the colonists' initial sense of difference from the Negro was founded not on a single characteristic but on a congeries of qualities which, taken as a whole, seemed to set the Negro apart.... In Africa these qualities had for Englishmen added up to savagery; they were major components in that sense of difference which provided the mental margin absolutely requisite for placing the European on the deck of the slave ship and the Negro in the hold." Winthrop Jordan, *White Over Black: American Attitudes Toward the Negro, 1550–1812* (Williamsburg, VA: University of North Carolina Press, 1968), 91–98.

18. Fields, "Slavery, Race and Ideology," 99.

19. Karl Marx, *Capital: A Critique of Political Economy*, vol. 1, trans. Ben Fowkes (New York: Penguin, 1976), 915.

20. Cedric Robinson, *Black Movements in America* (New York: Routledge, 1997), 2–8.

21. Howard Zinn, *A People's History of the United States*, 72.

22. David Brion Davis, *The Problem of Slavery in the Age of Revolution, 1770–1823* (Ithaca, NY: Cornell University Press, 1975), 24 and 51; Benjamin Quarles, *The Negro in the American Revolution* (Chapel Hill, NC: University of North Carolina Press, 1961), 40–41.

23. Barbara Jeanne Fields, edited online transcript of presentation to

producers of PBS documentary *RACE*, California, March 2001, http://www.pbs.org/race/000_About/002_04-background-02-02. htm.

24. Frederick Engels, *Anti-Dühring: Herr Eugen Dühring's Revolution in Science* (1939; repr., New York: New World, 1976), 117.

25. From notes taken by Robert Yates, Secret Proceedings and Debates of the Federal Convention (Cincinnati: Alston Mygatt, 1838), 144–45.

26. Keyssar, *The Right to Vote*, 20–24.

27. Ibid., 336. Only Vermont, New Hampshire, and Georgia did not have explicit property requirements for voting rights.

28. Plough Jogger, cited in Howard Zinn, *The People Speak: American Voices, Some Famous, Some Little Known* (New York: Perennial, 2004), 5–6.

29. Quoted in Howard Zinn and Anthony Arnove, eds., *Voices of a People's History of the United States* (New York: Seven Stories Press, 2004), 627.

30. Eric Foner, "Blacks and the U.S. Constitution, 1789–1989," *New Left Review* 183 (September–October 1990): 65.

31. Michael Goldfield, *The Color of Politics: Race and the Mainsprings of American Politics* (New York: New Press, 1997), 70.

32. Ibid.

33. Ibid., 70–71.

34. "The Migration of Importation of such Persons as any of the States now existing shall think proper to admit, shall not be prohibited by the Congress prior to the Year one thousand eight hundred and eight, but a Tax or duty may be imposed on such Importation, not exceeding ten dollars for each Person." U.S. Constitution, art. 1, sec. 9.

35. "No person held to Service or Labor in one State, under the Laws thereof, escaping into another, shall, in Consequence of any Law or Regulation therein, be discharged from such Service or Labor, but shall be delivered up on Claim of the Party to whom such Service or Labor may be due." U.S. Constitution, art. 4, sec. 2.

36. "Representatives and direct Taxes shall be apportioned among the several States which may be included within this Union, according

to their respective Numbers, which shall be determined by adding to the whole Number of free Persons, including those bound
to Service for a Term of Years, and excluding Indians not taxed,
three fifths of all other Persons." U.S. Constitution, art. 1, sec. 2.

37. Quoted in Foner, "Blacks and the U.S. Constitution," 65.

38. John Ashworth, *Slavery, Capitalism, and Politics in the Antebellum Republic,* vol. 1, *Commerce and Compromise, 1820–1850* (Cambridge: Cambridge University Press, 1995), 29.

39. Alien and Sedition Laws, effected July 14, 1789, art. 4, sec. 2.

40. Ashworth, *Slavery, Capitalism, and Politics*, 29.

41. "By 1804, all Northern states had voted to abolish the institution of slavery within their borders. In most of these states, however, abolition was not immediate. Instead, gradual emancipation laws set deadlines by which all slaves would be freed, releasing individuals as they reached a certain age or the end of a certain work period. This situation left some African Americans lingering in bonded servitude. Pennsylvania passed its Act for the Gradual Abolition of Slavery in 1780. Yet, as late as 1850, the federal census recorded that there were still hundreds of young Blacks in Pennsylvania, who would remain enslaved until their 28th birthdays." Nicholas Boston and Jennifer Hallam, "Freedom and Emancipation, Historical Overview," for PBS documentary *Slavery and the Making of America*, http://www.pbs.org/wnet/slavery/experience/freedom/history.html.

42. Edgar McManus, *A History of Negro Slavery in New York* (Syracuse, NY: Syracuse University Press, 1966), 174–75.

43. To John Holmes, 22 April 1820, cited in Paul Leicester Ford, ed., *The Works of Thomas Jefferson*, vol. 12 (New York: Knickerbocker Press, 1905), 159.

44. Letter to F. Corbin, November 26, 1820, in *Letters and Other Writings of James Madison*, vol. 3 (Philadelphia: J. Lippincott & Co., 1865), 193–94.

45. Robin Blackburn, *The Overthrow of Colonial Slavery 1776–1848* (New York: Verso, 1988), 276.

46. Marx, *Capital*, vol. 1 925–26.

47. Lewis C. Gray, *History of Agriculture in the Southern United States*

to 1860, vol. 1 (Washington, D.C.: Carnegie Institute of Washington, 1933), 530.

48. Ibid., 483, 530–31.

49. The wealth of the combined Southern states was greater than that of France or Germany in 1860, and income for the wealthiest of the planter class—defined as owning fifty slaves or more—was more than sixty times the per capita income of the day. Robert William Fogel and Stanley L. Engerman, *Time on the Cross: The Economics of American Negro Slavery* (Boston: Little, Brown and Company 1974), 134 and 249. Yet only a few thousand families made up this planting elite, and over two-thirds of the white Southern population owned no slaves at all. Zinn, *People's History*, 236.

50. Zinn, *People's History*, 236.

51. James M. McPherson, *Battle Cry of Freedom: The Civil War Era* (New York: Oxford University Press, 1988), 8.

52. Manning Marable, *Black American Politics*, 145.

53. Philip S. Foner, ed., *The Life and Writings of Frederick Douglass*, vol. 4 (New York: International Publishers, 1955), 192.

54. Frederick Douglass, *My Bondage and My Freedom*, ed. William L. Andrews (Chicago: University of Illinois Press, 1987), 188.

55. Mike Davis, "Why the U.S. Working-Class Is Different," *New Left Review* 123 (September–October 1980): 17.

56. Marx, *Capital*, vol. 1, 414.

57. The Fugitive Slave Act of 1850, 31st Cong, 1st sess. (September 18, 1850), Statutes at Large of the United States of America, 1789–1873. 9 (1862): 462. The Fugitive Slave Act (FSA) was part of a series of laws referred to as the "Compromise of 1850." In this compromise, the antislavery advocates gained the admission of California as a free state, and the prohibition of slave-trading in the District of Columbia. The slavery party received concessions with regard to slaveholding in Texas and the passage of this law.

The FSA new law created a force of federal commissioners empowered to pursue fugitive slaves in any state and return them to their owners. No statute of limitations applied, so that even those slaves who had been free for many years could be (and were) returned.

The commissioners enjoyed broad powers, including the right to compel citizens to assist in the pursuit and apprehension of runaways; fines and imprisonment awaited those who refused to cooperate. A captured runaway could not testify on his own behalf and was not entitled to a court trial. The commissioners received a fee of 10 dollars for every slave returned; the fee was reduced to five dollars if the accused slave were released.

58. Earl Ofari, *The Myth of Black Capitalism* (New York: Monthly Review Press, 1970), 15.

59. Ibid., 16.

60. Marable, *Black American Politics*, 145.

Chapter Two: Abolitionism

1. Goldfield, *The Color of Politics*, 97.

2. Herbert Aptheker, *Abolitionism, A Revolutionary Movement* (Boston: Twayne Publishers, 1989), 41.

3. Ashworth, *Slavery, Capitalism, and Politics*, 128.

4. Ashworth, *Slavery, Capitalism, and Politics*, 129; Herbert Aptheker, *Abolitionism: A Revolutionary Movement*, 56. Aptheker cites an official report of the American Anti-Slavery Society in 1838 that 1,350 societies existed locally with "perhaps 250,000 members."

5. Benjamin Quarles, *Black Abolitionists* (New York: Oxford University Press, 1969), 10.

6. Ibid., 9.

7. Ibid., 10.

8. Ashworth, *Slavery, Capitalism, and Politics*, 126.

9. Historian Eric Foner, for example, argued, "I think there's a good argument to be made that, really, 1829 should be the beginning of this movement. And that was with the publication of David Walker's *Appeal*." "Eric Foner on David Walker," PBS interview on *Africans in America*, ResourceBank, Part 4: 1831–1865, http://www.pbs.org/wgbh/aia/part4/4;2982.html.

10. Sterling Stuckey, *Slave Culture: Nationalist Theory and the Foundations of Black America* (New York: Oxford University Press, 1987), 129.

11. "That this appeal was highly attractive [to ruling-class whites] might be demonstrated by the number of leading public figures who gave it [the Colonization Society] their support, including many who were acutely conscious of prevailing public sentiment. Adorning the Society's list of officers during the antebellum period were such men as James Madison, Andrew Jackson, Henry Clay, Daniel Webster, Stephen Douglas, William H. Seward, Richard Rush, John Marshall, Roger Taney, Francis Scott Key, General Winfield Scott, Mathew Carey, Edward Everett, Benjamin Silliman, Abbot Lawrence, William Appleton, and many religious leaders and college presidents." Leon F. Litwack, *North of Slavery: The Negro in the Free States, 1790–1860* (Chicago: University of Chicago Press, 1961), 24.

12. Stuckey, *Slave Culture,* 128. However, Walker did not oppose emigration for all Blacks. Those who could, he argued, should go to their "greatest earthly friends and benefactors—the English," as England had done more to mitigate the plight of Blacks "than all the other nations of the earth put together."

13. Introduction to "David Walker's *Appeal*," PBS, *Africans in America.*

14. Quoted in Litwack, *North of Slavery*, 244.

15. Henry Highland Garnet, "The Past and the Present Condition, and the Destiny of the Colored Race," 1848, reprinted in Howard Brotz, ed., *Negro Social and Political Thought, 1850–1920: Representative Texts* (New York: Basic Books, 1966), 201.

16. Alphonso Pinkney, *Red, Black, and Green: Black Nationalism in the United States* (New York: Cambridge University Press, 1978), 23.

17. Ibid., 24.

18. Ibid.

19. Ibid.

20. Ibid., 25.

21. Ibid.

22. Ibid., 25–26.

23. Ofari, *The Myth of Black Capitalism*, 17. "Cast our eyes about us and reflect for a moment, and what do we behold! Every thing that presents to view gives evidence of the skill of the white man.... And yet, with all these living truths, rebuking us with scorn, we strut about, place our hands akimbo, straighten up ourselves

to our greatest height, and talk loudly about being 'as good as any body.' How do we compare with them? Our fathers are their coachmen, our brothers their cookmen, and ourselves their waiting-men.... The world is looking upon us, with feelings of commiseration, sorrow, and contempt. We scarcely deserve sympathy, if we peremptorily refuse advice, bearing upon our elevation." Martin Delany, *The Condition, Elevation, Emigration, and Destiny of the Colored People of the United States* (1852; repr., New York: New York Times and Arno Press, 1968), 42–43.

24. Delany asked: "Where is a more fit place [for Negroes] to seek new homes than in the land of their fathers and mothers, especially provided for them by nature?" Quoted in August Meier, *Negro Thought in America 1880–1915: Racial Ideologies in the Age of Booker T. Washington* (Ann Arbor: University of Michigan Press, 1966), 65.

25. Ofari, *Myth of Black Capitalism*, 18.

26. Ibid.

27. *Life and Times of Frederick Douglass, Written by Himself* (Boston: DeWolfe & Fiske Co., 1892), 177.

28. Quoted in Robert L. Allen, *Reluctant Reformers: Racism and Social Movements in the United States* (Washington, D.C.: Howard University Press, 1974), 40.

29. Litwack, *North of Slavery,* 246.

30. Ibid., 241.

31. In his autobiography, *The Life and Times of Frederick Douglass*, Douglass wrote of his break with Garrison: "After a time, a careful reconsideration of the subject convinced me that there was no necessity for dissolving the union between the northern and southern States; that to seek this dissolution was no part of my duty as an abolitionist; that to abstain from voting was to refuse to exercise a legitimate and powerful means for abolishing slavery; and that the Constitution of the United States not only contained no guarantees in favor of slavery, but on the contrary, was in its letter and spirit an anti-slavery instrument, demanding the abolition of slavery as a condition of its own existence, as the supreme law of the land." Douglass, *The Life and Times of Frederick Douglass*, 266.

32. Ibid., 223–24.

33. Frederick Douglass, "The Meaning of July Fourth for the Negro" (July 5, 1852), Rochester, New York; printed in Zinn and Arnove, *Voices of a People's History,* 186.

34. Robert S. Levine, *Martin Delany, Frederick Douglass, and the Politics of Representative Identity* (Chapel Hill, NC: University of North Carolina Press, 1997), 6.

35. From Philip Foner, *The Life and Writings of Frederick Douglass,* vol. 4, *Reconstruction and After* (New York: International Publishers, 1955), 103–13.

36. Wilson Jeremiah Moses, *The Golden Age of Black Nationalism, 1850–1925* (New York: Oxford University Press, 1978), 45.

37. Litwack, *North of Slavery,* 246.

38. Levine, *Martin Delany, Frederick Douglass,* 287.

39. Quarles, *Black Abolitionists,* 235.

40. Frederick Douglass, "John Brown: An Address," given at Harpers Ferry, West Virginia, May 30, 1881, in *Frederick Douglass: Selected Speeches and Writings,* ed. Philip S. Foner (Chicago: Lawrence Hill Books, 1999), 633–48, 648.

Chapter Three: The Civil War

1. James M. McPherson, *Battle Cry of Freedom: The Civil War Era* (New York: Oxford University Press, 1988), 245.

2. By this term, I mean the "replacement of a pre-capitalist regime of some sort followed by a social transformation—legal forms and so on—which clears the ground for the development of capitalism," Duncan Hallas, "The Bourgeois Revolution," *Socialist Review* 105 (January 1988): 17.

3. Goldfield, *The Color of Politics,* 138.

4. Karl Marx, "The Civil War in the United States," in Karl Marx and Frederick Engels, *Collected Works,* vol. 19 (London: Lawrence & Wishart, 1984), 150.

5. Peter Camejo, *Racism, Revolution and Reaction, 1861–1877* (New York: Monad Press, 1976), 20.

6. Bob Peterson, "Write the Truth," *Rethinking Schools* 16, no. 4 (Summer 2002): http://www.rethinkingschools.org/archive/

16_04/Writ164.shtml. Those who owned slaves: George Washington, Thomas Jefferson, James Madison, James Monroe, Andrew Jackson, John Tyler, James K. Polk, and Zachary Taylor. Those that didn't: John Adams, John Quincy Adams, Martin Van Buren, William Harrison, Millard Fillmore, Franklin Pierce, James Buchanan, and Abraham Lincoln.

7. James M. McPherson, *Drawn with the Sword* (New York: Oxford University Press, 1996), 13.

8. Ibid., 15.

9. McPherson, *Battle Cry of Freedom*, 92–93.

10. Speech at political rally, quoted in Litwack, *North of Slavery*, 276.

11. Ibid., 277.

12. Ibid.

13. Robinson, *Black Movements in America*, 71.

14. Greeley founded the *New York Tribune* in 1841 and was its editor until his death in 1872. Greeley used the paper to campaign against slavery. Among the newspaper's contributors was Karl Marx.

15. Robinson, *Black Movements in America*, 71.

16. James M. McPherson, *Abraham Lincoln and the Second American Revolution* (New York: Oxford University Press, 1991), 41.

17. Eric Foner, *Reconstruction: America's Unfinished Revolution* (New York: Harper & Row, 1988), xxii–xxiii.

18. McPherson, *Abraham Lincoln*, 41.

19. Raya Dunayevskaya, *Marxism and Freedom: From 1776 to Today* (New York: Bookman Associates, 1958), 82–83. Marx borrowed the phrase from the abolitionist Wendell Phillips, who said of Lincoln: "I will tell you what he is. He is a first-rate second-rate man." Phillips also wrote, "I do not say that McClellan is a traitor, but I say this, that if he had been a traitor from the crown of his head to the sole of his foot...he could not have carried on the war in more exact deference to the politics of that side of the Union. And almost the same thing may be said of Mr. Lincoln—that if he had been a traitor, he could not have worked better to strengthen one side, and hazard the success of the other." Wendell Phillips, "The Cabinet," *Speeches, Lectures, and Letters*, vol. 1 (Boston: Lee and Shepard, 1894), 457 and 450.

20. Marx, "The Civil War," 51.

21. McPherson, *Abraham Lincoln*, 42.

22. Robinson, *Black Movements in America,* 68.

23. Emancipation Proclamation, January 1, 1863; Presidential Proclamations, 1791–1991; Record Group 11; General Records of the United States Government; National Archives.

24. Richard Hofstadter, *The American Political Tradition: and the Men Who Made It* (New York: Knopf, 1948), 131.

25. Eric Foner, *Reconstruction,* 1.

26. Robinson, *Black Movements in America,* 76. Of the approximately 189,000 Blacks in uniform in the Union Army and Navy, 33,000 enlisted from the free states. The slaves were by far the more numerous. Ira Berlin and his coauthors report that: "The border states of Delaware, Maryland, Missouri, and Kentucky accounted for a total of nearly 42,000, more than half from Kentucky. Tennessee contributed 20,000; Louisiana, 24,000; Mississippi, nearly 18,000; and the remaining states of the Confederacy accounted for approximately 37,000." Ira Berlin, Barbara J. Fields, Steven F. Miller, et al., eds., *Slaves No More: Three Essays on Emancipation and the Civil War* (New York: Cambridge University Press, 1992), 203 and 206.

27. Dunayevskaya, *Marxism and Freedom,* 82.

28. Quoted in Camejo, *Racism, Revolution and Reaction*, 28.

29. Speech given March 2, 1863, in Rochester, New York, reprinted in Frederick Douglass, "Men of Color, To Arms!" *Douglass Monthly* V, no. VI (March 1863): 1.

30. McPherson quoted in Zinn, *A People's History of the United States*, 194.

31. Quoted in Joseph T. Glatthaar, *Forged in Battle* (New York: Free Press, 1990), 206. The Copperheads were Northern supporters of the South, mostly organized in the Democratic Party.

32. See Iver Bernstein, *The New York City Draft Riots* (New York: Oxford University Press, 1990).

33. W. E. B. Du Bois, *Black Reconstruction in America, 1860–1880* (1935; repr., New York: Free Press, 1992), 80.

Chapter Four: Reconstruction and Populism

1. C. Vann Woodward, *American Counterpoint: Slavery and Racism in the North-South Dialogue* (Boston: Little, Brown, and Co., 1964), 259.

2. C. Vann Woodward, *Origins of the New South, 1877–1913* (Baton Rouge, LA: Louisiana State University Press, 1951), 211.

3. For example, see Allen, *Reluctant Reformers*.

4. Jack M. Bloom, *Class, Race and the Civil Rights Movement* (Bloomington, IN: Indiana University Press, 1987), 19.

5. Eric Foner, *Reconstruction*, 124–25.

6. Ibid., 183.

7. Robinson, *Black Movements in America*, 85.

8. Eric Foner, *Reconstruction*, 180; Marable, *Black American Politics*, 144.

9. "Certainly, the South's profitable and constantly diversifying economy was an enviable one. Between 1840 and 1860, labor productivity in service and manufacturing doubled the comparable increase in agricultural production; cotton production itself had doubled between 1850 and 1860, and cotton profits for planters were substantially above normal; slave labor was 70 percent more productive than free agricultural labor, and during the spring and summer, and fall, slaves worked an average work week of 57 to 60 hours. In addition, slaves constituted nearly 80 percent of the South's artisan class. Consequently, as Robert W. Fogel observes, 'The southern plutocrats were considerably richer, on average, than their northern counterparts (by a factor of roughly 2 to 1)…. Nearly two out of every three males with estates of $100,000 or more lived in the South in 1860. This distribution of wealth was achieved despite the population of the white South (nearly 6 million) being less than one-third that of the North (more than 21 million).' The Civil War, however, would end the Southern elite's dominance of wealth: by 1870, 80 percent of the super rich would now be northerners." Robinson, *Black Movements in America*, 69.

10. Eric Foner, *Reconstruction*, 199.

11. Ibid., 199–202.

12. Ibid., 342.

13. Robinson, *Black Movements in America*, 87.

14. Eric Foner, *Reconstruction*, 426.

15. Camejo, *Racism, Revolution and Reaction*, 75–76.

16. Ibid., 76.

17. Eric Foner, *Reconstruction*, 31.

18. Camejo, *Racism, Revolution and Reaction*, 72.

19. Ibid., 80–87.

20. Du Bois, *Black Reconstruction*, 206.

21. Bloom, *Class, Race and the Civil Rights Movement*, 30.

22. Ibid.

23. Ibid.

24. Ibid.

25. Camejo, *Racism, Revolution and Reaction*, 88.

26. Eric Foner, *Reconstruction*, 96–98.

27. Camejo, *Racism, Revolution and Reaction*, 89.

28. Quoted in *Harvey Wasserman's History of the United States* (New York: Four Walls Eight Windows, 1988), 81.

29. Allen W. Trelease, *White Terror: The Ku Klux Klan Conspiracy and Southern Reconstruction* (New York: Harper & Row, 1971), xlvii.

30. Bloom, *Class, Race and the Civil Rights Movement*, 33.

31. Camejo, *Racism, Revolution and Reaction*, 97.

32. Manning Marable, *Blackwater: Historical Studies in Race, Class Consciousness and Revolution* (1981; repr., Niwat, CO: University of Colorado Press, 1993), 54–55.

33. Bloom, *Class, Race and the Civil Rights Movement*, 23.

34. Ibid., 27–28.

35. Quoted in Zinn and Arnove, *Voices of a People's History*, 231.

36. Bloom, *Class, Race and the Civil Rights Movement*, 36.

37. Ibid.

38. August Meier and Elliott Rudwick, *From Plantation to Ghetto*, 3rd ed. (1966; repr., New York: Hill and Wang, 1976), 195.

39. *Wasserman's History of the United States*, 71.

40. Ibid., 71.

41. Zinn and Arnove, *Voices*, 226; *Wasserman's History of the United States*, 71.

42. *Wasserman's History of the United States,* 89.

43. Ibid., 88–89.

44. Bloom, *Class, Race and the Civil Rights Movement,* 40.

45. Ibid., 40.

46. Ibid., 40.

47. Ibid., 40–41.

48. The Populist Party elected a governor in Tennessee, five of ten Congressmen from Virginia, eight of nine from North Carolina, two of seven from Mississppi, and four of eleven from Kentucky. Bloom, *Class, Race and the Civil Rights Movement,* 41.

49. *Wasserman's History of the United States,* 92.

50. Bloom, *Class, Race and the Civil Rights Movement,* 57–58.

51. Michael Kazin, *The Populist Persuasion: An American History* (New York: Basic Books, 1995), 42.

52. *Wasserman's History of the United States,* 93.

53. Ibid., 105.

54. Bloom, *Class, Race and the Civil Rights Movement,* 43.

55. "The origin of the term 'Jim Crow' applied to Negroes is lost in obscurity. Thomas D. Rice wrote a song and dance called 'Jim Crow' in 1832, and the term had become an adjective by 1838. The first example of 'Jim Crow law' listed by the Dictionary of American English is dated 1904. But the expression was used by writers in the 1890's who are quoted on the following pages." C. Vann Woodward, *The Strange Career of Jim Crow* (New York: Oxford University Press, 1974), 7.

56. *Wasserman's History of the United States,* 107–10.

57. Robert H. Brisbane, *The Black Vanguard: Origins of the Negro Social Revolution, 1900–1960* (Valley Forge, PA: Judson Press, 1970), 25.

58. Quoted in Allen, *Reluctant Reformers,* 79–80.

59. Quoted in Manning Marable, "Why Black Americans Are Not Socialists," in Phyllis Jacobson and Julius Jacobson, *Socialist Perspectives* (Princeton: Karz-Cohl Publishers, 1983), 65.

60. Allen, *Reluctant Reformers,* 75.

61. August Meier and Elliott Rudwick, eds., *The Making of Black America,* (New York: Atheneum, 1969) vol. 2, 69.

62. Michael Reich, *Racial Inequality: A Political-Economic Analysis* (Princeton: Princeton University Press, 1981), 236–37.

63. Bloom, *Class, Race and the Civil Rights Movement,* 48.

64. Quoted in Herbert Aptheker, *Afro-American History: The Modern Era* (New York: Citadel Press, 1972), 20.

65. John F. Keller, *Power in America: The Southern Question and the Control of Labor* (Chicago: Vanguard Books, 1983), 151–52.

66. Ibid., 151.

67. Bloom, *Class, Race and the Civil Rights Movement,* 53.

68. Aptheker, *Afro-American History,* 105.

69. Ibid., 107

Chapter Five: Accommodation, Racism, and Resistance

1. Wilson Jeremiah Moses, *The Golden Age of Black Nationalism, 1850–1925* (New York: Oxford University Press, 1978), 59.

2. Ibid., 67.

3. Ibid., 69.

4. Alexander Crummell, *Civilization and Progress: Selected Works of Alexander Crummell on the South,* ed. J. R. Oldfield (Charlottesville, VA: University Press of Virginia, 1995), 41.

5. Moses, *Golden Age,* 69 and 73.

6. Pinkney, *Red, Black, and Green,* 29.

7. Ibid., 30.

8. Ibid., 31.

9. See Lawrence Grossman, *The Democratic Party and the Negro: Northern and National Politics 1868–1892* (Chicago: University of Illinois, 1976).

10. Ofari, *The Myth of Black Capitalism,* 33–34.

11. Rod Bush, *We Are Not What We Seem: Black Nationalism and Class Struggle in the American Century* (New York: New York University Press, 1999), 72.

12. Manning Marable, *W. E. B. Du Bois: Black Radical Democrat* (Boston: Twayne Publishers, 1986), 42.

13. Ibid.

14. Brisbane, *The Black Vanguard*, 30.

15. Marable, *Du Bois*, 42.

16. Ibid.

17. Washington, "The Negro and the Labor Unions," 757; Brisbane, *The Black Vanguard*, 32.

18. Philip S. Foner, *Organized Labor and the Black Worker, 1619–1973* (New York: Praeger, 1974), 79.

19. Washington, "The Negro and the Labor Unions," 757.

20. Brisbane, *The Black Vanguard*, 31.

21. Marable, *Du Bois*, 43.

22. Quoted in August Meier, "The Paradox of W. E. B. Du Bois," in *The Segregation Era, 1863–1954*, ed. Allen Weinstein and Frank Otto Gattell, (New York: Oxford University Press, 1970), 99.

23. Ibid.

24. Ibid., 100.

25. Ibid., 102.

26. Quoted in Marable, *Du Bois*, 60.

27. Philip S. Foner, *American Socialism and Black Americans: From the Age of Jackson to World War II* (Westport, CT: Greenwood Press, 1977), 195.

28. Philip Foner, *Organized Labor*, 83–84, 97.

29. Philip S. Foner and Ronald L. Lewis, eds., *The Black Worker: A Documentary History from Colonial Times to the Present*, vol. 4, *The Black Worker During the Era of the American Federation of Labor and the Railroad Brotherhoods* (Philadelphia: Temple University Press, 1979), 194.

30. Michael Reich, *Racial Inequality: A Political-Economical Analysis* (Princeton, NJ: Princeton University Press, 1981), 241.

31. Ibid.

32. Sterling D. Spero and Abram L. Harris, *The Black Worker: The Negro and the Labor Movement* (New York: Columbia University Press, 1931), 358—59.

33. Philip Foner, *Organized Labor*, 84.

34. Ibid.

35. Philip S. Foner, *The History of the Labor Movement in the United States*, vol. 8, *Postwar Struggles* (New York: International Publish-

ers, 1988), 194–95.

36. Huey Latham, Jr., quoted in Foner, *Postwar Struggles*, 195.

37. Philip Foner, *Postwar Struggles*, 195.

38. For a representative argument of this case, see Roediger's *Wages of Whiteness*, in which he argues that "Black emancipation, battlefield heroism and citizenship thus ensured that white workers could never again see African-Americans or themselves in just the same way. However, more than enough of the habit of whiteness and of the conditions producing it survived to ensure that white workers would be at best uncertain allies of Black freedom and would stop short of developing fully new concepts of liberation for themselves as well." David. R. Roediger, *Wages of Whiteness: Race and the Makings of the American Working Class* (New York: Verso, 1991), 177.

39. Article on lynching in the news brief section of the *Christian Reader* (August 11, 1892), in *The Civil Rights Movement: An Eyewitness History*, ed. Sanford Wexler (New York: Facts on File, 1993), 22.

40. Fields, "Slavery, Race and Ideology ," 95–118.

41. Reich, *Racial Inequality*, 252–53; Gunnar Myrdal, *An American Dilemma: The Negro Problem and Modern Democracy* (New York: Harper & Brothers, 1944), 285.

42. Pinkney, *Red, Black, and Green*, 37.

Chapter Six: The Rise of Marcus Garvey

1. Philip Foner, *Postwar Struggles*, 22.

2. Ibid.

3. William M. Tuttle, Jr., *Race Riot: Chicago in the Red Summer of 1919* (New York: Atheneum, 1970), 14; Philip S. Foner, *American Socialism and Black Americans: From the Age of Jackson to World War II* (Westport, CT: Greenwood Press, 1977), 290.

4. Quoted in Brisbane, *The Black Vanguard*, 76.

5. Philip Foner, *Organized Labor and the Black Worker,* 131.

6. Philip Foner, *American Socialism and Black Americans*, 288.

7. Ibid., 289.

8. See Tuttle, *Race Riot.*

9. *C. L. R. James's 80th Birthday Lectures,* eds. Margaret Busby and Darcus Howe (London: Black Rose Press, 1984), 58.

10. Marable, *Du Bois,* 116.

11. Brisbane, *The Black Vanguard,* 96.

12. Peter Alexander, *Racism, Resistance and Revolution* (London: Bookmarks, 1987), 59.

13. Pinkney, *Red, Black, and Green,* 43–44.

14. Ibid., 43.

15. Judith Stein, *The World of Marcus Garvey: Race and Class in Modern Society* (Baton Rouge: Louisiana State University Press, 1986), 31–32.

16. Robert A. Hill, "The First England Years and After, 1912–1916," in *Marcus Garvey and the Vision of Africa,* ed. John Henrik Clarke, 38–70 (New York: Vintage, 1974), 63–64.

17. Marable, *Du Bois,* 114.

18. Ibid., 117.

19. Ibid.

20. Ibid.

21. Stein, *The World of Marcus Garvey,* 55–65.

22. Ibid., 61.

23. Brisbane, *The Black Vanguard,* 85.

24. Stein, *The World of Marcus Garvey,* 84.

25. Brisbane, *The Black Vanguard,* 88.

26. Leon Trotsky, *On Black Nationalism and Self Determination* (New York: Pathfinder, 1978), 50.

27. Pinkney, *Red, Black, and Green,* 48.

28. Stein, *The World of Marcus Garvey,* 63.

29. Ibid., 154.

30. Pinkney, *Red, Black, and Green,* 48.

31. *Philosophy and Opinions of Marcus Garvey,* vol. 2, Amy Jacques Garvey, ed., 2nd ed. (1925; repr. London: Frank Cass & Co., 1967), 69–70.

32. Bush, *We Are Not What We Seem,* 101.

33. Ibid., 72.

34. Pinkney, *Red, Black, and Green,* 55; "Marcus Garvey: Life and Les-

sons," The Marcus Garvey and UNIA Papers Project, UCLA, 1995, http://africawithin.com/garvey/garvey_lifeintro.htm.

35. "Marcus Garvey: Life and Lessons."

Chapter Seven: The Socialist, Communist, and Trotskyist Parties

1. Philip Foner, *American Socialism and Black Americans*, 4.

2. David H. Herreshoff, *The Origins of American Marxism: From the Transcendentalists to Daniel De Leon* (New York: Monad Press, 1967), 62.

3. Philip Foner, *American Socialism and Black Americans*, 6.

4. Ibid.

5. Philip S. Foner and Brewster Chamberlin, *Labor Movement in the United States: A History of the American Working Class From Colonial Times to 1890* (Westport, CT: Greenwood Press, 1977), 6.

6. Philip Foner, *American Socialism and Black Americans*, 6.

7. Ibid., 37.

8. Ibid., 6.

9. Ibid., 9.

10. Ibid., 14–15.

11. Marx, *Capital,* vol. 1, 414.

12. Isaac Myers, "Finish the Good Work of Uniting Colored and White Workingmen," in Philip Foner and Robert James Branham, eds., *Lift Every Voice: African American Oratory. 1987–1900* (Tuscaloosa and London: University of Alabama Press, 1998), 485.

13. Mike Davis, *Prisoners of the American Dream: Politics and Economy in the History of the U.S. Working Class* (New York: Verso, 1986), 27.

14. Quoted in Tim Wohlforth, *The Struggle for Marxism in the United States* (New York: Bulletin Publications, 1968), 11.

15. Philip Foner, *American Socialism and Black Americans*, 61.

16. Ibid., 58.

17. Oakley C. Johnson, *Marxism in United States History Before the Russian Revolution (1876–1917)* (New York: Humanities Press, 1974), 71.

18. Philip Foner, *American Socialism and Black Americans*, 65.

19. Philip Foner, *Organized Labor*, 53.

20. Quoted in ibid., 53.

21. Philip Foner, *American Socialism and Black Americans,* 72.

22. Ibid., 76.

23. Quoted in ibid., 77.

24. Ibid., 73.

25. Ibid.

26. L. Glen Seretan, *Daniel De Leon: The Odyssey of an American Marxist* (Cambridge, MA: Harvard University Press, 1979), 99.

27. Leon Trotsky, *My Life* (New York: Charles Scribner's Sons, 1971), 274. Babbitt is the central character in a story by Sinclair Lewis about the boring life of a disgruntled, middle-aged real estate salesman.

28. Philip Foner, *American Socialism and Black Americans*, 105–06.

29. Ira Kipnis, *The American Socialist Movement, 1897–1912* (1952; repr., Chicago: Haymarket Books, 2004), 278–79.

30. Trotsky, *My Life*, 275.

31. Philip Foner, *American Socialism and Black Americans*, 111.

32. Ibid., 114–15.

33. *Writings and Speeches of Eugene V. Debs* (New York: Hermitage Press, 1948), 64–65.

34. Philip Foner, *American Socialism and Black Americans,* 111–12.

35. Ibid., 114.

36. Ibid., 258.

37. Kipnis, *American Socialist Movement*, 428.

38. Philip Foner, *Organized Labor,* 108.

39. Ibid., 114.

40. Ibid., 115.

41. Ibid., 116.

42. Ibid.

43. Ibid., 116–17.

44. Ibid., 117.

45. Ibid., 119.

46. Ibid., 111–12.

47. Kipnis, *American Socialist Movement*, 420.

48. Philip Foner, *American Socialism and Black Americans*, 306.

49. Quoted in Trotsky, *On Black Nationalism*, 10.

50. Ibid., 10–11.

51. Carl E. Schorske, *German Social Democracy: 1905–1917, The Development of the Great Schism* (Cambridge, MA: Harvard University Press, 1955), 77.

52. Ibid., 69–70.

53. Rosa Luxemburg, *Rosa Luxemburg Speaks,* ed. Mary-Alice Waters (New York: Pathfinder, 1971), 304 and 329.

54. Quoted in Ronaldo Munck, *The Difficult Dialogue: Marxism and Nationalism* (London: Zed Books, 1986), 72–73.

55. Lenin, "Report of the Commission on the National and the Colonial Questions," *Collected Works*, vol. 31, 240.

56. Lenin, "The Discussion on Self-Determination Summed Up," *Collected Works*, vol. 22, 346.

57. Lenin, "The Right of Nations to Self-Determination," *Collected Works*, vol. 20, 411–12.

58. Ibid., 412.

59. Munck, *Difficult Dialogue,* 74.

60. Lenin, "The Revolutionary Proletariat and the Right of Nations to Self-Determination," *Collected Works*, vol. 21, 407–14.

61. Riddell, *Workers of the World*, 288–89.

62. Second Congress of the Communist International, "Theses on the National and Colonial Question," *Minutes of the Proceedings*, vols. 1 and 2 (London: New Park, 1977), sec. IIe.

63. John Reed, *Ten Days That Shook the World* (New York: Boni and Liveright, 1919).

64. Philip S. Foner and James S. Allen, *American Communism and Black Americans: A Documentary History, 1919–1929,* vol. 1 (Philadelphia: Temple University Press, 1987), 8.

65. Ibid., 6.

66. Ibid., 7.

67. Quoted in Theodore Draper, *American Communism and Soviet Russia* (New York: Viking, 1960), 321.

68. Jane Degras, ed., *The Communist International, 1919–1943*, vol. 1, *1914–1922* (New York: Oxford University Press, 1956), 401.

69. Foner and Allen, *American Communism and Black Americans,* 20.

70. Draper, *American Communism and Soviet Russia*, 332.

71. Naison, *Communists in Harlem*, 13.

72. Ibid.

73. Quoted in Foner, *Organized Labor,* 148–49.

74. Lee Sustar, "Self-Determination and the Black Belt," *Socialist Worker* (U.S.), November 1985, 4.

75. Marable, "The Crisis of the Black Working Class," 130–161.

76. Trotsky, *On Black Nationalism*, 47–48.

77. It should be noted that some of the CP's campaigns against "racism" internally were an excuse to purge its ranks.

78. Historian Dan T. Carter writes "the last thing the NAACP wanted was to associate with a gang of mass rapists" in his *Scottsboro: A Tragedy of the American South* (Baton Rouge: Louisana State University Press, 1994), 52. See also Kelley, *Hammer and Hoe*, 80.

79. Naison, *Communists in Harlem*, 61.

80. Philip Foner, *Organized Labor,* 231.

81. Draper, *American Communism and Soviet Russia*, 513-14.

82. Quoted in Cedric J. Robinson, *Black Marxism: The Making of the Black Radical Tradition* (London: Zed Books, 1983), 278.

83. Philip S. Foner, *American Communism and Black Americans: A Documentary History,* vol. 2, *1930–1934* (Philadelphia: Temple University Press, 1991), p. xxii.

84. Quoted in Philip Foner, ibid., xxii.

85. Paul D'Amato, "The Communist Party and Black Liberation in the 1930s," *International Socialist Review* 1 (Summer 1997).

86. Trotsky, *On Black Nationalism*, 26.

87. Ibid., 24–25.

88. Ibid., 29.

89. Ibid., 25–26. Trotsky's theory of permanent revolution, outlined in his essays *The Permanent Revolution* and *Results and Prospects*, has many elements that cannot be discussed here. But the relevant element that Trotsky is referring to here is his analysis that the working class of an oppressed nation fighting for national liberation will raise its demands *as a class*. In that way, it can seek to go beyond the limits of a national liberation struggle to fight for socialism. See Trotsky, *The Permanent Revolution* (New York:

Pathfinder Press, 1969).

90. Ibid., 30.

91. Ibid.

92. Quoted in ibid., 34.

93. Qoted in Tony Martin, *The Pan-African Connection: From Slavery to Garvey and Beyond* (Dover, Massachusetts: Majority Press, 1983), 174.

94. Trotsky, *On Black Nationalism,* 41.

95. Ibid., 46.

96. Ibid., 47–48.

97. Ibid., 48.

98. Ibid., 59.

99. Ibid., 50.

100. Ibid., 53.

101. Ibid., 64.

102. *New International* 5, no. 12 (December 1939).

103. C. L. R. James, "The Revolutionary Answer to the Negro Problem in the U.S.A.," resolution presented at the Socialist Workers Party (USA) conference in 1948, available online at the C. L. R. James Internet Archive, http://www.marxists.org/archive/james-clr/works/1948/revolutionary-answer.htm.

104. Duncan Hallas, *Trotsky's Marxism and Other Essays* (Chicago: Haymarket Books, 2003), 91.

105. Trotsky, *On Black Nationalism*, 55.

106. Ibid., 62.

107. Hallas, *Trotsky's Marxism*, 91.

108. Trotsky, Internal Bulletin, Workers' Party (USA), 1944.

109. C. L. R. James, *Notes on Dialectics: Hegel–Marx–Lenin* (Westport, CT: Lawrence Hill and Co., 1980), 117.

Chapter Eight: The Roots of the Civil Rights Movement

1. Manning Marable, "The Crisis of the Black Working Class: An Economic and Historical Analysis," *Science and Society* XLVI, no. 2, (Summer 1982): 130–61.

2. Philip Foner, *Organized Labor,* 272.

3. Marable, "Crisis," 136.

4. Cedric Robinson, *Black Movements in America,* 129; Foner, *Organized Labor,* 259 and 264.

5. Manning Marable, *Race, Reform, and Rebellion* (Jackson, MS: University Press of Mississippi, 1984), 14.

6. Ibid., 17–18.

7. Ibid., 18.

8. Ibid., 31.

9. Ibid., 28–29.

10. Ibid., 29–30.

11. Philip Foner, *Organized Labor,* 269.

12. Taylor Branch, *Parting the Waters: America in the King Years, 1954–63* (New York: Simon and Schuster, 1988), 22.

13. Bloom, *Class, Race and the Civil Rights Movement,* 137.

14. Editorial, "Civil Rights After the Till Murder," *American Socialist* 2, no. 11 (November 1955): 3.

15. "Trial by Jury," *Time,* October 3, 1955, 19.

16. Telegraph from Mamie Bradley to President Eisenhower, 2 September 1955, Eisenhower Archives online, http://www.eisenhower.archives.gov/dl/Civil_Rights_Emmett_Till_Case/TelegramMamieBradleytoDDE1955Sept2.pdf.

17. Letter from Max Rabb to Jim Hagerty, October 23, 1956, Eisenhower Archives online http://www.eisenhower.archives.gov/dl/Civil_Rights_Emmett_Till_case/MaxRabbtoHagertyOct23_1956.pdf.

18. Letter from J. Edgar Hoover to Herbert G. Brownwell, September 6, 1955, available from PBS website for *The Murder of Emmett Till,* http://www.pbs.org/wgbh/amex/till/filmmore/ps_reactions.html.

19. *Jackson Daily News* [Mississippi], September 25, 1955. Available online at http://www.crimelibrary.com/notorious_murders/famous/emmett_till/13.html.

20. Bloom, *Class, Race and the Civil Rights Movement,* 140.

21. Michael Eric Dyson, *I May Not Get There with You: The True Martin Luther King, Jr.,* (New York: Free Press, 2000), 107.

22. Bloom, *Class, Race and the Civil Rights Movement,* 141.

23. Ibid., 142.

24. Ibid.

25. Ibid.

26. C. Vann Woodward, *The Strange Career of Jim Crow* (New York: Oxford University Press, 1979), rev. ed., 165–66.

27. Bloom, *Class, Race and the Civil Rights Movement*, 152.

28. J. Harvie Wilkenson III, *From Brown to Bakke: The Supreme Court and School Integration, 1954–1978* (New York, Oxford University Press, 1979), 63.

29. Ibid., 65.

30. Ibid.

31. Harvard Sitkoff, *The Struggle for Black Equality*, rev. ed. (New York: Hill and Wang, 1993), 64.

32. Clayborne Carson, *In Struggle: SNCC and the Black Awakening of the 1960s* (Cambridge, MA: Harvard University Press, 1981), 20.

33. Marable, *Race, Reform, and Rebellion*, 68.

34. Ibid., 68–69.

35. Lee Sustar, "How the Fight for Rights Was Radicalized," *Socialist Worker* (U.S.), May 1987.

36. Ronald Steel, *In Love with the Night: The American Romance with Robert Kennedy* (New York: Simon and Schuster, 2000), 159.

37. Sustar, "Fight for Rights."

38. Marable, *Race, Reform, and Rebellion*, 76.

39. August Meier and Elliott Rudwick, *From Plantation to Ghetto*, 3rd ed. (New York, Hill and Wang: 1976), 288.

40. Quoted in Clayborne Carson et al., eds., *The Eyes on the Prize Civil Rights Reader: Documents, Speeches, and Firsthand Accounts from the Black Freedom Struggle, 1954–1990* (New York: Penguin, 1991) 163–65.

41. Quoted in Marable, *Black American Politics*, 95.

42. Carson, *In Struggle*, 175. Carson describes the new left as "an amorphous body of young activists seeking new ideological alternatives to conventional liberalism."

43. Doug McAdam, *Freedom Summer* (New York: Oxford University Press, 1988), 25.

44. Marable, *Race, Reform, and Rebellion*, 91.

45. Quoted in Lance Selfa, "The Mississippi Freedom Summer," *Socialist Worker* (U.S.), June 1989.

46. Lance Selfa, *The Democratic Party and the Politics of Lesser Evilism* (Chicago: International Socialist Orgnization, 2004), http://www.internationalsocialist.org/pdfs/democrats_lesserevillism.pdf.

47. Quoted in Selfa, "Freedom Summer."

48. Marable, *Race, Reform, and Rebellion*, 93.

Chapter Nine: The Politics of Malcolm X

1. Richard Wright, *12 Million Black Voices* (New York: Thunder's Mouth Press, 1941), 112.

2. Bloom, *Class, Race and the Civil Rights Movement*, 196.

3. See Pinkney, *Red, Black, and Green*, 159–60. The membership numbers were kept secret: *Ebony* magazine estimated them to be 100,000 by 1970, and the paper, *Muhammad Speaks*, had a circulation of 600,000 at its height, although that number does not, of course, necessarily represent members.

4. C. Eric Lincoln, *The Black Muslims in America*, 3rd ed. (Trenton, NJ: Africa World Press, 1994), 88.

5. Ibid., 91. Answering the question of a hostile reporter, Malcolm X retorted: "Nine or ten states would be enough."

6. *The Hate That Hate Produced, Newsbeat*, presented by Mike Wallace and Louis Lomax (New York, WNTA-TV, 10–17 July 1959).

7. Brisbane, *The Black Vanguard*, 216.

8. Pinkney, *Red, Black, and Green*, 67.

9. Bloom, *Class, Race and the Civil Rights Movement*, 194.

10. Ibid., 194–95.

11. *The Autobiography of Malcolm X*, as told to Alex Haley (New York: Grove Press, 1964), 274.

12. Bloom, *Class, Race and the Civil Rights Movement*, 194.

13. Ibid.

14. George Breitman, *The Last Year of Malcolm X: The Evolution of a Revolutionary* (New York: Schocken Books, 1967), 9.

15. Ibid., 16.

16. Ibid., 17. Breitman states that NOI members were told privately

that a mass campaign "would only antagonize the authorities and make it worse for the brothers in court."

17. Ibid., 10–11.

18. *Autobiography of Malcolm X*, 200.

19. Ibid., 293–94.

20. Breitman, *Last Year*, 19.

21. Ibid., 19–20.

22. Ibid., 20.

23. George Breitman, ed., *Malcolm X Speaks: Selected Speeches and Statements* (New York: Merit Publishers, 1965), 38.

24. Ibid., 38–39.

25. Ibid., 39.

26. Ibid., 215.

27. Ibid., 69.

28. *Autobiography of Malcolm X*, 368.

29. Breitman, *Malcolm X Speaks,* 70.

30. Ibid., 232–33.

31. Ibid., 21–22.

32. Ibid., 228–29.

33. George Breitman, ed., *The Assassination of Malcolm X* (New York: Pathfinder, 1976), 46–48.

34. Breitman, *Last Year,* 45–46.

35. Editorial, "Malcolm X," *New York Times,* February 22, 1965.

36. Marable, *Race, Reform, and Rebellion*, 101.

37. Ibid.

38. Ibid.

39. Breitman, *Malcolm X Speaks*, 25–26.

Chapter Ten: Black Power

1. J. H. Clarke, *Malcolm X: The Man and His Times* (New York: Macmillan Co., 1969), 209.

2. Bloom, *Class, Race and the Civil Rights Movement*, 199.

3. Sitkoff, *Struggle for Black Equality,* 185–86.

4. Fred R. Harris and Roger W. Wilkins, eds., *Quiet Riots: Race and Poverty in the United States* (New York: Pantheon Books, 1988), 6.

5. Bloom, *Class, Race and the Civil Rights Movement*, 204.

6. Ibid.

7. Ibid.

8. Ibid., 208.

9. *Report of the National Advisory Commission on Civil Disorders* (Washington, D.C.: Government Printing Office, 1968), 1.

10. Ibid.

11. Harris and Wilkins, *Quiet Riots*, 3-4.

12. Bloom, *Class, Race and the Civil Rights Movement*, 200.

13. Lyndon B. Johnson, "To Fulfill These Rights," Commencement Speech at Howard University, Washington, D.C., June 4, 1965, available online at the Lyndon Baines Johnson Library archives, http://www.lbjlib.utexas.edu/johnson/archives.hom/speeches.hom/650604.asp.

14. Daniel Patrick Moynihan, *The Negro Family: The Case for National Political Action*, Office of Policy Planning and Research, U.S. Department of Labor (Washington, D.C.: U.S. Government Printing Office, 1965).

15. Sitkoff, *Struggle for Black Equality*, 199.

16. Roy Wilkins, "Whither 'Black Power'?" *Crisis* 73, no. 7 (August–September 1966): 353–54.

17. David J. Garrow, *Bearing the Cross: Martin Luther King, Jr., and the Southern Christian Leadership Conference* (New York: William Morrow and Co., 1986), 497.

18. Sitkoff, *Struggle for Black Equality,* 109–10.

19. Ibid., 200.

20. Ibid., 195.

21. Stokely Carmichael and Charles V. Hamilton, *Black Power: The Politics of Liberation in America* (New York: Random House, 1967), 146.

22. Robert L. Allen, *Black Awakening in Capitalist America: An Analytic History* (Garden City, NY: Anchor Books, 1969), 164.

23. Marable, *Race, Reform, and Rebellion*, 108.

24. Ibid., 108–09.

25. Allen, *Black Awakening*, 146.

26. Ibid., 146. Bundy had earlier come to national recognition as a

national security adviser to John F. Kennedy and Lyndon Johnson during the Vietnam War.

27. Lee Sustar, "Carving out a Niche in the System" *Socialist Worker* (U.S.), March 1988.

28. Allen, *Black Awakening*, 54.

29. Ibid., 168–69.

30. Ibid., 169–70.

31. Ibid., 165.

32. Ibid., 6–7.

33. Ibid., 250.

34. Bloom, *Class, Race and the Civil Rights Movement*, 203–04.

35. Ibid., 212.

36. Garrow, *Bearing the Cross*, 580.

37. Ibid., 537.

38. Ibid.

39. Michael Eric Dyson, "No Small Dreams: The Radical Evolution of MLK's Last Years," *LiP Magazine* online, January 20, 2003. Available at: http://www.lipmagazine.org/articles/featdyson_mlk_p.htm.

40. Ibid.

41. "Martin Luther King, Jr., "Why I Am Opposed to the War in Vietnam," speech given at the Ebenezer Baptist Church, Atlanta, GA, April 16, 1967. Quoted in James Cone, "Martin Luther King, Jr., and the Third World," *The Journal of American History* 74, no. 2 (September 1987): 455–67.

42. Garrow, *Bearing the Cross*, 440.

43. David J. Garrow, *The FBI and Martin Luther King, Jr.: From "Solo" to Memphis* (New York: W. W. Norton, 1981), 214.

44. Dyson, *I May Not Get There with You*, 86.

45. Ibid.

46. Quoted in Zinn and Arnove, *Voices*, 424–25.

47. Dyson, "No Small Dreams."

48. V. I. Lenin, *State and Revolution* (1917; repr., New York: International Publishers, 1932), 7.

Chapter Eleven: The Black Panthers and DRUM

1. Philip S. Foner, ed., *The Black Panthers Speak* (Philadelphia: J.B. Lipincott, 1970), xvii.

2. Ibid., xxi.

3. "What We Want, What We Believe," October 1966 Black Panther Party Platform and Program, reprinted in ibid., 1–4.

4. Bush, *We Are Not What We Seem*, 201.

5. Philip Foner, *Black Panthers Speak*, 50.

6. Ibid., 51.

7. Ibid., 107.

8. Bobby Seale, *Seize the Time: The Story of the Black Panther Party and Huey P. Newton* (New York: Random House, 1968), 72.

9. Jack Weinberg and Jack Gerson, "SDS and the Movement," in Michael Friedman, ed., *The New Left of the Sixties* (Berkeley, CΛ: Independent Socialist Press, 1972), 180–228.

10. Philip Foner, *Black Panthers Speak*, 44.

11. Ibid., xiii.

12. "Re: Counterintelligence Program/Black Nationalist Hate Groups," Federal Bureau of Investigation Memorandum, May 4, 1968, 3–4.

13. U.S. Senate, Select committee to Study Governmental Operations with Respect to Intelligence Activities, *Summary Detailed Staff Reports on Intellegence Activities and the Rights of Americans,* final report, 94th Congress, 2nd sess., 1976, Book 3, 187–88.

14. Ibid., 188.

15. Ibid., 213–14.

16. See Ward Churchill and Jim Vander Walls, eds., *Agents of Repression: the FBI's Secret Wars Against the Black Panther Party and the American Indian Movement*, 2nd ed. (Cambridge, MA: South End Press, 2002), 98–99.

17. Eldridge Cleaver, "On the Ideology of the Black Panther Party," (San Francisco: Black Panther Party, 1970), available at http://www.etext.org/Politics/MIM/bpp/bppideology1970.html.

18. Dan Georgakas and Marvin Surkin, *Detroit I Do Mind Dying: A Study in Urban Revolution,* 2nd ed. (Cambridge, MA: South End Press, 1998), 20.

19. Bush, *We Are Not What We Seem*, 208.
20. Dan Georgakas, "Revolutionary Struggles of Black Workers in the 1960s," *International Socialist Review* 22 (March–April 2002): 59–64.
21. Ibid., 64.
22. Ibid.
23. Allen, *Black Awakening*, 139.

Chapter Twelve: Making Race a Central Wedge Issue

1. Among the supporters for Jackson's strike-breaking were Dr. Martin Luther King, Sr., father of the slain civil rights leader, the heads of the local NAACP and Urban League chapters, and a host of business leaders tied to the Chamber of Commerce. Austin Scott, "Sanitation Workers' Strike in Atlanta Loaded with Ironies," *Washington Post*, April 17, 1977.
2. Lindsey Gruson, "Philadelphian's Careers at Stake as Hearings Approach on Police Bombing," *New York Times*, October 7, 1985.
3. Adoph L. Reed, Jr., *The Jesse Jackson Phenomenon: The Crisis of Purpose in Afro-American Politics* (New Haven, CT: Yale University Press, 1986), 14–15.
4. See Dyson, *I May Not Get There With You*, 93–99.
5. Jesse Jackson, "Jesse Jackson's Policy Towards Business," *Business Week*, June 1, 1987.
6. Keeanga-Yamahtta Taylor, "Civil Rights and Wrongs: Racism in America Today," *International Socialist Review* 22 (November–December 2003): 32.
7. Marable, *Black American Politics*, 266.
8. "The Rainbow Continues to Grow—It Takes Time," interview with Jesse Jackson, *U.S. News and World Report*, April 23, 1984: 34.
9. Goldfield, *Color of Politics*, 309.
10. In a televised chat with Bob Dole, Goldwater declared, "We're the new liberals of the Republican Party." Kathryn Q. Seelye, "Politics: Bob Dole," *New York Times*, February 26, 1996.
11. Goldfield, *Color of Politics*, 311.
12. Ibid., 310.

13. Kevin Phillips, *The Emerging Republican Majority* (New Rochelle, NY: Arlington House, 1969), 37.

14. Ibid., 236–38.

15. Quoted in Martin Carnoy, *Faded Dreams: The Politics and Economics of Race in America* (New York: Cambridge University Press, 1995), 210.

16. Ibid., 213–14.

17. Eugene Robinson, "Mondale Echoes Carter Attack on Reagan," *Washington Post*, September 19, 1980.

18. Goldfield, *The Color of Politics,* 314.

19. "Reagan's Comments on Race Draw Sharp Fire," *St. Louis Post-Dispatch*, January 14, 1989.

20. Quoted in Marable, *Race, Reform, and Rebellion*, 201–02.

21. Juan Williams, "Civil Rights Commissioner Says He Plans to Cool His Rhetoric," *Washington Post*, May 13, 1985.

22. Editorial, "Racism is Back," *Economist*, November 16, 1991: 15.

23. Kevin Phillips, *The Politics of Rich and Poor: Wealth and the American Electorate in the Reagan Aftermath* (New York: Random House, 1990), 32.

24. Ibid., 43.

25. Peter Goldman, "Carter's Trip of the Tongue," *Newsweek*, April 19, 1976: 14.

26. Kenneth Woodward, "Showdown in Plains," *Newsweek*, November 22, 1976: 81.

27. Goldfield, *The Color of Politics*, 313–14.

28. Sitkoff, *The Struggle for Black Equality*, 215.

29. Marable, *Black American Politics*, 250.

30. Goldfield, *Color of Politics*, 312–16.

31. Dan Balz, "White Men Reassert their Force in the Electorate," *Washington Post,* December 26, 1984.

32. John Dillin, "Democratic Party analysts take measure of special-interest group splintering," *Christian Science Monitor*, December 26, 1984.

33. "[What the founders of the DLC] wish to be rid of is some of the New Deal and Great Society baggage that seems irrelevant 50 and 20 years on." "Spring in the air—and in the step of the Demo-

crats," *Economist*, March 23, 1985.

34. Phil Gailey, "Dissidents Defy Top Democrats; Council Formed," *New York Times*, March 1, 1985.

35. Sheila D. Collins, *The Rainbow Challenge: The Jackson Campaign and the Future of U.S. Politics* (New York: Monthly Review Press, 1986), 292.

36. Clint Bolick, "Clinton's Quota Queens," *Wall Street Journal*, April 20, 1993.

37. "Issues, Answers in the Clinton-Dole Debates: Excerpts from the Debates," *USA Today*, October 17, 1996.

38. Salim Muwakkil, "Failed Crime Bill Sold Out Reform for Punishment," *Chicago Sun-Times*, August 16, 1994. Leslie Phillips, "Democrat's Goal: Change 8 Votes," *USA Today*, August 15, 1994.

39. Lance Selfa, "Eight Years of Clinton-Gore: The Price of Lesser-Evilism," *International Socialist Review* 13 (August–September 2000): 12.

40. Upon hearing the court's decision on the contested election, Gore declared, "Now the U.S. Supreme Court has spoken. Let there be no doubt, while I strongly disagree with the court's decision, I accept it. I accept the finality of this outcome.... And tonight, for the sake of our unity of the people and the strength of our democracy, I offer my concession." Susan Martin and David Ballingrud, "Long run to the White House," *St. Petersburg Times*, December 14, 2000.

Conclusion

1. Summarizing the findings of the *2005 State of Black America* report, Marc Morial, Urban League president, points out: "Since the 1960s, one of the success stories is the growth of the African-American middle class—those who are college-educated, participating throughout the American economy and growing in stature and influence." Morial added, "But what we face is that these successes of 40 years are being eroded. The danger is the great backslide that can occur." Erin Texeira, "New Report Details Black Inequality, Persistent Wealth and Health Care Gaps," *Associated Press*, April 5, 2005.

2. Carnoy, *Faded Dreams*, 14–16. (emphasis added)

3. David A. Bositis, *Black Elected Officials: A Statistical Summary*, Joint Center for Political and Economic Studies, 2001, 5.

4. T. Boston, "Racial Equality and Class Stratification," *Review of Radical Political Economics* 17, no. 3 (Fall 1985): 56.

5. Marable, *Black American Politics*, 153.

6. Selfa, *Politics of Lesser Evilism*, 60–64.

7. "Blacks Need Capital, Jackson Says: Learning Economics, Technology, Essential Investments," *Seattle Times*, June 11, 2001.

8. Salim Muwakkil, "Jesse Jackson's New Crusade: It's all about the Benjamins," *In These Times*, March 20, 2000. Muwakkil rightly points out: "...Jackson's capitalist embrace is nothing new. His latest capitalist adventures are continuations of his previous concerns about economic equity and corporate reciprocity. He has long argued that inner-city and rural communities were ripe for the kind of investment U.S. corporations reflexively target elsewhere in the world. Even while working with King's Southern Christian Leadership Conference (SCLC), Jackson brought an economic focus to civil rights concerns; he headed the group's Operation Breadbasket, which badgered inner-city supermarkets to employ local residents and stock products made by Black-owned companies. When Operation PUSH broke away from SCLC in 1971, Jackson again asserted the primacy of free market economics in the freedom struggle. 'To a considerable extent, Jackson's current strategy is a throwback to Operation PUSH's "corporate covenants" of 20 years ago,' Manning Marable, director of Columbia University's Institute for Research in African-American Studies, writes in a recent column.

"Civil rights groups are increasingly focusing their agendas on issues of economic justice. Jackson again appears to be leading the way with his various 'projects' encouraging market investments. One aspect of the Wall Street Project is to use churches to evangelize an economic message, transforming debt-ridden Black consumers into solvent stockholders. 'Too many working poor people choose a bear lottery over a bull market,' Jackson explained in a recent interview. 'They choose floating gambling boats over stable banks. They must be brought into the age of economic enlightenment.'"

9. Karl Marx, *The German Ideology* (New York: International Publishers, 1947), 64.

10. Herbert Hill, "Race, Ethnicity and Organized Labor: The Opposition to Affirmative Action," *New Politics* 1, no. 2 (Winter 1987): 36.

11. Manning Marable, "Which Way for the Black Movement?"*Against the Current* (May 1984).

12. Gregory Meyerson, "Rethinking Black Marxism: Reflections on Cedric Robinson and Others," *Cultural Logic: An Electronic Journal of Marxist Theory and Practice* 3, no. 2, Spring 2000, http://eserver.org/clogic/3-1%262/meyerson.html

Meyerson continues: "As I will show, the incorrect understanding of the primacy of class does carry with it for critics of historical materialism both the devaluation of 'race' and 'gender' as explanatory categories and their devaluation as real people, women and people of color. So when the charge is made against Marxism that it makes race and gender secondary, there is always the sense that race and gender are being treated at once as analytical categories and citizens—with the implication that Marxism in theory is the corollary of a deprivation of rights in practice. On this view, race, gender, class are co-primary, interacting, intersecting and, to reiterate the confusion I see between the triad as analytical category and person, in dialogue.

"...In my view, and this is surely controversial, but it also puts Marxism on its strongest footing, the primacy of class means not only that class is the primary determinant of oppression and exploitation but the only structural determinant. 'Race' and gender (this essay focuses on racism but has implications for gender) are not structural determinants. There is racist and sexist ideology. And there is a racial and gendered division of labor, whose severity and function vary depending on where one works in the capitalist global economy. Both ideology and the division of labor are understood here to be functional for class rule—facilitating profit making and social control. Class rule is itself a form of class struggle. This latter point is crucial. Class rule is never automatic or easy, and there is constant resistance, both to class rule itself and its symptoms."

13. Allen, *Reluctant Reformers*, 211.

14. Ibid., 235–36.

15. For a discussion of the weaknesses of Lenin's theory, see Tony Cliff, "The Economic Roots of Reformism," *Neither Washington nor Moscow: Essays on Revolutionary Socialism* (London: Bookmarks, 1982), 108–17.

16. Ibid., 109.

17. Martin Glaberman, "Class Is a Missing Element," *New Politics* 1, no. 3 New Series (Summer 1987): 59.

18. Michael Reich, "The Economics of Racism," in Edwards, Reich, and Weisskopf, eds., *The Capitalist System* (Englewood Cliffs, NJ: Prentice-Hall, 1972), 316, 318.

19. Victor Perlo, *Economics of Racism U.S.A.: The Roots of Black Inequality* (New York: International Publishers, 1975), 168.

20. Hal Draper, *Karl Marx's Theory of Revolution*, vol. 2, *The Politics of Social Classes* (New York: Monthly Review Press, 1978), 66.

21. Ibid.

22. Ibid., 74.

23. Tony Cliff, *Building the Party: Lenin 1893–1914* (Chicago: Haymarket Books, 2002), 71–72.

24. Trotsky, *On Black Nationalism*, 28.

25. Breitman, *Assassination of Malcolm X*, 55–56.

26. Ibid., 42.

27. Chris Harman, "The Summer of 1981: A Post Riot Analysis," *International Socialism* 14, series no. 2 (Autumn 1981): 28.

28. Lenin, *Right of Nations to Self-Determination*, 411–12.

29. Chris Harman, *The Fire Last Time: 1968 and After*, 2nd ed. (London: Bookmarks, 1998), see 351–55 for a fuller discussion.

30. For a discussion of these issues, see Celia Petty, Deborah Roberts, and Sharon Smith, *Women's Liberation and Socialism* (London: Bookmarks, 1987).

31. Marable, "Why Black Americans Are Not Socialists," 70.

Index

About Haymarket Books

Haymarket Books is a nonprofit, progressive book distributor and publisher, a project of the Center for Economic Research and Social Change. We believe that activists need to take ideas, history, and politics into the many struggles for social justice today. Learning the lessons of past victories, as well as defeats, can arm a new generation of fighters for a better world.

We take inspiration and courage from our namesakes, the Haymarket Martyrs, who gave their lives fighting for a better world. Their 1886 struggle for the eight-hour day, which gave us May Day, the international workers' holiday, reminds workers around the world that ordinary people can organize and struggle for their own liberation. These struggles continue today across the globe—struggles against oppression, exploitation, hunger, and poverty.

Also from Haymarket Books

Subterranean Fire: A History of Working-Class Radicalism in the United States

Sharon Smith • This accessible, critical history of the U.S. labor movement examines the hidden history of workers' resistance from the nineteenth century to the present.   *ISBN 193185923X*

The Communist Manifesto: A Road Map to History's Most Important Political Document

Karl Marx and Frederick Engels, edited by **Phil Gasper** • Includes the full text of the *Manifesto*, with commentaries, annotations, and additional works by Marx and Engels.   *ISBN 1931859213*

Literature and Revolution

Leon Trotsky, edited by **William Keach** • A new, annotated edition of Leon Trotsky's classic study of the relationship between politics and art.

   ISBN 1931859213

Women and Socialism: Essays on Women's Liberation

Sharon Smith • The fight for women's liberation is urgent—and must be linked to winning broader social change.   *ISBN 1931859116*

The Meek and the Militant: Religion and Power Across the World

Paul Siegel • Examines the historical roots of religion around the world, it origin and persistence, and how it has acted as a bulwark of the social order, but also as a revolutionary force.   *ISBN 1931859248*

Order these titles online at www.haymarketbooks.org or call 773-583-7884. Distributed to the trade by Consortium Book Sales and Distribution.